Modern Sport Ethics

Recent Titles in the
CONTEMPORARY WORLD ISSUES
Series

Books in the **Contemporary World Issues** series address vital issues in today's society such as genetic engineering, pollution, and biodiversity. Written by professional writers, scholars, and nonacademic experts, these books are authoritative, clearly written, up-to-date, and objective. They provide a good starting point for research by high school and college students, scholars, and general readers as well as by legislators, businesspeople, activists, and others.

Each book, carefully organized and easy to use, contains an overview of the subject, a detailed chronology, biographical sketches, facts and data and/or documents and other primary source material, a forum of authoritative perspective essays, annotated lists of print and nonprint resources, and an index.

Readers of books in the Contemporary World Issues series will find the information they need in order to have a better understanding of the social, political, environmental, and economic issues facing the world today.

Modern Sport Ethics

A REFERENCE HANDBOOK

Second Edition

Angela Lumpkin

ABC-CLIO™

An Imprint of ABC-CLIO, LLC

Santa Barbara, California • Denver, Colorado

1/4/18
ww
$60.00

Library of Congress Cataloging-in-Publication Data

Names: Lumpkin, Angela, author.
Title: Modern sport ethics : a reference handbook / Angela Lumpkin.
Description: Second Edition. | Santa Barbara, California : ABC-CLIO An Imprint of ABC-CLIO, LLC, [2017] | Series: Contemporary World Issues | Includes bibliographical references and index.
Identifiers: LCCN 2016034038 (print) | LCCN 2016046451 (ebook) | ISBN 9781440851155 (acid-free paper) | ISBN 9781440851162 (Ebook)
Subjects: LCSH: Sports—Moral and ethical aspects.
Classification: LCC GV706.3 .L84 2017 (print) | LCC GV706.3 (ebook) | DDC 796.01—dc23
LC record available at https://lccn.loc.gov/2016034038

ISBN: 978-1-4408-5115-5
EISBN: 978-1-4408-5116-2

21 20 19 18 17   1 2 3 4 5

This book is also available as an eBook.

ABC-CLIO
An Imprint of ABC-CLIO, LLC

ABC-CLIO, LLC
130 Cremona Drive, P.O. Box 1911
Santa Barbara, California 93116–1911
www.abc-clio.com

This book is printed on acid-free paper ∞

Manufactured in the United States of America

Contents

Preface and Acknowledgments

Examples of unethical conduct in amateur sport are reported nonstop by the print, electronic, and social media. These unethical practices are associated with an overemphasis on winning and commercialism that have taken amateur sport away from the ideals of playing sports for the inherent joy and personal satisfaction of challenging oneself against a respected opponent or a performance standard. Cheating to gain unfair advantages, gamesmanship ploys, the use of performance-enhancing drugs, recruiting scandals, academic misconduct associated with athletes, discriminatory practices against females and African Americans, and other breaches of principled behavior have become everyday realities in sports. Many fans, who increasingly want to be entertained as they cheer their favorite teams, have come to accept and cheer questionably ethical actions as normative behavior and the way the game should be played to help secure the all-important victory.

For well over a century, millions in the United States have claimed youth, interscholastic, intercollegiate, and Olympic sports teach positive values. Yet, many people argue sport ethics is a contradictory combination of words or an oxymoron. For ethical conduct to characterize sports, coaches, players, administrators, parents, and fans need to teach, model, and reinforce character development and positive values. To address ethical challenges like taunting, disrespect for opponents and officials, and cheating, this handbook on sport ethics emphasizes sportsmanship, respect for the game, fair play, and making morally reasoned decisions as essential to ensuring positive values and character will be taught, learned, and demonstrated.

Chapter 1 includes a historical context for examining sport ethics, specifically how character development and sports are linked. A description of ethics, ethical theories, and moral reasoning helps the reader gain a deeper understanding of the interface between amateur sport, ethical conduct, and morality in sports. Achieving positive values through sport programs sponsored by educational institutions is challenged by unethical behaviors. Numerous examples of gamesmanship and violence, violations of academic eligibility rules, sport dropout due to physical and psychological burnout, cheating, and the use of performance-enhancing drugs demonstrate the adverse effects of unethical behaviors in sports. Specific suggestions are described to show how character education can reduce unethical actions in sports.

Chapter 2 examines contemporary issues, controversies, and problems confronting all levels of sports in the United States. This chapter stresses that an overemphasis on winning is a leading culprit contributing to unethical actions in sports. Specific ethical problems threatening the achievement of positive outcomes in youth, interscholastic, and intercollegiate sports are presented. Recommendations for teaching positive values to youth, adolescent, and young adult athletes are offered. Ethical issues in sport transcend national boundaries, and unethical behaviors are found throughout the world. The Olympic Games are described historically with an emphasis on these controversies: amateurism; nationalism and politics; racism and human rights; sexism and discrimination against females; bidding scandals; unethical behavior of officials; and use of performance-enhancing drugs and doping scandals. Examples of gamesmanship, cheating, gambling, and fixing outcomes of the selection host nations and competitions show how unprincipled behaviors have become commonplace in international sports. Given the global interconnectedness of sport, codes of ethics have been enacted to guide athletes, coaches, officials, and fans in acting in morally appropriate ways, essential if sport is to achieve the lofty goals of friendship, respect, and fair competition.

Chapter 3 includes essays from scholars to bring diverse voices in discussing ethical issues in sports. Each perspective adds insights in exploring the pros and cons of ethical concerns that plague sports at all competitive levels.

Chapter 4 personalizes this examination of sport ethics by providing 39 biographical sketches of athletes, coaches, and leaders whose ethical conduct in sport has been worthy of emulation. Each profile shows how teaching and modeling positive values has made a difference in the lives of those who subsequently demonstrated positive values in sports. This chapter also describes 139 sport and sport-related organizations placed into brief historical context. For each of the national governing bodies, the international sport federation is listed. Whenever a sport organization emphasizes ethical conduct, this is stated.

Chapter 5 includes 3 documents, 12 figures, and 13 tables that provide evidence of existing ethical problems as well as positive approaches for addressing them. These data and documents provide key facts or statistics to help readers understand important ethical issues in sports. These entries are placed into historical context. The reader is challenged to draw morally reasoned conclusions about ethical issues in sports using the facts and evidence presented.

Chapter 6 provides over 150 citations of reference works, books, magazine and journal articles, other print works, DVDs, databases, and Internet sites, each with an annotation describing its relationship to sport ethics. These print and nonprint resources are the best available for learning more about and staying current with the latest challenges to ethical morality in sports and possible ways to recapture the moral fabric of amateur sports.

Chapter 7 provides the reader with a chronology of significant events starting with the beginning of the modern Olympic

Games to the present that have illustrated unethical and ethical conduct in sports. Thirty-eight examples chronicle the erosion of positive values; 12 examples applaud the highest levels of principled behaviors. All of these examples are provided chronologically to contextualize unethical actions in sport.

The glossary provides brief definitions of over 44 key terms associated with ethical conduct in sports.

Acknowledgments

Parents are the first teachers who begin the process of developing and modeling moral values for their children. I would like to express my deepest appreciation to my parents, Carol and Janice Lumpkin, who taught me what was morally right and helped me learn an ethical code of behavior that has shaped who I am as a person. I dedicate this book to honor them in appreciation for their guidance and love.

Modern Sport Ethics

Introduction

Sport ethics has been called an oxymoron because many believe sport and ethics are incongruent or contradictory. Sport describes competitive physical activities governed by rules. These competitions usually involve one or more opponents playing for fun and/or reward. Involvement in sport often begins early as balls are some of the first toys given to children, with parents often teaching their children how to throw, catch, and kick. Playing sports and attending sport competitions are frequently shared between children and parents as enjoyable bonding experiences. Many children realize the significance placed on sports; plus, sports are often integrated with friends, food, and fun. Also, everyone is surrounded by mediated sports on television, radio, the Internet, and social media.

Brief Origin of Sport

Even though the exact origin of rule-governed sport is unknown, it is generally assumed individuals in prehistoric, Chinese, Native American, and other early civilizations engaged in competitive sporting activities. Sports in early eras were usually

---

These Princeton University athletes were members of the U.S. team in the first modern Olympic Games held in Athens, Greece, in April 1896. Olympic athletes initially and for nearly a century were required to be amateurs competing for the love of the game based on the British Amateur Sport Ideal. (AP Photo)

linked with religion, war, and rites of passage into adulthood. While competitions may have been recreational, the early Mayan civilization took their ball matches more seriously than most, since the losers were often killed.

Most historians credit the Greeks with formalizing competitive sports based on historical documents recounting warrior/athlete competitions. These competitions began as informal, spontaneous displays of athletic prowess but later evolved into Panhellenic festivals, including the ancient Olympic Games. Athletic competitions in early Greece were held in honor of various gods and linked directly with religious observances. These festivals included competitions in which athletes ran, jumped, wrestled, boxed, threw the discus and javelin, drove chariots, and rode horses as they demonstrated their skills as warriors.

Sport for men in subsequent civilizations was associated with military preparedness, such as during the Middle Ages in jousting, and in Germany, Sweden, and Denmark in gymnastics and fencing. The British were instrumental in promoting sport competitions through colonization, leading to the worldwide spread of soccer, rugby, field hockey, rowing, tennis, badminton, golf, boxing, and horse racing. The British and other predominately European immigrants brought their love of sports to what became the United States of America.

Sports in the early years in the United States were primarily recreational in nature as individuals of all ages played various ball games. While a few females became sport enthusiasts, mostly males competed in baseball, cricket, bowling, pool, horseshoes, rowing, fox hunting, horse racing, running, boxing, and other physical activities. Baseball, which had become the favorite ball-and-stick game in rural pastures and on city streets and benefited from a set of written rules, was spread during the Civil War as soldiers wearing blue and those wearing gray played in military encampments and prison camps. As the popularity of baseball as a participant sport grew nationwide, it became professionalized when Harry Wright paid the

Cincinnati Red Stockings' players in the late 1860s. With professional baseball players helping to popularize the game, baseball truly became the national pastime as many males (and a few females) played pickup, and later organized, games.

The baseball nine, as a team was called on mostly men's college campuses, was soon supplanted in popularity by the football eleven. As football, a uniquely American game that evolved from rugby and soccer, gained supremacy in colleges, it fostered the construction of stadiums seating thousands. Newspapers promoted games between teams representing Yale and Princeton as their annual contest became a highlight on the social calendar. Male collegians also played baseball and tennis, rowed, ran track, boxed, and engaged in gymnastics, although these sports were never as popular as football. Designed as a winter sport to be played between football and baseball seasons, basketball remained on the periphery on most campuses until after World War II. While played on most campuses, more importantly, it was spread worldwide by the Young Men's Christian Association (YMCA). Basketball did, however, become the most popular participatory sport for females at women's colleges. These women also informally played baseball, field hockey, tennis, and golf, shot archery, fenced, ran track, rowed, and engaged in gymnastics.

Boys' high school sports followed the lead of college sports, with an emphasis on the team sports of football, baseball, and basketball and track and field. Economic factors limited the breadth of sport programs but did not deter the enthusiasm displayed by communities in cheering for their local teams. In some small towns, girls' basketball at times rivaled the popularity of boys' basketball. The girls, however, usually played by rules restricting their movement to a portion of the court due to societal perceptions that the full-court game was too vigorous for females.

Organized youth sports for boys can be traced back to the 1920s, when local communities began to establish teams, especially summer baseball teams, to prevent juvenile delinquency and promote local businesses (as sponsors). Illustrations of the beginnings of national competitive sport programs included American Legion baseball in 1925, Pop Warner Football in 1929, Little League Baseball in 1939, and Biddy Basketball in 1951.

Youth, scholastic, collegiate, and Olympic sports mushroomed in fan popularity, participation, and competition in the years after World War II due to economic prosperity, expanding educational opportunities, and the media. Radio, free-to-air television, cable television, and the Internet joined the print media in publicizing sports and dramatically increased the revenues associated with sports. With greater financial benefits to coaches and institutions, most often associated with winning, however, have come ethical concerns.

What Is Ethics?

Ethics is the study of morals, moral values, and character. A person's morals are those motives, intentions, and actions that are right and good, rather than wrong or bad. Moral values communicate the relative worth each individual associates with virtuous behaviors like honesty, respect, and responsibility (Lumpkin, Stoll, and Beller 2012). People's moral values characterize who they are and what they will do. Family, religion, peers, and societal influences help shape moral values.

In sport and other aspects of life, people usually make decisions and act based on their moral values. Even though it is assumed people's lives reflect what they believe is right and wrong, there is the possibility they may act differently in their personal lives than they do in their professional roles or differently depending on the situation. For example, sometimes when confronted with problems, individuals may fail to rationally analyze the issues, think through the ramifications of different resolutions, or act based on their moral values. Time constraints may lead to hasty actions that under other circumstances would not go against the expectations of others, rules, or laws. Sometimes self-interest or personal advantage may cloud a person's judgment leading to actions with unintended consequences. Peer pressures or unique circumstances may lead to people acting in ways that harm others.

Given these issues and possibly as a way to address these challenges, ethical pluralism suggests taking multiple approaches to the same problem—that is, values may be situational, contextually based, or absolute. Considering the five ethical theories briefly described in the following section could help each person understand how differently people may view the same situation.

Ethical Theories

Utilitarian theory, or *utilitarianism*, states that the ultimate standard of what is morally right is dependent on the greatest amount of good for the greatest number of people—that is, there is no specific standard of right because it depends on the circumstances and resultant consequences. Individuals adopting utilitarianism make ethical decisions based on what they think the anticipated short- or long-term consequences will be for most people. The goal is to maximize utility, or the amount of satisfaction, benefit, or enjoyment, for most individuals. The challenge, however, is determining exactly what this collective human welfare could be. For example, if a collegiate athlete maintains his or her eligibility by receiving an unearned grade from a professor and subsequently helps the team win a championship, this would benefit the team, institution, and maybe thousands of fans. It could be argued this produces the most benefit, thereby offsetting the fact that the other students in the course did not receive preferential treatment in the grades they received.

The theory of *ethical relativism* argues that each individual determines what is true, so all points of view are equally valid. Since people believe different things are true, there are no moral

absolutes and no definitive right or wrong. The relativist claims
social norms and cultures differ, so morals evolve and change.
A relativist might believe Caucasian males deserve preferential treatment in athletics because they are more skilled, even
though females do not receive similar treatment. For example,
the ethical relativist would not have supported the banning of
South Africa, due to its apartheid practices, from the Olympic
Games from 1964 to 1992, because discrimination against ethnic groups was acceptable in South Africa at that time. Most
reject the theory of ethical relativism because underlying moral
values relative to the treatment of others are violated.

Situational ethics is an ethical theory that takes into account
the context of a situation or an act when judging whether it is
ethical. Proponents of this theory willingly permit casting aside
absolute moral standards. In the absence of a universal standard or law, what matters is the outcome or consequences; so,
the end justifies the means. Possibly the following contrasting
realities can help illustrate the application of situational ethics.
In a pickup game of basketball played among friends, everyone
is expected to call his or her own fouls or acknowledge knocking the ball out-of-bounds. Caring about one's friends and
maybe getting to keep playing with the group leads to these
actions. But, once an organized game is played with officials,
most athletes will not admit to the same fouls or violations
as the end goal of winning is more important than expressing
concern for opponents. Situational ethics has been extended
by many athletes and coaches to mean trying to get away with
(i.e., not penalized by the officials) as many actions on the field
or court as possible to gain competitive advantages.

Non-consequential (*Kantian*) theory states that there is an
absolute moral code of behavior. Whatever is morally right is
always right, and wrong behavior is always wrong. In its strictest
application, an inherent rightness, or a categorical imperative,
exists and can be applied consistently and without partiality
in every situation. It is the moral duty of an individual to do
what is morally right without regard to the circumstances. In

application of this theory, if a volleyball player touches the ball as it goes out-of-bounds, he or she is morally obligated to admit touching the ball, even though it results in the loss of a point. This emphasis on doing one's duty builds moral courage because the universal standard applies without exception. This belief in inherent rightness, while making it easier to resist compromises to ethical standards, is sometimes challenged when there are conflicting duties, such as loyalty to teammates and conformity with the rules.

Justice as fairness, another ethical theory, advocates guaranteeing equal rights and equality of opportunity while providing the greatest benefit to those least advantaged. The justice part of this theory states that not everything has to be equal as long as each person has an equal opportunity to succeed or reach a desired outcome. This is balanced by fairness to ensure those least advantaged will be provided additional benefits in addressing existing disparities. For example, Title IX of the 1972 Education Amendments requires that all students in educational institutions have equal opportunities to participate in sports and are provided with equivalent treatment, benefits, and opportunities. Justice mandates an end to discriminatory treatment. Fairness, however, means equal opportunity, not necessarily spending equal dollars or offering the same number of teams.

Although not an ethical theory, it is important to include a brief overview of *moral development*. The study of moral development examines how and through what processes people learn and develop morally, even when confronted with psychological and social detractors. Social learning theorists advocate that moral values are learned and developed through a cognitive-developmental approach—that is, experiences with parents, other adults, peers, environmental influences, and the process of socialization progressively shapes moral values. These individuals learn principles of right and wrong and develop their reasoning abilities. Some philosophers have suggested moral judgments advance from a lower-level focusing on obedient actions performed to avoid punishment through following rules for self-interest and in conformity to the expectations of parents, peers, and society in general. Ideally, individuals will advance to an adherence to universal ethical principles (Kohlberg 1981).

Moral Reasoning

Those who adhere to principle-based morality advocate using moral reasoning, which is the process of evaluating personal values and developing a consistent, impartial set of moral principles by which to live (Lumpkin, Stoll, and Beller 2012). The first step in reasoning morally is moral knowing. This means an individual cognitively learns about moral issues and how to resolve them. The second step is moral feeling, which describes what each person believes along with the beliefs, values, and principles guiding interactions with others. The third step is moral acting, which describes how each individual behaves based on what is known and believed (Kohlberg 1981). Thus, to reason morally, a person identifies what is known about moral values, believes in these values, and, most importantly, has the moral courage to act based on these values.

As will be examined in this book, there are problems with the moral reasoning of athletes. For example, Beller and Stoll (1995) found that the moral reasoning of youth, interscholastic, and intercollegiate athletes is less consistent, impartial, and reflective than that of nonathletes. Other studies have shown lower levels of moral reasoning characterize collegiate athletes in revenue-producing sports; athletes in team sports show less moral reasoning than do athletes in individual sports; and male athletes behave less morally than do female athletes (Beller and Stoll 1995; Bredemeier and Shields 1995; Rudd and Stoll 2004; Silva 1983). Of particular concern is that the longer athletes participate in sport, the lower their moral reasoning (Bredemeier 1995; Rudd and Stoll 2004)—that is, as athletes progress through youth, school, college, and professional athletics, they demonstrate less moral courage to reason morally and act based on moral values.

One possible explanation for lower scores on moral reasoning inventories may be the application of groupthink to sport. Groupthink occurs when group or team members expect or mandate conformity from individuals who may want to make morally right decisions but are silenced or pressured to support a united decision or outcome. The cultures of some sports that emphasize doing whatever it takes to win, such as throwing at a batter in retaliation for a teammate having been hit with a pitch, illustrate groupthink. To apply this concept further, groupthink may lead to the expectation of "taking out" an opponent in football or ice hockey in order to play against a lesser-skilled opponent and thus increase the possibility of winning. Groupthink may lead to the use of performance-enhancing drugs as teammates seek to enhance their physical abilities to help win championships.

Some athletes try to make it seem unethical actions are really ethical—that is, they may claim there is no rule against their actions, no one will ever know, or everyone else does it. Some athletes state their actions are not unethical since no one was harmed or no fouls were called or penalties assessed. Or, they may argue that while rules of the sport were violated, the amount of good accomplished overshadowed the small amount of harm—the ends justify the means (Stoll and Beller 2006). Some athletes use what has been called bracketed morality (Bredemeier and Shields 1995) to justify acting unethically in sport to win or gain advantages. Bracketed morality occurs when athletes suspend their moral values used in everyday life and cause harm to others or act immorally within a competitive situation. Yet, outside of sport, these individuals behave in congruence with their moral values. Given the behaviors of some athletes, is it possible they are attempting to justify their unsportsmanlike actions? Do others perceive their actions as unfair, dishonest, disrespectful, and against the rules?

Obstacles and fallacies in moral reasoning can lead to unethical behaviors in sport. Table 1.1 provides several examples to illustrate how athletes, coaches, or others in sport may justify their actions.

Table 1.1 Fallacies in Moral Reasoning in Sport

Fallacy	Description of This Fallacy	Sport Examples of Fallacy
Ad hominem	Attacking the person rather than the argument, such as by name-calling	A coach who has been violating recruiting rules lashes out against the person who reported these violations by calling him or her a whistleblower whose word cannot be trusted.
Appeal to ignorance	Claiming something is right just because it has not been shown to be wrong	An athlete who has been accused of using performance-enhancing drugs claims there is no evidence to prove he or she has used these drugs.
Appeal to force	Supposing "might makes right" or the biggest, strongest, or greatest number must be right	Since every lineman in football holds, then holding is just an accepted part of how the game is played.
Appeal to tradition	Resisting change because it is not the way things have typically been done	College coaches have always been given preferential admissions for their star recruits, so everyone is supposed to agree there is no reason to change this successful practice.
Bandwagon effect	Appealing to what everyone is doing or popular opinion; related to groupthink	Taunting members of opposing teams by fans is a part of the home court advantage.
Circular reasoning or begging the question	Using one thing to justify or support the same thing	Football teams bring in most of the revenue so, of course, they should be able to spend whatever they want on their teams.
Dogmatism	Affirming a person's subjective certainty (i.e., closed mindedness) is the only solution	In baseball, everyone accepts the pitcher is expected to throw at a batter who is crowding the plate.
Equivocation	Using words incorrectly or those with the wrong meaning to prove a point	Since the coach is in control, he or she can do whatever it takes to motivate athletes.

Fallacy	Description of This Fallacy	Sport Examples of Fallacy
Fallacy of authority	Claiming something is true just because it was stated or done by someone with authority	This product must be as good, because my favorite player endorses it.
False cause	Assuming one event always causes a second event	Ms. Smith is too demanding in her English course, which is why three key players on the team are failing her course.
Single cause	Claiming a simple cause to a complicated problem	Requiring an athlete who misses classes to run laps in the early morning to motivate him or her to attend classes.
Slippery slope	Assuming a specific action, if not continued, will inevitably lead to a bad outcome	Without a demanding off-season conditioning program, athletes will not work diligently and enhance their fitness and skills to help win more games next season.
Straw argument	Attacking one aspect or a minor point of an argument	Since so many men's teams have been eliminated, this proves Title IX is flawed and should not be enforced.

Brief Historical Context for Amateur Sport and Character Development

Before exploring the issue of whether or not there has been an erosion of values in sport as suggested by the examples in Table 1.1, it is important to establish whether or not sport can and should teach character and moral values. Socrates, Plato, Aristotle, and other Greek philosophers revered those who attained their highest potential as shown through their superiority in knowledge. This process of demonstrating excellence and virtue, or *arete*, also was applied to prowess in athletic contests. The victorious athlete was respected and honored by the Greeks because he demonstrated his superiority over all challengers. This was particularly the case when upper-class men, the nobility, trained for war and occasionally competed in athletics, not necessarily for lucrative prizes, but to prove their superior abilities and prowess.

Greek athletes also professionalized sport. After centuries of competing with the goal of displaying their athletic superiority, warrior/athletes were replaced by specialists who, rather than develop as all-around athletes who could run, jump, throw, and engage in hand-to-hand combat, trained in the specific event they believed they could dominate. Most of these athletes were motivated by the praise and financial rewards received if they won. The benefits of winning, however, led some athletes to sell their skills to the highest bidder instead of competing as representatives of their home cities. Eventually, because the rewards were valued so highly, some athletes cheated and bribed opponents to let them win. These and other corruptions led to the elimination of the Olympic Games around AD 400.

By the nineteenth century, British upper-class males, who were leaders of the dominant international power at the time, were competing in sports in elite schools, universities, and private clubs. They claimed sports taught socialization skills, initiative, loyalty, cooperation, sportsmanship, self-discipline, and leadership, which were viewed as important characteristics for the ruling class. This concept was called the British Amateur Sport Ideal because it was believed social and moral values were learned, practiced, and reinforced through sport.

Many upper-class males in Great Britain praised those who played at their games (i.e., the amateur), while disparaging those who worked at sport for financial gain (i.e., the professional). Through this differentiation, upper-class males separated themselves from those who depended on victory for a living or as a supplement to their incomes. Upper-class males advanced this ideal of "playing the game for the game's sake" by attending exclusive educational institutions and building private clubs, such as the All England Lawn Tennis and Croquet Club (Wimbledon), which excluded those without the financial means and status to join. Working-class males who were eager to play sports for pay were viewed as social inferiors in the economically stratified society of Great Britain.

The British ideal of teaching character and moral values through sports influenced sport worldwide. Among the strongest advocates was Frenchman Pierre de Coubertin, the founder of the modern Olympic Games, who sought to use sport to promote world peace and friendship. When the modern Olympic Games were begun in 1896, de Coubertin and the International Olympic Committee (IOC) perpetuated the British (and Greek-influenced) ideal that sport should be played for the sheer joy of participation and competition, rather than for remuneration. This policy led to the early exclusion of working-class athletes from the Olympic Games, because they could not afford to stop working to train. For more than 80 years, IOC regulations stipulated that athletes had to verify their amateur status to be eligible to compete.

Since the 1980s, though, most Olympic athletes have been professionals because they have trained and competed year-round and supported themselves through appearance fees, prize money, and income from other sport-related activities. In accepting this reality, the IOC permitted each international sport federation to determine eligibility rules for its athletes. Another contributing factor to this elimination of the amateur requirement was the attempt to level the playing field, so the United States and other nations would have a better chance to win the all-important medal count.

Athletics in Educational Institutions

The concept of amateurism in sport has shaped educational sport in the United States as males and females in schools and colleges have played sports as a part of their extracurricular activities (i.e., as a supplement to their academic curriculum). For example, the National Federation of State High School Associations (NFHS) emphasizes that sport participation enhances the academic performance of athletes. This governing organization states high school athletes have higher grade point averages, lower drop-out rates, better daily attendance, and fewer discipline problems than do nonparticipating students (National Federation of State High School Associations 2016).

School administrators, coaches, and parents believe the over 7.8 million high school athletes, in addition to enhancing their sport skills and physical fitness, learn sportsmanship, self-discipline, and teamwork. This view of interscholastic sports harkens back to the British Amateur Sport Ideal, especially given the fact that the NFHS disallows any high school athlete from receiving financial benefits other than those provided by schools, leagues, or state associations.

The National Collegiate Athletic Association (NCAA) has always viewed college athletes as amateurs and athletic programs as integral to each member institution's educational mission (Falla 1981). The NCAA has attempted to maintain a clear distinction between college athletics and professional sports. The line between the amateur and professional, however, has changed dramatically as a look at the evolution of athletic scholarships, or grants-in aid, reveals (Sack 2005). When founded in 1906, the NCAA viewed the awarding of athletic scholarships as a violation of amateurism based on the premise that athletics were extracurricular activities for students to engage in during their free time and played for the love of the game. Despite this, in 1929 the Carnegie Foundation reported in *American College Athletics* that most colleges subsidized athletes in violation of NCAA rules (Savage, Bentley, McGovern, and Smiley 1929). Even though in 1948 the NCAA adopted the Principles for the Conduct of Intercollegiate Athletics (called the Sanity Code) that specifically banned athletic scholarships, several colleges continued to give them. After unsuccessful attempts to enforce this ban, and because of the widespread practice of paying the educational and living expenses of athletes in violation of the NCAA's amateur code, in 1957 the NCAA permitted the awarding of athletic scholarships in its rules. This change was tantamount to sanctioning a practice previously defined as professionalism (Sack 2005).

The NCAA now defines a professional athlete as someone who receives any type of payment for athletic participation other than what its regulations allow. Even though by the late 1900s the British and the IOC realized amateurism had become historically obsolete and a hypocritical myth, there remains a persistent belief that youth, interscholastic, and intercollegiate sports in the United States should be played by amateurs. This is not the model internationally, however, because seldom do educational institutions sponsor and provide sport teams for students. Rather, individuals participate in a variety of sports through independent clubs having no connection with schools and colleges.

Another challenge facing amateur sport in colleges is a commercialized arms race (The Drake Group 2016; Knight Commission on Intercollegiate Athletics 2001). In an attempt to keep up with conference members or highly ranked teams, institutions are continuously building new and more elaborate athletic facilities for practices, physical conditioning, and competition, or at least making renovations to improve athletic facilities. These expansive and increasingly plush facilities are used to impress potential recruits with the latest and greatest accommodations and possibly to appease the athletes who spend many hours using these facilities. With no constraints on spending, other than how much private funding can be raised, the millions spent on athletic facilities continue to escalate annually. Many schools are modeling their interscholastic sport programs, especially football, after this commercialized concept of building bigger and more elaborate facilities.

Sport for over a century has been used to promote schools and colleges. Since sport is the beneficiary of free publicity in the media, institutions of higher education have used athletics to influence political favor in state capitals and as a key factor in athlete (student) recruitment. Being able to brag about having outstanding facilities for athletes and luxury boxes for wealthy fans of football and basketball teams gives departments of athletics significant power and influence on their campuses.

It could be claimed that intercollegiate athletics has become a model for the transmission of economic, rather than educational, values.

The Knight Commission on Intercollegiate Athletics was formed to examine abuses threatening the integrity of intercollegiate athletics and the institutions in which they operate. Based on its examination of numerous areas, such as recruiting and revenues, this Commission recommended a "one-plus-three" model for reform (Knight Commission on Intercollegiate Athletics 1991). Its report suggested presidential control should lead the way for academic integrity, financial integrity, and certification. The Knight Commission added two progress reports in 1992 and 1993 (Knight Commission on Intercollegiate Athletics 1992, 1993). A decade after its initial call for reform and action, this Commission reported that despite some reform efforts, the problems in big-time intercollegiate athletics had grown, rather than diminished (Knight Commission on Intercollegiate Athletics 2001). In "Restoring the Balance Dollars, Values, and the Future of College Sports," the Knight Commission on Intercollegiate Athletics in 2010 advocated for greater transparency in reporting athletic spending, rewarding making academic values a priority, and treating college athletes primarily as students, not as professional athletes. Despite these reports and associated publicity, academic abuses, an expensive arms race, heightened commercialization based on television and corporate interests, and a widening chasm between educational values and intercollegiate athletics persisted and expanded. The Commission characterized some aspects of intercollegiate athletics as corrupt due to extensive unethical conduct. To address these serious issues, the Commission recommended academic reforms, a reduction in the arms race, and a de-emphasis on commercialization.

The Drake Group, Inc., established in 1999, defends "academic integrity in higher education from the corrosive aspects of commercialized college sports" (The Drake Group 2016). Through position papers and advocacy, this group seeks to lead reform efforts to encourage athlete and faculty personal and intellectual growth and integrity. The Drake Group position statements include "O'Bannon, Amateurism, and Viability of College Sport," NCAA Division I Restructure," "Student Fee and Institutional Subsidy Allocations to Fund Intercollegiate Athletics Position Statement," "Athlete Academic Protection Responsibilities," and others.

Despite the issues identified by the Knight Commission and The Drake Group, many still claim sport builds character and teaches moral values. Sport competitions and seeking to win are not the culprits. Rather, could it be that an overemphasis on winning, monetary outcomes, and moral relativism have overtaken more positive outcomes in importance?

Morals vs. Winning

Since sport heroes may harm their reputations and risk their livelihoods through their unethical actions, why do they take such huge risks? Some athletes may decide the financial and personal benefits from winning significantly overshadow the lesser likelihood of being caught. Erosion in character may occur if immoral actions become more important than, and conflict with, moral values, or when a person lacks the moral courage to do what is right. Some athletes, coaches, and fans believe "winning isn't everything; it's the only thing." Without moral values as guides, the emphasis on winning at all levels of sport can lead to increased unethical and unsportsmanlike behaviors. Within the next paragraphs, frequent occurrences in sport will be briefly described in questioning whether or not these actions are ethical or unethical. These include taunting and intimidation, gamesmanship and violence, eligibility, elimination, cheating, gambling, and using performance-enhancing drugs.

Has Winning in Sports Become Too Important?

Given the overwhelming evidence that winners are richly rewarded, it is easy to understand why pressures to win increase. Parents and coaches may begin by encouraging children to play sports, but too often the adults forget the ages of youthful athletes and begin to push, prod, berate, yell, punish, and demean them when they do not perform like professional athletes. Pressures to win may be physical, such as when a coach ignores an injury and plays an athlete to help win a game, despite the potential for a permanent injury. Or, athletes may hide their injuries from coaches and parents because they are fearful of harsh comments questioning their commitment to the team or constant reminders about the financial and time investments in their sport development made by these adults.

Pressures to win also may be psychological, such as when a coach questions an athlete's effort or heart in trying to motivate him or her to play better. When the stakes are higher, such as in a championship game, the pressures from coaches, parents, and fans intensify. One sad example of the destructive consequences of such pressures to win in high school occurred several years ago in Pennsylvania. In the suicide note left by a sophomore quarterback, he stated that after leading his team to the state championship, he could not deal with the pressures of having to repeat as champions two more years. Of course, there also are the self-imposed pressures athletes feel. The intensity of these pressures to win is related to numerous factors, such as the athlete's perceptions of and reactions to pressures from parents, coaches, and fans; confidence or lack of confidence in the athlete's abilities to succeed; and the attraction of the anticipated status and financial benefits accompanying winning.

The pressures to win on youth, interscholastic, and intercollegiate athletes are disproportionate to the likelihood of achieving the desired outcome. For example, in every team sport there are as many nonwinners as there are winners on the scoreboard. In an individual sport such as golf or track and field, there is one winner and numerous nonwinners. The word loser was intentionally not used because of its negative connotation—that is, calling an athlete a loser is so derogatory it may lead to a verbal or physical response. As long as adults involved with sport praise and reward winners and ignore or disapprove of those who do not win on the scoreboard, many athletes and coaches may choose to do almost anything to win. Some athletes and coaches engage in unethical behaviors so they can avoid the negativity associated with not winning.

But, it might be asked, if it is not about winning, then why keep score? An essential differentiation needs to be made between winning (at any cost?) and seeking to win while playing ethically. To illustrate this point, Harold Abrahams in the movie *Chariots of Fire* is questioned about whether he is placing too much emphasis on winning. He responds that he is not trying to win at any cost, but he is seeking to win within the rules.

At best, for every winner there is at least one nonwinner. In contrast, seeking to win remains a viable objective whenever athletes compete. The athlete who is seeking to win tries to play as skillfully as possible. However, despite diligent preparation and effort, this may not result in a victory. So, if competing in sports is not primarily about winning, what are the goals? Shared goals for youth, interscholastic, and intercollegiate sports include having fun, developing sport skills, building character, and learning life lessons.

Maybe one way to help keep winning in perspective is to conceptualize it differently. Winning could be defined as competing against one's self to become the best athlete possible—that is, learning sport skills and using these skills during competitions allow an athlete to measure his or her performance against a personal standard or potential. Another benchmark could be improvement as athletes continue to develop and expand their sport skills. Sometimes athletes compete against a standard like the clock, a course, or a specific distance. In this context, the process of seeking to win is characterized by exerting maximal effort, learning from mistakes, and appreciating incremental progress.

Despite these alternative perspectives, the emphasis placed on winning remains. When sport stresses and rewards only winning, problems emerge at all levels of competition. These include cheating, gamesmanship and violence, discriminatory actions, and the use of performance-enhancing drugs, which will be discussed in the next sections.

Gamesmanship and Violence

Gamesmanship describes creative or even devious strategies and methods used to help win. While technically these actions are not against written sport rules, are they ethical? Gamesmanship is often about getting inside the head of an opponent to gain advantages. Many believe the emphasis on winning, especially as popularized through the electronic and print media, is a major contributing factor in the increase in gamesmanship in sport. For example, many athletes accept that taunting is just a part of the game. So, is the objective of sport to outperform other athletes, or is it to psyche out opponents so they perform at lower levels than they are capable?

Coaches and athletes acknowledge sport instruction books provide information about fundamental skills and playing strategies but are silent about how to be effective in gamesmanship—rather, when the mental side of sport is discussed, it focuses on motivation, confidence, relaxation, and self-control. So, gamesmanship must be learned from coaches, teammates, and others within the context of sports. But, are these role models teaching positive or negative lessons?

One common approach to gamesmanship is to attempt to break the flow or concentration of an opponent. Some baseball players have been accused of using slow play as an intentional distraction to their opponents. A batter may slowly walk to the plate, take considerable time to get set in the batter's box, step out after each pitch, and only step back in after several adjustments to his batting gloves or parts of his uniform, and often ask for a time-out just prior to the pitcher's delivery. In college and professional football, coaches wait until the last possible moment to call a time-out, often causing the field goal kicker to have to kick again since he had already begun his kicking motion before the whistle stopping play was heard. A glaring stare at an opponent after making a successful move in wrestling may help in breaking his concentration.

Another gamesmanship strategy is to try to get opponents to overthink or underthink their play. Athletes may allege a specific sport is just not their best or they are not very skilled in this sport in trying to get opponents to let up or not play as well as possible. Another ploy often used in tennis occurs when players ask their opponents if there are weaker strokes that they would like more setups for during the warm-up prior to matches. In baseball, catchers try to get umpires to call pitches strikes by "framing pitches," and baserunners on second try to steal catchers' signs to pitchers. Flopping, or faking being fouled, occurs in basketball, soccer, and football. Some defend actions such as these by stating there are no criteria or lines drawn about whether these actions are or are not acceptable. Simply stated, athletes and coaches engage in gamesmanship to help win because they think they can get away with it without being penalized or there is no specific rule against their actions.

Taunting, which derides or mocks another person, is another frequently used type of gamesmanship. Taunting often comes from fans who criticize the play of opponents, call them names, or yell to try to throw them off their games. A large number of athletes and fans believe taunting is just a part of the game. Some fans assume the price of admission gives them the right to mock or jeer opponents, since this is part of the home court (or field) advantage. For example, sometimes yelling "air ball" occurs when an athlete on the visiting team misses the rim entirely on a shot attempt. Despite the hurtful nature of taunting in youth, scholastic, and collegiate sports, seldom have taunting policies been adopted and enforced. One impressive exception, however, was the Wisconsin Interscholastic Athletic Association in 2015 that banned taunting chants, such as "air-ball," directed at opponents or their spectators during games as disrespectful and unsporting behavior (Bieler 2016).

A few years ago at a men's intercollegiate basketball game, the fans held up pictures of Duke University's J.J. Redick's mother and sister and yelled disparaging comments about them at him. Some argued this was unsportsmanlike; others claimed it was their right as fans to do whatever they could to distract the Atlantic Coast Conference's leading scorer at the time and maybe help the home team win. Taunting such as this continues to escalate as fans at lower levels of sport mimic intercollegiate and professional sports fans. For example, a casual observer at a youth soccer or basketball game might be shocked to hear the words some parents, siblings, and friends shout at children on the other teams, coaches, and officials.

Some athletes seem to take pleasure in taunting opponents when they score touchdowns, hit home runs, or dunk basketballs. At what point do individual and team celebrations intentionally humiliate or demean opponents? Some would argue that running up the score on an over-matched opponent is a form of taunting; others would defend running up the score as sending a clear message of superiority telling opponents they must improve.

Moral suasion to change this form of gamesmanship has failed to eliminate taunting, with sport behaviors continuing to deteriorate and get more abusive. As a result, sport governing organizations and educational institutions have established policies limiting what can be said and done. Codes of ethics and personal conduct contracts are illustrations of initiatives to eliminate taunting and emphasize sportsmanship.

Trash talkers often challenge their opponents using boasts about their skills or insults about opponents' abilities. For example, an athlete might mockingly ask, "Is that the best you got?" as if to suggest that the trash talker is such a better player, and there is no way the opponent can stop him or her from scoring. Trash talkers, who may believe this is one of sport's most beloved practices, use this gamesmanship ploy to psyche out or get into the heads of their opponents and maybe throw them off their games. Many athletes are able to ignore or disregard trash talking and focus on playing well; others are bothered, distracted, and insulted. Whenever these latter reactions occur, the trash talker has succeeded in gaining an advantage to help win, which was the goal.

One objective of taunting and trash talking is intimidation, or behaviors intended to keep opponents from performing as skillfully as they potentially could. Physical and psychological intimidation has become normal actions for some athletes. A hard foul on a shooter, a crushing tackle on a wide receiver, a pitcher throwing a high and tight fastball to a batter, and a laser forehand hit toward the head of a player at the tennis net are examples of how athletes seek to instill doubt or force timidity in opponents. Is this good strategy, playing fair, trying to injure an opponent, and/ or intimidation?

Intimidation includes intentional behaviors that cause a person to fear imminent injury or harm. Some athletes seek to intimidate through violent tackles and other physical contacts that send the message of "don't mess with me or you'll get hurt." The label of a dirty player or enforcer is associated with intimidation because this player has earned a reputation for intentionally hurting opponents. A disdainful stare is often used to intimidate a less-confident opponent. Verbal abuse, including taunting and trash talking, also can be used to intimidate.

Psychological intimidation is shrewder than physical intimidation. Is trying to get inside someone's head to throw him or her off just how the game is played? While Larry Bird and Michael Jordan were two of the all-time greatest players in the National Basketball Association (NBA), they also were two of the most prodigious trash talkers in trying to intimidate their opponents. Are their examples of trash talking what youth, interscholastic, and intercollegiate athletes should follow?

Some coaches use intimidation to try to motivate athletes as they pressure, threaten, or coerce them. For example, a coach may use negative feedback, obscene language, and physical punishments in hopes of changing an athlete's performance or effort. Coach Mike Rice was fired in 2013 when a video of practice showed him verbally and physical abusing Rutgers University basketball players. Naismith Memorial Hall of Fame coach Bobby Knight has been praised as an outstanding coach, yet many have questioned his use of vulgarity and in-your-face confrontations with athletes on his teams.

Because of the significant power differential, coaches attempt to control the behaviors of their athletes in ways that could be considered physically or verbally abusive. For example, in 2015 football players at the University of Illinois complained of violent confrontations with and pressures from head football coach Tim Beckman not to report injuries and obtain medical treatment. Under the threat of punishments, less playing time, loss of grants-in-aid, or expulsion from the team, most athletes feel forced to follow coaches' directives. With quitting their sports as the only perceived alternative, many athletes are so intimidated they will violate sport rules or sport governing association rules, engage in unethical behaviors, or harm their bodies by playing while injured or training excessively.

Coercion, especially if linked with a threatened loss of favor with the coach, has resulted in some athletes being sexually abused by their coaches. A coach's intimidating control may begin when a highly skilled athlete comes under the influence of a coach who promises the likelihood of a college grant-in-aid, gold medal, or professional sport contract if this athlete will do what the coach says. Coaches spend considerable time with and have easy access to children and adolescents because they are trusted by parents and athletes. So, extra practice times to further develop an athlete's skills can provide opportunities for a predatory coach to begin inappropriate touching, often leading to sexual assault. In addition, coaches must be held accountable for sexually harassing their athletes. In the case of Anson Dorrance, the women's soccer coach at the University of North Carolina at Chapel Hill, he and the institution settled a lawsuit out of court because of his inappropriate behaviors relative to the sexual activities of members of his teams.

Until recent years, behaviors by coaches were seldom questioned because the cultures in various sports gave coaches almost total control over the lives of their athletes. As a result of intimidating and harassing behaviors by coaches, sport organizations and educational institutions have taken steps to reduce the abuse of power by coaches. Development and enforcement of codes of conduct and signed contracts of expected behaviors are examples of setting boundaries for the appropriate use of power by coaches.

One more issue related to intimidation is the increasing level of violence in sports. Violence is directly related to what coaches teach and/or permit their athletes to do, what officials allow, and what is modeled by athletes at higher levels of competition. Since coaches stress aggressive play, especially in contact and collision sports, they may permit, encourage, and even teach their athletes to be so aggressive they engage in violent actions—that is, coaches, through their verbal and nonverbal cues, shape and largely control how athletes play. Depending on whether violent hits are the standard expectation or disapproved by the coach, athletes will learn to respond accordingly by engaging or not engaging in violent play.

While rule books are quite clear about allowable and non-allowable actions by athletes, officials determine how each game is called. So, the oft-heard comment that the officials are "letting them play" is actually stating few penalties are being assessed for hard contact. The escalation of such actions to the point of violence often results because many athletes believe right is defined as whatever is not penalized. Athletes are highly influenced by what they see professional and collegiate athletes do on television (and on YouTube), as violent actions by professional and collegiate athletes are mimicked by younger athletes. Violent actions of athletes are more likely to occur when they see their violent actions help the team win, and violence is cheered by fans. These benefits in the minds of impressionable athletes far outweigh the possibility of getting penalized.

The emphasis on winning has led to an increase in violence among parents, fans, and athletes outside of the actual game. For example, sadly, Thomas Junta beat Michael Costin to death in a fight after a youth hockey practice in which the sons of both men participated. Out-of-control actions such as this have become all-too-frequent occurrences, such as parents attacking young athletes, their coaches, the officials, and other fans. Coaches have attacked officials, opposing athletes, and fans. A T-Ball coach offered a player $25 if he would hit an autistic teammate in the face with a ball in an attempt to sideline him from a playoff game, so the coach would not have to play the injured (and poor-skilled) youth. These violent acts happen because those involved have forgotten sport is only a game, not a life-or-death situation.

Athletes, especially in sports in which physical contact is integral to the game, sometimes have a difficult time drawing the line between adhering to the rules and breaking not only the letter of the rules but also the spirit of the rules. The spirit of the rules refers to playing the game without resorting to gamesmanship or strategies designed to exploit the rules to gain unfair advantages. Constitutive rules govern how a specific sport should be played and differentiate it from other sports. Proscriptive rules forbid or prohibit certain actions, such as undercutting in basketball or clipping in football. Often these rules have been developed and are enforced to reduce and prevent violent actions that cause serious injuries and harm athletes. Some proscriptive rules have been added to address behaviors such as hockey players using their sticks as weapons and athletes brawling or fighting. Sportsmanship rules have been added in an attempt to thwart out-of-control actions, such as when a soccer player receives a red card (resulting in disqualification) for repeatedly tripping opponents or 15-yard penalties in football for unsportsmanlike conduct such as targeting (in college football) or helmet-to-helmet hits that often cause concussions in professional football.

Is violence on the rise in sports because athletes view opponents as objects to be removed in the headlong pursuit of victory? It is easier to intentionally harm another person when he or she is viewed as an object, rather than a human being. For example, in 1994 the cronies of Tonya Harding hit her rival, Nancy Kerrigan, in the knee to incapacitate her so she would be unable to compete in the United States Figure Skating Championships, which was the qualifying event for selecting figure skaters for the Olympic Games. In 2006, Mitch Cozad, backup punter at the University of Northern Colorado, stabbed the starting punter in his kicking leg to increase Cozad's chances of getting to play. Such actions seem to indicate individuals will resort to violence if it will benefit them personally.

Has the seriousness of injuries increased because some coaches urge athletes to be more aggressive? For example, John Chaney, former basketball coach at Temple University, in 2005 directed an athlete on his team to rough up an opponent. ESPN's SportsCenter often shows and celebrates vicious hits in football and ice hockey. In 2015, Los Angeles Dodger Chase Utley slid hard and late into second base and flipped the New York Mets' shortstop Ruben Tejada, who broke his leg on the play. While Utley claimed he was just trying to break up a potential double play, his controversial slide (which led to a rule change prior to the 2016 season making the runner and batter automatically out for a similar action in putting another athlete in danger of a serious injury. These examples seemingly reinforce that violence is central to how these games should be played. Is it any wonder impressionable young athletes mimic their sport heroes? During the telecast of a collegiate bowl game in 2008, the broadcasters in discussing a video of a youth football game praised one athlete who violently blindsided and knocked out his opponent.

In thinking about violence in sport, it is important to ask why violence is permitted in sports, why it is taught, why it is condoned, and why it is rewarded. Violence is used to intimidate and thereby gain competitive advantages. Violence increases whenever proscriptive and sportsmanship rules are not enforced—that is, athletes learn quickly what they can and cannot get by with and then act accordingly. For example, basketball players are coached to see how the game is being officiated and then to adjust their actions accordingly. So, if holding or hand-checking is not being penalized, athletes are coached to engage in these actions as aggressively as allowed. The bottom line is that overly aggressive and violent actions have become more acceptable; deciding where to draw the line between ethical and unethical behavior has become blurred for many athletes, coaches, and fans.

Violence is taught by some coaches, teammates, and parents because it is perceived it can help in gaining competitive advantages. What else would lead a father to sharpen the exposed edges of his son's football helmet in order to injure opponents and get the opposing team's best players off the field because they are bleeding? It is argued that some fans want to see hockey players drop their sticks and fight, deadly crashes on the racetrack, or incapacitating hits in football. Some sport managers admit they permit and encourage violence because it sells. Athletes realize that sometimes violent behaviors in sport are rewarded. A hard slide into the shortstop to break up an attempted double play and hacking the low post player on his or her way up for an easy two points are considered by many to be good aggressive plays. Is there a point at which actions like these violate the letter and spirit of the rules?

It is argued by many that gamesmanship, including taunting and trash talking, intimidation, and violence signal a decline in sportsmanship and illustrate a general loss of civility in sport. Is an emphasis on playing by the letter and spirit of the rules needed? Can ethical behaviors in sport replace gaining advantages in any ways possible to help win?

Eligibility

Some people may question how eligibility issues relate to sport ethics. In youth sports, there are age and weight categories specifying who can or cannot play on teams so competition is fair and equitable. However, it seems for every rule, such as age limits or number of years playing interscholastic sports, there are attempts to get around these rules. For example, some parents choose to gain developmental advantages for their sons by holding them back a grade in elementary or middle school so they will be physically more developed when competing in interscholastic sports. Is attempting to gain this physical advantage ethical?

A huge issue in interscholastic sports today deals with recruiting. Private schools and special interest or magnet schools, which do not have defined attendance areas as do public schools, are free to recruit skilled athletes to attend their schools and offer scholarships. Some people argue this is unethical because of the unfair advantages gained by teams with recruited athletes. Another controversial issue in schools is whether "no pass, no play," a policy requiring a specified level of academic achievement to be eligible to play, discriminates against adolescents based on socioeconomic status and associated learning opportunities.

The most controversial issue surrounding eligibility in colleges also relates to academics. As coaches identify prospective athletes who they want to play on their teams, they may learn recruits have low grade point averages or earned low scores on standardized admission tests. Many coaches seek and obtain preferred admissions for marginally prepared students based on the argument that these adolescents deserve educational opportunities. It may be more likely these coaches simply believe these highly talented athletes can help their teams win. Once these students are admitted, despite tutoring and other academic support services, many students struggle academically and fail, primarily because they did not have the requisite preparation for college-level work.

Intercollegiate athletic associations require these athletes make normal progress toward their chosen program of study to maintain eligibility to compete. This sometimes results in athletes being given unearned grades and athletes taking a smorgasbord of courses that do not lead to degrees, such as at the

University of North Carolina at Chapel Hill (Wainstein, Jay, and Kukowski 2014). The low graduation rates associated with sport teams at some institutions illustrates this ethical issue.

Elimination

In some cases, there may be ethical issues associated with the elimination of athletes from sports. Young athletes, when asked why they participate in sports, consistently respond that having fun is most important. Several studies and researchers have stated that 50 to 70 percent of youth have self-selected, for physical and psychological reasons, out of sports by age 13. These young athletes say they drop out because they are not having fun anymore, are not getting to play or to play a preferred position, have limited input because programs are controlled by parents and coaches, are tired of the intensity of their training, and are bothered by receiving so much negative feedback.

Many middle and secondary school students are cut from teams or choose not to even try to make teams because they perceive they lack the skills. Some adolescents have grown tired of coaches or parents pushing them too hard in sports, such as through the expectation to concentrate on only one sport year-round, even at times when they have been injured due to overtraining. Other young athletes do not want to deal with the expectations of their communities to lead their teams to championships or parents who pressure them to succeed because of huge financial investments in their training programs.

Most students in high school do not play on sport teams. They have already opted out or been cut in the narrowing of the sport funnel as fewer participation opportunities are provided. This elimination process is significant at the collegiate level with between 2.6 percent (wrestling) and 11.9 percent (lacrosse) of scholastic athletes playing sports in college, while only 1.6 percent (football), 1.2 percent (men's basketball), and 0.9 percent (women's basketball) advance from college to the

National Football League (NFL), NBA, and Women's National Basketball Association (WNBA) respectively (NCAA 2016). Some college athletes leave sports because of year-round training, coaches' demands for improved performance, and pressures to win. To address the issue of dropout, maybe athletes, parents, and coaches should agree on the purpose of sports at each level. Is it for fun, fitness, character development, competitions primarily among the highly skilled, or primarily to win?

Cheating

An overemphasis on winning is the primary culprit, many suggest, that leads to cheating in sports. While seeking to win is one reason why sports are played, is it how the victory is sought after and attained that is the issue? It seems the goal for some athletes and coaches is to try to outwit the officials. For others, it is how to circumvent rules for personal advantage. Cheating takes many forms, such as copying a classmate's paper or exam to help maintain eligibility or giving a college athlete or family member financial benefits not permitted by the rules to influence the athlete's decision about which college to attend. Is it cheating to claim to catch a pass you know hit the ground first or fake an injury to stop the clock so the kicker can attempt a potential game-winning field goal?

Possibly the most widespread controversy related to winning is what is or is not fair, honest, ethical, or right within sport. Some athletes and coaches believe it is cheating only if you get caught. They feel no ethical obligation to play by the rules, unless they are forced to comply. For example, Bill Belichick and the New England Patriots were suspected of stealing signs from opposing teams for years. In 2007, Belichick and the Patriots were caught videotaping hand signals from defensive coaches from the New York Jets. They were fined by the NFL commissioner for intentionally defying a policy statement that such cheating would not be tolerated. In 2015, the NFL fined the New England Patriots $1 million and a first-round pick in

2016 and fourth-round pick in 2017 because team personnel were found to have deliberately deflated footballs during the 2015 American Football Conference Championship Game. Patriots' Quarterback Tom Brady was initially suspended for four games, but the NFL Players Association appealed on his behalf and a U.S. district court judge erased this suspension. However, in 2016, a U.S. appeals court reinstated his four-game suspension.

The driving force for cheating within sport is to gain competitive advantages—that is, some athletes and coaches behave as if they will do whatever it takes to win. This may mean intentionally teaching, learning, and executing actions in violation of the rules. For example, a football coach may teach offensive linemen how to hold defensive linemen in ways less likely to be flagged by officials. Athletes may learn and practice these techniques until they become so proficient their holding helps win more games. Three questions could be asked to determine if this is cheating or not (Blanchard and Peale 1988). First, is using techniques to hold an opponent permitted within the rules? Second, is the use of these techniques fair to all concerned? Third, does using these holding techniques make each athlete feel morally good about himself or herself? If the answer to any of these questions is "no," is this cheating?

What about this situation? Near the end of a closely contested basketball game, athletes on the team with fewer points intentionally foul opposing athletes hoping free throws will be missed and possession of the ball can be regained and more points scored to try to win. Is this cheating since there is an intentional rule violation in opposition to the spirit of the rules? Is this an acceptable form of gamesmanship since fouling is permitted along with awarding of free throws to the person fouled? While the strategy used in the NBA called "Hack a Shaq," which is named for 15-time All-Star Shaquille O'Neal who struggled with his free throw shooting, is allowed by the rules, does this demonstrate sportsmanship or ethical conduct? Are these good strategies to use when seeking to win? Should the game be played to use the rules in attempting to gain advantages? and Is playing the game this way right or ethical?

Many coaches and athletes claim certain behaviors are acceptable, and even expected, due to a sport's unique culture; others not engaged in a particular sport simply may not understand how the game is played. For example, fighting in ice hockey is often perceived as just a part of the game, but it is not in football. A runner attempting to score and knocking over the catcher who has the ball is the expectation in baseball, while knocking down a defender on the way to the basket is not. The goalie in soccer advancing ahead of the line to narrow the angle for a penalty kick is perceived by many to be gaining a strategic advantage, while trying to serve from inside the baseline in tennis would not be. Accidentally moving a golf ball is a penalty stroke for an intercollegiate golfer, but typically it is not for the weekend duffer. Is fighting in ice hockey, knocking over the catcher, reducing the angle in soccer, or failing to assess a penalty stroke cheating?

For some athletes, coaches, and fans, whether something is cheating depends on whether this action can be done without getting caught. Others state there is no such thing as cheating inside of sport because as long as athletes and coaches are willing to live with the consequences of rule violations, then it is justifiable to try almost anything. Cheating becomes even more valued if athletes or coaches are not penalized for rule violations that help their teams win. Some would argue cheating is permissible because they are playing by the letter of the rules as enforced by the officials (i.e., no penalty, no harm).

If the objective of the game is to see how effectively coaches and athletes can break sport rules to their advantage, is this cheating? The spirit of the rules dictates fair play, sportsmanship, and honesty. Sportsmanship calls for playing within the rules as written with firm resolve. Athletes who behave ethically play by the spirit of the rules and will not violate the rules strategically to gain advantages.

Cheating also includes actions violating regulations of sport governing organizations, such as those dealing with recruiting and eligibility. The purpose of these rules is to equalize competition so outcomes are based on skilled performances, not on who can find ways to entice more of the best athletes to play for one team. But, many coaches and athletes circumvent these regulations because they believe it will increase the possibility of winning. For example, Kelvin Sampson, former basketball coach at the University of Oklahoma and Indiana University, made hundreds of impermissible phone calls to prospective recruits. Was this cheating?

Violations of recruiting regulations also occur at the youth and interscholastic levels. Some youth sport coaches recruit the most highly skilled athletes for travel teams or when forming teams to represent communities in elimination tournaments, often through gifts like athletic shoes, apparel, and equipment. Some interscholastic coaches use financial benefits to influence families to move or change the legal guardians of athletes so they will live in a required attendance area associated with these coaches' teams. When select teams, private schools, public magnet schools, or foreign-exchange programs are involved, the family may not have to move so an athlete is eligible to play on a certain team or coach, but recruiting is still happening. Some would argue such actions cause no harm because an athlete should be able to maximize his or her competitive opportunities. Others claim the recruitment of youth and adolescents is cheating because it violates the spirit of the rules.

Sport is replete with violations of eligibility rules at all levels of sport. In youth sport, cheating often involves age requirements, which are set to equalize competition between youth at different developmental levels. For example, one father falsified his son's birth certificate, which enabled Danny Almonte to pitch his team to third place in the Little League World Series in 2001, although he was 14 years old (two years too old). To qualify for teams with weight limitations or compete in a lower weight category in wrestling, some athletes are encouraged by coaches to change their developmentally appropriate weight through unsafe measures, such as running in rubber suits and not hydrating properly. The rationale given for such dangerous practices is these athletes or their teams will increase their chances of winning.

In interscholastic sports and intercollegiate athletics, cheating is often associated with giving unearned grades or changing the grades of some athletes to keep them eligible. Despite pages of regulations governing intercollegiate athletes, a few coaches knowingly play athletes who have not met the required standards of academic eligibility, such as transfer admissibility, minimum number of hours passed with earned grades, progress made toward earning meaningful degrees, and declaration of majors. Some argue, however, that athletes who struggle academically should be granted exemptions to these academic standards because they were not adequately prepared for college-level work when admitted. Some believe so strongly these rules are unjust they feel justified in breaking them to keep their athletes eligible to help win games.

Since coaches' jobs depend on winning, rule-breaking behaviors are sometimes overlooked by sport managers, encouraged by fans, and condoned by schools and colleges. For example, the sexual assaults by football players at many colleges are often covered up or not punished by coaches, and complicit athletic directors and even presidents, as happened at Baylor University between 2012 and 2015. Athletes often know they will not be held responsible for their aberrant behaviors by coaches who will mishandle sexual assault reports to keep their athletes on the team. Similarly, athletes also know their coaches are violating recruiting rules, such as at the University of Mississippi, and academic eligibility standards, such as at Syracuse University. Athletes realize that if coaches will seemingly do anything to win, they are more likely to cheat. These athletes are learning cheating and deception are accepted as the way the game is played.

Some athletes and coaches claim that if they are not cheating, then they are not trying hard enough to win. Have unethical actions been accepted as just the way the game is played?

Sometimes cheaters gain advantages and are praised for their creativity and rewarded for winning as long as what they do is not harmful or dirty. Is any cheating right? Since many coaches cheat during recruiting, such as by giving inducements or making too many contacts with recruits, are the best recruiters those who cheat in signing the best recruits without getting caught?

Has cheating increased because winning has become so important? For example, did Major League Baseball (MLB) ignore the known use of steroids and other performance-enhancing drugs because teams' revenues were increasing? Have the cultures of some sports accepted cheating, such as stealing signs, videotaping other teams' signals, and hand-checking on defense in basketball, as good strategies? That is, does today's apparent condoning of cheating in sport mean athletes, coaches, and fans have developed a tolerance to cheating like a drug abuser builds up a tolerance for a physically dependent drug like cocaine or heroin? If this is the case, is this ethical?

Gambling

One specific example of cheating is gambling, such as when athletes are enticed by gamblers to fix the outcomes of games. By controlling the point spread, readily available in numerous media, athletes and gamblers can make money. (Point-shaving occurs when gamblers pay athletes to manipulate the spread between the projected scores of two teams to enable the gamblers to win their bets.) Bookmakers and gamblers paid 33 basketball players from seven colleges, including City College of New York (winner of the 1950 National Invitational Tournament [NIT] and the 1950 NCAA championship) and the University of Kentucky, to shave points in 49 games. Most of the players received suspended sentences, while the fixers and gamblers served time in prison. City College of New York de-emphasized basketball. The Southeastern Conference banned the University of Kentucky, winner of the NCAA basketball championship in

1948, 1949, and 1951, from conference play, and other institutions were urged by the NCAA not to play the team; as a result, Kentucky canceled its 1952–1953 season. The NBA banned all of the players involved from playing in its league. Most, but not all, people view fixing games as unethical.

Green Bay Packer and the league's Most Valuable Player (MVP) as running back Paul Hornung and Detroit Lions All-Pro defensive tackle Alex Karras were suspended for the 1963 season for gambling on NFL games. Former Cincinnati Red All-Star and manager Pete Rose was banned for life from MLB for gambling on baseball games, including those in which he played and managed. Professional football player Michael Vick, who owned the property housing Bad Newz Kennels, was found guilty with accomplices of the torture and brutal execution of dogs. Vick was found to have engaged in betting over $40,000 on the outcome of illegal dog fights. He served 548 days in prison. The NFL suspended him indefinitely for killing dogs and gambling, but reinstated him after his release from prison.

NBA referee Tim Donaghy provided information to gamblers, bet on NBA games, and may have affected the outcome of games through his officiating calls during his 13 seasons as a NBA official. When such actions occur, they are typically condemned. But is gambling wrong when it is a small wager among friends on the golf course, or if a person joins an online pool during March Madness?

Having discussed several problems and controversies characteristic of several levels of sport, the next discussion examines issues specifically confronting youth, interscholastic, and intercollegiate sport. Each section will begin with a description of the goals, or the rationale for why individuals believe sport should exist at these levels. Next, specific problems will be discussed to demonstrate how they threaten the integrity of sport. Finally, recommendations will be offered for addressing the issues as sports at these three levels seek to achieve potential benefits in morally responsible ways.

Discriminatory Actions and Societal Factors

Sport potentially offers a welcoming environment for the blending together of people and their experiences. Sport has been praised for being a melting pot as immigrant groups used sport to become assimilated into the culture of the United States. The question about whether sport leads society or sport reflects society has been discussed for years. For example, when Jackie Robinson began playing for the Brooklyn Dodgers in 1947, baseball was applauded for integrating the national pastime before many people in their daily lives were as welcoming. However, it also could be argued that the integration of professional baseball, football, and basketball occurred because it was financially beneficial (i.e., to field the best teams to make the highest profits, the teams needed the best talent available, which included African Americans). While sport overall can be a socializing influence, its success historically in accepting all athletes on an equitable basis has been less praiseworthy. Some argue unethical behaviors in sport reflect a general erosion of moral values in society.

Social class, while not as stratified as in other countries, remains a significant reality of life in the United States. A person's socioeconomic heritage influences what sports may be played due to access to equipment, facilities, coaching, and competitions. For example, basketball is called the city game because only a ball and goal are required; competitors are readily available, and then the game is on. This is quite different from golf, which requires a set of clubs, continuing supply of balls, greens fees for playing courses, and money to travel to competitions. Most of the best golfers come from families with the financial resources to support playing this sport; basketball players come from all socioeconomic strata, although the numbers playing basketball are disproportionate from those less well-off financially. From an ethical perspective, it could be asked if this situation is right, just, or fair. While interscholastic sports have removed some of the financial barriers for playing tennis, swimming, or wrestling, athletes who play certain sports largely reflect the limitations of their socioeconomic status.

Race, ethnicity, and racism remain controversial issues in sports, even though many of the discriminatory practices of the past have been eliminated. While the exclusion of African Americans and members of other races and ethnicities from some sports is viewed as discriminatory today, at one time their exclusion reflected attitudes held by many individuals in the United States. Some segregated sport opportunities were enjoyed by African Americans and other ethnic minorities, while sometimes Caucasian teams welcomed all athletes on equitable terms. For example, it took an entire season, but the Caucasian and African American athletes and coaches finally came to respect each other in a newly integrated high school in Virginia as chronicled in the movie *Remember the Titans*.

While most discrimination against ethnic minority athletes has been eliminated relative to making teams, earning playing time, getting grants-in-aid, and securing living accommodations, some residual racism persists. For example, in 2014 NBA commissioner Adam Silver forced Los Angeles Clippers' owner Donald Sterling to sell the team because of his racist comments. Also in 2014, racism was part of the bullying and racial slurs directed toward Jonathan Martin by Richard Incognito of the Miami Dolphins. Racial slurs and epithets are sometimes heard in taunting and trash talking, especially in international soccer matches.

Some ethnic minority athletes enter college through preferred admissions or are less prepared than their peers, often as a result of socioeconomic barriers at home or their educational programs ill-prepared them for college-level work. While many benefit from the academic support services provided athletes, some athletes still are unable (or unwilling) to earn degrees.

Some doors remain barred to ethnic minorities because of prejudice, as progress to fully integrate the coaching and management ranks of sport has been much slower than athletes' acceptance onto teams. In contrast with the number of athletes, especially in basketball, football, and track and field, relatively few ethnic minorities have been hired as head coaches, athletic directors, and in other sport management roles. Many argue Caucasians who make hiring decisions are reluctant to hire, and even interview, ethnic minority coaches and sport managers. Justice and fairness and federal laws demand opening vacancies to the best qualified candidates and hiring practices eliminate discriminatory treatment.

Just like for ethnic minorities, females continue to struggle to gain full acceptance as athletes, coaches, and sport managers (Acosta and Carpenter 2014). While some females have broken through the glass ceiling restricting their opportunities, sport remains predominately a man's world. At times, sexism continues to affect societal attitudes toward the role of and sport opportunities provided to females.

Females in the United States were usually excluded from sports until the twentieth century, although there were exceptions, such as in women's colleges. Societal attitudes restricted most females to their homes and the fulfillment of domestic responsibilities. Even during the early decades of the twentieth century, females were seldom competitive athletes. Exceptions to this exclusion included a limited number of Caucasian women at private clubs where they engaged in golf, tennis, and swimming, some African American females who attended segregated schools and colleges, like Tennessee State, and some girls' basketball teams sponsored by rural schools. While the women's rights movement helped lead the way for the elimination of many discriminatory practices in society, historically sport lagged behind, rather than led the way, in its acceptance of females as equals to males.

The role of females in sport continues to be shaped by males who direct, coach, and report on all levels of competition. Many males believe females are not as interested in sport or lack the expertise to coach, manage, and lead sport programs. For example, men who are most often the scholastic and collegiate athletic directors hire coaches. For example, 77.7 percent of directors of athletics in NCAA institutions are males (Acosta and Carpenter 2014). More often than not, they have chosen to hire males. For example, in NCAA institutions, 56.6 percent of the head coaches of women's teams are males (Acosta and Carpenter 2014). Maybe this is because more men apply, men are more qualified, or it is perceived female candidates are less interested, unqualified, or not likely to continue in sport given family responsibilities. Or, maybe females are discriminated against because many in the "'old boys' network" simply do not want to hire and work with them.

A breakthrough for females began in the 1970s as changing perceptions and federal laws resulted in a dramatic increase in playing opportunities for females in youth, interscholastic, and intercollegiate sport. Sometimes it required lawsuits or the threats of legal action before sport governing organizations permitted females to play alongside males. Other sport organizations began to initiate teams and programs in response to increased interest expressed by females.

Title IX of the Education Amendments of 1972 states no person can be discriminated against or precluded from participation in any interscholastic or intercollegiate sport program. As a direct outcome of this federal legislation, schools greatly expanded their sport offerings for girls and began to treat them more fairly, such as by providing teams, uniforms, equipment, coaches, access to facilities, and travel expenses, where once these were available only to boys. Since this law requires schools to cease historical practices of relegating girls to the stands to watch or the sidelines to cheer, these females could now dream of receiving grants-in-aid to fund their education and having professional careers in sports. Still, though, a few states provided interscholastic sport teams for females in nontraditional seasons, while males continued to play during traditional seasons. The rationale for this practice was to maximally use facilities. The courts found this practice discriminated against females because they were disadvantaged in being recruited or having the opportunity to receive grants-in-aid.

While Title IX significantly impacted intercollegiate athletic programs, it was much more controversial. When this legislation was passed, intercollegiate athletics was almost exclusively the domain of males. Most males perceived Title IX as a threat to the status quo of having control over all the money, facilities, and benefits associated with sport. The first reaction of some directors of athletics, coaches, and the NCAA was so negative that some males attempted to get Congress to prevent the application of this law to athletics. These attempts met no success. Several regulations, interpretations, clarifications, and lawsuits have reinforced this law, which requires equal opportunities in educational institutions, including athletics for both sexes.

Specifically, this legislation requires equal opportunity in interscholastic sport and intercollegiate athletics in three areas: (a) financial assistance, which must be substantially equal to the ratio of male to female athletes; (b) equivalent treatment, benefits, and opportunities in program areas, such as the provision of equipment and supplies, travel and per diem allowance, and provision of locker rooms, practice and competitive facilities, and recruitment; and (c) the interests and abilities of male and female students must be equally and effectively accommodated (U.S. Department of Justice 1972).

Since 1979 when these three areas were described in the Final Policy Interpretations (U.S. Department of Education 1979), significant progress has been achieved by female athletes in schools and colleges. In some institutions, however, there has been resistance to providing equal opportunities for females with residual discriminatory practices. In almost all colleges, males continue to receive more funding for recruiting, athletic scholarships, and operations than females.

The most controversial requirement in Title IX deals with meeting the interests and abilities of male and female students. Institutions are given the option to choose between one of three ways to comply with this requirement: (a) demonstrate that the participation opportunities are substantially proportionate to the undergraduate student enrollment; (b) demonstrate a continuing practice of program expansion in response to developing interests and abilities of the underrepresented sex; or (c) show the interest and abilities of the members of the underrepresented sex have been fully and effectively accommodated (U.S. Department of Education 2003).

The first of these, which has been called a safe harbor, has been adopted by many institutions because it was believed to be easier to demonstrate. The problem with this option is proportionality has been accused of being the same as a quota—that is, since the percentage of athletes by sex is expected to mirror the percentage of undergraduate students by sex, some institutions have eliminated men's teams claiming Title IX was the causal factor. Athletes and coaches from these teams have argued in their lawsuits that this was reverse discrimination. The courts have consistently disagreed by stating Title IX does not require and does not support the elimination of men's teams as a way to provide substantially proportionate participation opportunities for both sexes. The use of roster management by limiting the number of male athletes, and especially walk-ons who are not recruited, also is not congruent with the spirit of Title IX, which supports increased opportunities for the underrepresented sex, not a reduction in the opportunities for the other sex. The other two options are equally effective ways to comply with ensuring equal participation opportunities. Both have been used by institutions as they continue to expand athletic opportunities for females, unless they have already met their interests and abilities (U.S. Department of Education 2010).

In summary, although social class is initially influenced by economics, an adult's social class has less to do with circumstances of birth than with abilities, opportunities, and what is done with these. Still, societal factors, including race and sex, continue to present ethical challenges to sport as some discriminatory treatment persists. Athletes know when coaches, sport administrators, and fans treat others disparately due to their socioeconomic status, race, ethnicity, and sex. To ensure equitable treatment, adults can model that each person is respected on the basis of personal merit, not on some characteristic of birth or other circumstance. Behaving in morally acceptable ways demands this.

Moral Callousness

Whenever athletes, coaches, and fans justify taunting, intimidation, violence, cheating, use of performance-enhancing drugs, and related behaviors, they may be illustrating moral callousness (Kretchmar 2005). This term describes how people harden their feelings, like forming calluses on the hands from manual labor, so they no longer feel their actions are morally wrong. For example, athletes may justify their use of performance-enhancing drugs by stating that all other athletes are using these drugs, so they have no choice but to use them to compete on a level-playing field or have a chance to win. Or, coaches may rationalize violating recruiting regulations by claiming other coaches are cheating in recruiting, therefore, their cheating must be acceptable, too. When asked, athletes and coaches who violate the rules in these or similar ways may rationalize they have done nothing morally wrong.

To further illustrate this concept of moral callousness, many athletes, when asked, acknowledge their coaches teach them how to cheat. For example, some coaches teach basketball and football players how to gain advantages, such as through holding, in ways difficult to detect. Some soccer goalies are taught how to advance past the goal line on penalty kicks, even though the rules prohibit it. Basketball players who shoot free throws at higher success rates may be taught how to take the places of their fouled teammates who are less accurate shooters. Some coaches alter playing fields in ways that benefit their teams and teach their players to take advantage of how their fields have been changed. Many coaches tell their athletes never to tell an official about knocking the ball out-of-bounds or not catching a pass, if the officials' incorrect calls are in their team's favor.

The concept of moral callousness suggests that over time individuals can grow hardened, such as when athletes make less morally reasoned decisions the longer they are involved with sports (Bredemeier 1995; Rudd and Stoll 2004). To emphasize how intentionally fouling at the end of the game to stop the clock may illustrate moral callousness, consider how the game was played decades ago. This type of rule violation did not occur, and the intentional grabbing or hacking of an opponent to prolong the game would have been viewed as unsportsmanlike. Has the perception changed because this strategy might help win the game? What about when a football player fakes an injury near the end of a game to get the clock stopped? Some affirm this is cheating, while others argue this is just good strategy. Has moral callousness in some sports changed intentional rule violations into good strategies?

Is sport ethics an oxymoron? Has there been a moral drift toward the acceptance of more unethical behaviors in sport? Or, can moral values and character be developed in and through sport? The next section will explore the interface between amateur sport, ethical conduct, and importance of character and moral values in sports.

Synergy between Character Development and Sport

Athletic ability and sport achievement are highly esteemed in this country, as verified by multimillion-dollar salaries and 24/7 mediated sport. Another reason for this status is the belief sport teaches moral values and life lessons. Many people realize behaviors learned in sport, whether good or bad, will last a lifetime. These individuals state sport has the potential to teach social values like cooperation and teamwork and moral values like integrity, respect, and justice. Parents want their children to participate in sport programs to help them learn these values.

Character education includes teaching athletes and coaches moral reasoning or knowing what is right, valuing what is right, and doing what is right. Initiating this process could begin with encouraging athletes and coaches to question what the media, other athletes, and other coaches may suggest is right. Since humans frequently model what they see, athletes and coaches may never have been challenged to ask why certain behaviors in many sports seem integral to and characteristic of them. For example, is it morally defensible for a wrestling or gymnastics coach to expect a normally maturing athlete to drop weight, such as through eating too little, wearing a rubber suit while working out, or failing to hydrate properly? Does sport give coaches the right to use obscene language and verbal abuse to motivate athletes?

Cognitive dissonance is the discomfort or tension felt when there is a discrepancy between what is known or believed to be morally right and new information or interpretations. When confronted with new information and asked to accommodate new ideas, conflict between right and wrong occurs and increases with importance and impact of the decision and inability to rationalize and explain away conflict. This cognitive dissonance leads athletes and coaches to examine what is the right thing to do in sports. The key to understanding cognitive dissonance necessitates that athletes and coaches question situations and issues to learn to differentiate between what is morally right and wrong through formal and informal processes. For example, intervention programs, such as those described next, could have a positive, long-term effect on moral reasoning.

Athletes can be educated about what character is, what it looks like, and how to live principled lives. Steps coaches and parents can take to help achieve the goal of building character include: (a) modeling what character is, shaping and continuing to mold moral values, and consistently reinforcing and praising the ethical behaviors of young athletes; (b) teaching what it means to treat opponents, officials, and teammates honorably and respectfully while following the letter and spirit of the rules; (c) modeling how to behave when faced with morally challenging situations; (d) shaping players' thinking so effort, hard work, and doing one's best are more important than winning; and (e) reinforcing how character is displayed in sport, such as through sportsmanship and fair play, and how moral values can be applied in other aspects of life.

Four moral values of justice, honesty, responsibility, and beneficence will be described to illustrate how their underlying principles can contribute to the development of character. Justice means treating others with fairness, such as through the distribution of benefits, equitable application of policies and procedures, equity in punishments, and appropriate compensation whenever harm or unfairness has been suffered. A universal rule of conduct associated with justice is: do not violate the rules of the game. So, the athlete who tries to gain competitive advantages without getting penalized by an official is violating this principle. Honesty is about keeping promises, telling the truth, and being trustworthy. Honest athletes and coaches adhere to the principle of do not cheat or lie, even if they believe a rule may be flawed or it would be to their advantage to cheat or lie. Responsibility encompasses fulfilling one's duty and being a person who can be counted on to carry out what is expected. In order not to act irresponsibly, an athlete as a dependable teammate puts the team ahead of selfish interests. Beneficence refers to playing fairly or doing good. The beneficent athlete does not intentionally harm an opponent, helps prevent a teammate from getting into a fight, avoids a potentially volatile situation, and does good by being a role model for ethical behavior (Lumpkin, Stoll, and Beller 2012).

In addition to moral values like these four, a socially valued, moral virtue is a deeply held trait or disposition that causes a person to act morally. Moral virtues especially relevant to sports include civility, cool-headedness, courage, loyalty, modesty, persistence, and teamwork. When displaying these virtues, athletes can learn to be confident, dependable, determined, disciplined, eager to learn, enthusiastic, and poised. Athletes with these virtues are more likely to work hard, put the team first, learn from mistakes and failures, become mentally tough, develop and show moral courage by being willing to stand up for what is right, and win and lose with class.

Coaches of young athletes, with the support of parents, keep winning in perspective while establishing team cultures that nurture and develop moral values and moral virtues. They establish rituals and procedures, such as beginning each practice with comments emphasizing character, using trigger words and actions as reminders for ethical behaviors that should be repeated, such as thanking the passer for an assist and utilizing teachable moments to reinforce moral values. Through the process of transforming the culture in a sport—winning is redefined (not focused on the scoreboard); players' efforts (not the outcome) are rewarded; specific, measurable, attainable, rewarding, and timely goals are set to stretch each player to work harder; and symbolic rewards are given to reward effort and achieving personal growth in character.

Athletes can be highly competitive, yet still demonstrate sportsmanship. Respecting opponents, officials, teammates, and the letter and spirit of the rules describes sportsmanship. It also includes gracefulness in losing, inevitably a part of sport, while working diligently to win. Learning sportsmanship can be an important precursor to learning about living. It includes integrity to win with humility and lose without making excuses, throwing things, or starting fights. With these moral values and moral virtues as desirable outcomes, next comes a discussion about how to develop character.

Successful Programs That Help Develop Moral Values and Character

There are numerous organizations and efforts focused on developing character through sport, possibly in response to how the moral reasoning of athletes lessens as the competitive level increases. Three examples will be briefly described. First, Character Counts, the approach to character education established by the Josephson Institute of Ethics, promotes six pillars of character in schools and communities: trustworthiness, respect, responsibility, fairness, caring, and citizenship. It uses these six pillars as the foundation for its sportsmanship campaign, Pursuing Victory with Honor. Second, the Champions of Character program offered by the National Association of Intercollegiate Athletics seeks to instill an understanding of the core character values in sport of respect, responsibility, integrity, servant leadership, and sportsmanship. It provides practical tools for athletes, coaches, and parents to use in modeling exemplary character traits. Third, the Positive Coaching Alliance seeks to transform youth and high school sports so athletes have positive, character-building experiences. Through partnerships among sport managers, coaches, athletes, parents, officials, and organizations, the goal of athletes' learning life lessons through sports remains central to building better athletes, better people.

Resolving Ethical Dilemmas

Programs like these seek to help athletes make reasoned decisions in sport. When faced with ethical dilemmas, it is important to understand the process that leads to behaving morally. The starting point is to define and interpret the situation by identifying the issue or issues and gathering the facts (who did what). In this data-gathering process, it is helpful to explore what actions are possible, who and how people might be affected by a specific course of action, and how these individuals possibly would react depending on what might occur.

In the analysis phase, each person tests what is right and wrong in comparison with his or her moral values. Three informal tests can help in deciding what a person believes is the morally right action to take. The "stench test" describes a negative, gut-level reaction to the situation—that is, if a person feels an action is wrong, then he or she does not do it. The "media test" suggests that if a person would be uncomfortable if the planned action or decision were to be reported in the national or local media, then he or she does not do it. The "mom test" offers that if a person is considering violating the moral values of someone cared about, then he or she does not do it (Blanchard and Peale 1988). In addition, during the analysis phase, it is important to identify any colliding values, because at times two right values may conflict. For example, what should be done when telling the truth would hurt a teammate's feelings and possibly be perceived as disrespectful? Whenever this may occur, the challenge is to determine how to prioritize or stack these values to resolve the dilemma. A caution, however, is to make sure moral values trump personal preferences. Finally, each person decides whether to act morally. It takes moral courage to take the morally right action.

Several principles can help in resolving ethical dilemmas. First, it is essential to keep winning in perspective. It is important to educate coaches, athletes, sport managers, and fans about values, such as sportsmanship, and stress playing the game by the letter and spirit of the rules. Helpful in this educational process could be to develop, publicize, and enforce codes of conduct. To make these codes effective, however, penalties should be assessed whenever unethical behaviors occur. When sport managers keep winning in perspective, they will choose to hire and retain coaches based on integrity and modeling of moral values (not based on their win-loss records). Coaches, athletes, and others who are committed to sport helping to build character will choose to follow the rules of sport governing organizations.

Conclusion

Sport ethics may have become an oxymoron. But, the current erosion in moral values and character development through sport does not have to be accepted as an inevitable result. In some instances, sport has become morally bankrupt as numerous examples of unethical behavior threaten fair play, sportsmanship, and character development. Some young athletes can become selfish and undisciplined, and act unethically when they realize principles of fairness and integrity are not enforced. However, when parents and coaches teach, model, shape, and reinforce moral reasoning and influence learning morally sound lessons for life, athletes can learn about and strengthen their character. Moral values like integrity, respect, and responsibility are integral to sport when striving to perform to the best of one's abilities replaces an overemphasis on winning. Parents and coaches can emphasize pursuing victory with honor and playing the game by the letter and spirit of the rules.

As the outcome of the game hangs in the balance, so does integrity. Morally based actions can reflect the moral values integral to who each athlete is. As stated in the Olympic Creed, "The most important thing in life is not the triumph, but the fight; the essential thing is not to have won, but to have fought well" (International Olympic Committee 2015). After all, athletes would rather play, even on a losing team, than sit on the bench for a winning team, because it is actually playing a sport that is fun. Athletes playing to the best of their abilities while valuing others and the integrity of the letter and spirit of the rules are engaged in life-enriching activities.

References

Acosta, R. V., and L. J. Carpenter. 2014. "Women in Intercollegiate Sport: A Longitudinal, National Study—Thirty-Seven-Year Update, 1997–2014." Available at: http://acostacarpenter.org/2014%20Status%20of%20Women%20in%20Intercollegiate%20Sport%20–37%20Year%20Update%20-%201977–2014%20.pdf.

Beller, J. M., and S. K. Stoll. 1995. "Moral Reasoning of High School Student Athletes and General Students: An Empirical Study versus Personal Testimony." *Pediatric Exercise Science 7* (4): 352–363.

Bieler, D. 2016. "Wisconsin High Schoolers Banned from Chants Including 'Airball' and 'Scoreboard.'" Available at: https://www.washingtonpost.com/news/early-lead/ wp/2016/01/12/wisconsin-high-schoolers-banne d-from-chants-including-airball-and-scoreboard/.

Blanchard, K., and N. V. Peale. 1988. *The Power of Ethical Management*. New York: William Morrow.

Bredemeier, B. J. L. 1995. "Divergence in Children's Moral Reasoning about Issues in Daily Life and Sport Specific Contexts." *International Journal of Sport Psychology 26* (4): 453–463.

Bredemeier, B. J., and D. L. Shields. 1995. *Character Development and Physical Activity*. Champaign, IL: Human Kinetics.

Drake Group, The 2016. Available at: http://thedrakegroup. org/about/.

Falla, J. 1981. *NCAA: The Voice of College Sports*. Mission, KS: National Collegiate Athletic Association.

International Olympic Committee. 2015. "Factsheet The Olympic Movement." Available at: http://www.olympic. org/Documents/Reference_documents_Factsheets/The_ Olympic_Movement.pdf.

Knight Commission on Intercollegiate Athletics. 1991. "Keeping Faith with the Student-Athlete: A New Model for Intercollegiate Athletics." Available at: www.knightcommission. org/images/pdfs/1991–93_kcia_report.pdf.

Knight Commission on Intercollegiate Athletics. 1992. "A Solid Start." Available at: www.knightcommission.org/ images/pdfs/1991–93_kcia_report.pdf.

Knight Commission on Intercollegiate Athletics. 1993. "A New Beginning for a New Century." Available at: www. knightcommission.org/images/pdfs/1991–93_kcia_ report.pdf.

Knight Commission on Intercollegiate Athletics. 2001. "A Call to Action: Reconnecting College Sports and Higher

Education." Available at: www.knightcommission.org/images/pdfs/2001_knight_report.pdf.

Knight Commission on Intercollegiate Athletics. 2010. "Restoring the Balance Dollars, Values, and the Future of College Sports." Available at: http://knightcommission.org/images/restoringbalance/KCIA_Report_F.pdf.

Kohlberg, L. 1981. *The Philosophy of Moral Development: Moral Stages and the Idea of Justice.* New York: Harper and Row.

Kretchmar, R. S. 2005. *Practical Philosophy of Sport and Physical Activity*, 2nd ed. Champaign, IL: Human Kinetics.

Lumpkin, A., S. K. Stoll, and J. M. Beller. 2012. *Practical Ethics in Sport Management.* Jefferson City, NC: McFarland and Company, Inc.

National Collegiate Athletic Association. 2016. "Estimated Probability of Competing in College Athletics." Available at: www.ncaa.org/sites/default/files/2015%20 Probability%20Chart%20Web%20PDF_draft5.pdf.

National Federation of State High School Associations. 2016. "The Case for High School Activities." Available at: www. nfhs.org/articles/the-case-for-high-school-activities/.

Rudd, A., and S. Stoll. 2004. "What Type of Character Do Athletes Possess? An Empirical Examination of College Athletes versus College Non-Athletes with the RSBH Value Judgment Inventory." *Sport Journal 7* (2): 1–10.

Sack, A. L. 2005. "Amateur vs. Professional Debate." *Berkshire Encyclopedia of World Sport 1*: 44–49.

Savage, H., H. W. Bentley, J. T. McGovern, and D. F. Smiley. 1929. *American College Athletics.* New York: Carnegie Foundation for the Advancement of Teaching.

Silva, J. M. 1983. "The Perceived Legitimacy of Rule Violating Behavior in Sport." *Journal of Sport Psychology 5* (4): 438–448.

Stoll, S. K., and J. M. Beller. 2006. "Ethical Dilemmas in College Sport." In *New Game Plan for College Sport*, edited by R. E. Lapchick, 75–90. Westport, CT: Praeger.

U.S. Department of Education. 1979. "A Policy Interpretation: Title IX and Intercollegiate Athletics." Available at: www.ed.gov/about/offices/list/ocr/docs/t9interp.html.

U.S. Department of Education. 2003. "Open to All—Title IX at Thirty, the Final Report of the Secretary's Commission on Opportunity in Athletics." Available at: www.ed.gov/about/bdscomm/list/athletics/title9report.doc.

U.S. Department of Education. 2010. "Intercollegiate Athletics Policy Clarification: The Three-Part Test—Part Three." Available at: www2.ed.gov/about/offices/list/ocr/letters/colleague-20100420.pdf.

U.S. Department of Justice. 1972. "Overview of Title IX of the Education Amendments of 1972, 20 U.S.C. A§1681 ET.SEQ." Available at: www.justice.gov/crt/overview-title-ix-education-amendments-1972–20-usc-1681-et-seq.

Wainstein, K. J., A. J. Jay, III, and C. D. Kukowski. 2014. "Investigation of Irregular Classes in the Department of African and Afro-American Studies at the University of North Carolina at Chapel Hill." Available at: http://3q h929iorux3fdpl532k03kg.wpengine.netdna-cdn.com/wp-content/uploads/2014/10/UNC-FINAL-REPORT.pdf.

2 Problems, Controversies, and Solutions

Introduction

Sport is a multibillion-dollar industry with popularity across all ages, ethnicities, and socioeconomic strata. Relationships with various media have helped sport attain an unprecedented status in the United States and internationally—that is, the media promote sports, and sports increase the reach and popularity of various media. The reach of sport encompasses participation, products, and entertainment.

Millions of people participate in sports through Little League Baseball, Pop Warner Football, the Senior Games, the Olympic Games, and public and private sport organizations, clubs, schools, and colleges. Sport participation includes occasional golf outings with business associates, softball games at family reunions, pickup games of basketball with friends at recreation centers, and sport camps for children and adolescents. Relative to sport products, most households have sport equipment and clothing as well as collectibles associated with favorite teams. Millions of dollars are invested in outfitting athletes with equipment and uniforms, purchasing sport-related video games, and equipping homes and businesses with various electronics that enhance viewing of favorite teams and players.

Philadelphia Flyers and Pittsburgh Penguins players fight in the third period of a NHL hockey game on January 24, 2010. While fights in professional ice hockey games are commonplace and seemingly accepted as part of the culture of this sport, this does not mean that such actions are morally right. (AP Photo/Matt Slocum)

Sporting events are always available, with in-person and electronic spectating as people seek to be entertained day and night with an endless array of sports and demonstrate a seemingly insatiable appetite for sports.

Overlaying the pervasiveness of sport, however, are numerous challenges. Many perceive there has been a decrease in the integrity associated with sport because winning has become all important—that is, breaking rules to gain competitive advantages and a "winning is everything" mentality in many instances have replaced honesty, respect, sportsmanship, and fair play. Others, who claim playing a sport can and does teach character, argue this is a desired outcome because sport helps prepare people for life. To examine whether sport, character, and winning can coexist in positive ways, this chapter will examine controversies and problems across all levels of sport, followed by sections specifically analyzing youth, interscholastic, and intercollegiate sports. Recommendations for addressing the controversies and problems confronting sport will be offered.

Controversies and Problems across All Levels of Sport

Whenever winning becomes the sole purpose of sport, then everything else, including moral values and the development of character, seems threatened. The identity of the United States as a global power, it seems, is predicated on winning—politically, economically, and being No. 1 in sport. Not only is the team representing the United States expected to win the most medals in the Olympic Games, but athletes from this country are expected to win the Davis Cup (men) and Fed Cup (women) in tennis, Ryder Cup (men) and Solheim Cup (women) in golf, the America's Cup (this cup is named for the first yacht to win the trophy), and other international sport competitions. Pressures to win on some athletes, coaches, and sport managers may lead to actions violating sport rules or rules of sport governing organizations, as they justify behaviors by stating they just did these things to try to win.

But, why is winning such a powerful motivator that it can lead to unprincipled actions? The answer points directly to the benefits accruing to the victorious. Winners become sport heroes and heroines and enjoy the rewards of victory. For example, winners get carried off the field or court, have their pictures in various media, appear on ESPN's SportsCenter, and get invited to meet the president at the White House. The big man (and sometimes woman) on campus phenomenon thrives in schools and colleges as athletes who win are recognized by others, and their achievements are celebrated. By way of contrast, seldom is heard a word about athletes who compete to the best of their abilities and serve as role models of sportsmanship. The fact that people in this country love a winner is a lesson not lost on the young, who are constantly bombarded with evidence of the celebrity status and financial benefits enjoyed by those who win.

Youth Sport

Youth sport enjoys a somewhat idyllic status in the United States. Many parents, coaches, and other volunteers in youth sport claim laudatory and beneficial outcomes accrue to children who play sports. They state young athletes develop sports skills and physical fitness; learn how to play sports; learn and develop self-confidence, discipline, sportsmanship, and teamwork; and develop and maintain friendships. A perusal of purpose statements of community recreational programs and many youth sport organizations verifies these goals as established by adults.

The goals from athletes' perspectives, however, are not always the same as those listed by adults. Consistently, children emphasize the first and foremost goal is always to have fun. This should not be surprising since children love to play, which to them is fun. In addition, children say they want to learn sport skills through participating in sport, spend time with their friends, have something to do, and feel successful. Probably the more noteworthy difference is adults advocate that sports teach character and moral values, while this is absent from the children's list. This is not to say, however, that children are resistant to learning values. In fact, they are likely to learn whatever is taught, good or not so good.

Problems and Controversies in Youth Sports

The problems and controversies affecting youth sports will be discussed in three specific areas. First, there is a concern about children not having fun playing sports. Second, most children want to learn sport skills, and this is not always happening. Third, winning dominates most aspects of youth sports.

Taking the Fun Out of Sport

When children choose not to participate in sports, the primary reason given is often playing a sport is not fun. Young athletes are quite clear in wanting to have fun in sports, which they usually define as getting to play and not sitting on the bench. Children want to be actively engaged and avoid unpleasant experiences. Since too often coaches forget this obvious reality, it is no wonder children quit or do not join teams the next year as they choose to participate in activities that are more fun.

Children are often relegated to the bench because they are not as skilled, physically fit, or developmentally advanced as other children. None of these mean children do not want to play. Children are not nearly as concerned about dropping a fly ball or missing a tackle as their coaches and parents are. Many youth sport coaches believe winning a game is much more important than giving every child an equitable opportunity to play. So, most youth sport programs have established written rules requiring at least a minimum amount of playing time for each child in each game, because otherwise many children would not get to play—that is, instead of adults keeping winning in perspective by focusing on treating each child fairly, equitable playing time had to be required.

While ensuring playing time for each young athlete may be an important guarantee, just being in the game does not automatically make sport fun. Children also want to play their favorite positions. Not every child who wants to play quarterback or pitcher can do so all the time because others will have similar preferences; but, this should not mean children never get these opportunities. Similarly, children do not think it is fair to be forced to play certain positions, such as right field or on the offensive line, they do not enjoy. Sometimes, instead of allowing themselves to be relegated to these positions, they drop out of the sport. Also, anyone who has ever watched a youth sport game knows the attraction is the ball. So, if a child never gets to touch the ball, the fun may quickly disappear. Again, has playing the most skillful child in key positions emphasized winning over fun and skill development for all?

Children did not establish youth sport national championships—adults did. Yet, for every 10-year-old national champion, there are thousands of children who would much prefer to have fun just playing games with their friends. To illustrate the adult view of youth sports, this actually happened. One Saturday morning in a youth soccer program, parents arrived with their children for soccer games only to be told there were no officials. Instead of giving the children soccer balls to play with as they chose, the parents put their children back in their vehicles and drove away as if to say, "Obviously, children cannot have fun playing soccer without officials." An automobile advertisement shown in 2015 and 2016 pictured a father congratulating his son on winning the championship as they approach the car. As he opens the car door, the boy hands his trophy to his father, who is disgusted to read the engraved word "Participant." The father pries off the silver plate, turns it over, and with a marker writes the word "Champ." Once in the car, the father hands the trophy back to his son and says, "Here, Champ." Rather than winning trophies that quickly collect dust on shelves, should the goals of youth sports emphasize children having fun while being physically active and interacting socially with friends?

Children did not establish youth sport travel, elite, or select teams—adults did. These teams attract highly skilled players who are provided opportunities to compete against other talented athletes. Those who support these teams believe these competitions accelerate the skill development of those chosen, who, it is assumed, have the potential for sport stardom. There is, however, an ever-present threat of exploitation. Often, these young athletes are pressured to practice for and compete in the same sport year-round lest they fall behind, often leading to overtraining or overuse injuries. These young athletes may become consumed by the practices, competitions, travel, and pressures to win. The latter is particularly a problem with team sponsors expecting victories in return for their financial support, thus increasing the pressures to win, maybe at any cost.

Many athletes on travel, club, elite, or select teams lose opportunities to spend time with peers and interact with them in other sports and social activities. The costs associated with these teams may create problems for parents and other children who do not receive the same type of parental investments. Or, athletes without the financial means to join these teams may be excluded or receive benefits jeopardizing their eligibility to play sports in high school or college. Coaches and others involved with these travel, club, or select teams may influence the choices of educational institutions these athletes attend—as these adults advance their own careers. Has developing the skills of a few children on these teams replaced an emphasis on fun for all?

Learning or Not Learning Sport Skills

Some children learn skills that enable them to participate in and enjoy sports throughout their lives. But, this does not always happen. Most youth sport coaches have limited expertise in how to teach sport skills and especially how to teach them in developmentally appropriate ways to children. Youth sport coaches are largely volunteers and often parents who agree to help provide sport experiences for their children and other children. Often these volunteers have played sports in high school, and maybe college, or they may only have an interest in the sport they are coaching. As a result, these coaches often coach as they were coached or model their behaviors after those observed through the media.

Whenever youth sport coaches are poorly prepared for their roles, the children do not learn sport skills or they learn them incorrectly. The lack of coaching preparation may result in practices during which children are expected to engage in disorganized activities that are boring or potentially harmful and do not lead to skill development. Whenever practices are filled more with athletes getting yelled at by the coach than with getting to catch, hit, or kick balls, little skill is developed.

Often, youth sport coaches possess limited knowledge about effective instructional strategies, motivational techniques, or risk management. Even though these coaches frequently make mistakes due to their limited preparation, they still expect skillful play by young athletes. Coaches seldom are required to demonstrate their knowledge of the basics of their sport or how to prevent and care for injuries, and largely they coach their athletes without supervision, which may permit physical, psychological, and sexual abuse of children. These volunteers determine what types of experiences these young athletes will have and if they learn sport skills.

Winning as the Only Measure of Success

While not having fun or not learning sport skills causes many children to drop out of sport activities, an even more serious problem in youth sport may be the overemphasis on winning. Did children decide they needed manicured fields, uniforms modeled after those worn by professional athletes, and year-round practices and competitions in one sport to have fun and learn sport skills? No, but youth sport athletes enjoy these fields, uniforms, and organized programs as pickup games have largely become a relic of the past—that is, youth sports have become super-organized and imitators of professional sports.

Ask any youth sport program director about who causes their problems and for whom more and more rules must be written, and the answer is inevitably coaches and parents who have gotten over-invested in youth sport. When parents invest significant amounts of time and money, they often expect winning teams while forgetting the ages and skill levels of young athletes. Many controlling, and sometimes even abusive, adults have imposed their emphasis on winning and overly competitive proclivities on child's play. Some out-of-control parents verbally abuse and physically assault officials, coaches, and other parents. The movie *Kicking and Screaming* depicts an out-of-control parent humorously. Could it be some parents seem fixated on their children being winners, earning celebrity status, receiving college grants-in-aid, and becoming professional sport millionaires yet fail to remember sports are supposed to be fun for children and build character?

This adult compulsion for winning as the only measure of success in sport now permeates youth programs with adverse consequences, such as when adults engage in physical confrontations with officials, coaches, and opposing players whenever their team does not win or they believe it has been treated unfairly. Most children would not dedicate their childhood years to mastering backhands, jump shots, or balance beam routines without considerable urging from parents and coaches. These coaches and parents push children into sports based on a professional model as fun gets short shrift. The emphasis on winning keeps some children on the bench or away from positions more likely to impact the outcome of a game or competition. The bodies of the most highly skilled and developmentally advanced may be taxed to the point of overuse injuries and permanent incapacitation. Overtraining, in the guise of getting bigger, stronger, and faster, may lead to physiological and psychological issues, such as interruption of normal growth and maturation, eating disorders, and use of performance-enhancing drugs. If these stressors become unbearable, athletes burn out and leave sport entirely. Have youth sports become miniature versions of professional sports?

Some out-of-control coaches and parents yell, scream, and verbally abuse young athletes. A few coaches seek to build their reputations based on the winning percentages of their teams to help secure coaching positions at higher levels of sport. Some coaches and parents victimize young athletes when they pressure them relentlessly to win, often leading to physiological and psychological problems. When parents disproportionately focus their lives and resources on a highly skilled child hoping he or she will become a collegiate and professional athlete, this almost always causes financial and interpersonal problems in the family.

In seeking to keep parents under control, some youth sport programs have begun to require them to attend sessions about sportsmanship to help them keep winning in perspective. Codes of conduct for parents have been established and enforced. Some youth sport programs have initiated 24-hour rules (i.e., cooling off time before parents can talk with coaches) to hopefully reduce confrontations. Some programs have enforced silent days when parents are forbidden to speak during youth competitions. Occasionally, behaviors have become so abusive or unsportsmanlike parents have been removed from the stands and banned from attending future youth sport competitions. Such actions lead to questions about what moral values these parents are modeling.

Children seldom mention winning as a reason why they participate in sports. Young athletes learn from adults about the importance placed on winning. So, many respond they like to win because parents and coaches reward winning, such as when adults buy treats for athletes after winning but not after losing a game or lavish praise on the player whose play directly led to a win on the scoreboard. While young athletes soon forget scores, they do remember whether they had fun.

Teaching Values in Youth Sports

To emphasize having fun and learning sport skills, a few suggested changes might be considered. First, youth sport organizations could educate parents to help them model proper behaviors at competitions, de-emphasize winning, and keep children as the focus of all decisions. Second, coaches of young athletes could be taught the importance of, and held accountable for, playing every child in each game and in different positions during the season, teaching skills, strategies, and rules in developmentally appropriate ways, giving each child an equal opportunity to strive for success, and de-emphasizing winning. Third, the emphasis could be shifted from outcome to process—that is, winning as the singular goal could be replaced by seeking to win while doing one's best. This approach potentially can reinforce developing character, young athletes learning moral values, and young athletes making the right decisions in sport.

Keeping winning in perspective means playing hard and playing fairly, as coaches and parents can redefine winning so athletes do not focus solely on the scoreboard—that is, reward youngsters for effort and sportsmanship regardless of the outcome. In child-centered programs, coaches and parents will reinforce determination, persistence, and incremental progress through symbolic rewards more than tangible awards and the scoreboard.

Fair play, sportsmanship, teamwork, honesty, respect, responsibility, and integrity do not automatically result from participating in youth sport. Rather, it is important to focus on educating everyone involved with youth sport about these moral values. Coaches and parents can help shape the character of young athletes by ensuring sport experiences are fun, being supportive and encouraging, emphasizing treating opponents fairly and respectfully, reinforcing the importance of respecting the authority of coaches and officials, and modeling ethical behavior. Most importantly, if parents and coaches diligently teach, model, and reinforce these moral values, children will view them as integral to sport and how games are to be played.

Interscholastic Sport

Most people in the United States believe interscholastic sport is an important part of educational and extracurricular activities of adolescents. Public school sport programs are funded from state appropriations in ways similar to academic programs because it is claimed that through sport adolescents learn valuable lessons and enjoy positive outcomes. The goals of interscholastic sport programs are for adolescent athletes to develop sport skills and physical fitness; learn moral virtues like teamwork, cooperation, self-discipline, and sportsmanship; compete in organized, supervised, and safe environments; learn how to work as a member of a team; and enhance their academic work. An extended goal is to provide a shared activity for students, schools, and communities.

Interscholastic athletes want to enjoy their experiences, but not in the same way younger athletes emphasize having fun. These adolescents take more seriously the development of sport skills because sport at this level excludes them if they do not meet coaches' standards. Being a member of a team and enjoying associations with peers are important to many athletes. Most also begin to realize they may be playing in their last level of competitive sport as the ever-narrowing funnel of sport will most likely preclude their opportunity to play a college sport. A small minority of high school athletes, however, will work diligently to hone their skills in hopes of receiving grants-in-aid and advancing to the next competitive level.

Problems and Controversies in Interscholastic Sport

Some of the problems and controversies confronting youth sport also plague interscholastic sport, such as when athletes drop out when sports are no longer enjoyable and burn out due to physiological and psychological factors. Some parents and coaches require adolescent athletes to specialize in one sport. These adults emphasize that only through dedicated, year-round physical conditioning, skill development, and competition can an athlete realize his or her potential and maybe even qualify to play this sport in college. Sport specialization also may mean an athlete is forced to choose between playing on the school's team or competing in a sport like gymnastics in nonschool-sponsored competitions. This oftentimes places pressure on an adolescent athlete to choose between wanting to play and socialize with friends while representing his or her school and wanting to take advantage of competitive opportunities nationally and even internationally.

In addition to sport specialization, interscholastic sport is challenged by specific ethical problems and controversies associated with academics, eligibility, conduct, and the emphasis on winning. Each of these issues will be discussed along with possible ways to address them to keep character development a desired outcome.

Academics

The NFHS and schools throughout the United States have found that interscholastic athletes achieve at a higher level academically than do nonathletes. They report athletes attend classes more regularly and stay in school at higher levels as well. Like their peers who are actively involved with band, debate, or other extracurricular activities, athletes psychologically and socially benefit from being part of groups with shared interests (National Federation of State High School Associations 2016).

One reason why interscholastic athletes may do better academically is that many states, schools, or coaches have implemented "no pass, no play" policies. These typically require a minimal grade in each course or passing all courses to play sports. These policies, some of which were mandated at the state legislative level, were enacted because some athletes were not taking advantage of their educational opportunities. Where these policies exist, interscholastic athletes can no longer ignore their academic work and are encouraged to take a more conscientious approach to being a student first so they can earn the privilege of playing sports. Yet, some have argued these policies or laws discriminate against students with learning difficulties or those who may have had fewer or inferior educational opportunities. Some also claim that without sports as an incentive, some students will drop out of school.

A common issue related to academics is some athletes choose to cheat, rather than study, learn, and pass their courses. These athletes may be helped with cheating by classmates or have classmates do their homework assignments. Some coaches who also teach give unearned grades or influence other teachers to give passing grades to athletes, even though these athletes do not attend class, turn in assignments, or pass their tests. Some people emphasize that when this occurs, these athletes are being exploited academically because they are not learning essential knowledge for their adult lives. These athletes are cheating themselves of opportunities to qualify for college and the financial benefits associated with earning a college degree.

Athletes who get to keep playing without completing the prerequisite academic work are learning that athletic abilities can exempt them from academic rules and the responsibility to play by these rules. It is an easy transfer of this feeling of entitlement onto the court or field so sport rules are ignored or violated to gain advantages. Is this a lack of morally based decision making that could lead to a feeling of being above the law relative to drinking alcohol, violating traffic regulations, sexually assaulting females, and getting into physical altercations?

Eligibility

In addition to interscholastic athletes maintaining their eligibility academically, they must meet the requirements of their schools, leagues, and conferences. The legitimacy of athletes attending particular schools is the rule most often violated. For example, some exceptionally skilled basketball players may enroll at a different school each year in high school as they seek to play under an acclaimed coach, to compete against better competition, or to increase the likelihood of being recruited by coaches of the best college teams. Sometimes transfers between schools include private schools, because requirements about living in a specified attendance area do not apply. In other cases, creative, but not always allowable, approaches are used to change an athlete's legal guardian so this athlete can meet the technical details of a public school's eligibility requirement. The new schools attended seldom have anything to do with academics and everything to do with playing sports. Should such school transfers be allowed?

Another eligibility issue deals with the age of athletes. Most state high school associations have rules specifying the maximum age, usually 19 or 20, for the eligibility of athletes. These rules were enacted because older and more mature athletes would have physiological advantages in interscholastic sports. Similarly, these governing associations limit the number of years of competition in interscholastic sports so adolescents cannot continue to play year after year instead of making progress in attaining their diplomas.

Some parents decide to have their child, most often boys, repeat an elementary or middle school grade so he can gain a developmental advantage over other athletes. Thus, the concept of redshirting that often occurs in intercollegiate athletics has moved down to precollegiate athletics. The goal in the minds of parents is that their sons throughout high school will compete against boys who are one year younger and less mature physically. This advantage, they posit, could be just enough to lead to greater success for their sons. While it may be beneficial athletically, what are the implications academically, socially, or ethically?

Because state high school associations exist primarily to provide competitive opportunities and establish rules that govern athletic competitions, most are not staffed with enforcement personnel to monitor compliance with eligibility rules. Often violations go undetected, with games and championships won by teams and individuals who according to the rules were ineligible. When adolescent athletes observe that violations of the rules can lead to winning championships, what lessons are they learning?

Unethical Conduct

Interscholastic sport is not exempt from unethical conduct on the part of athletes, coaches, and fans. Sometimes these individuals have chosen to follow the examples of those involved with intercollegiate and professional sports, such as by engaging in taunting, cheating, and violence. Another example of unethical behavior is hazing, which is defined as meaningless, harassing, and humiliating actions toward others. Older team members sometimes use hazing to initiate new players into the team by requiring them to do tasks that often harass and humiliate them. While some argue hazing is harmless and just adolescents having fun, what allegedly is used to build team unity has become hurtful and degrading, such as seniors forcing freshmen or sophomores to consume inedible items and drink alcoholic beverages.

Sometimes hazing has included sexually harassing young adolescents. For example, in 2014, seven football players on a New Jersey high school football team were charged with hazing, sexually assaulting, and engaging in criminal sexual contact against teammates. Many guilty of hazing, but not all, have been disciplined and sometimes lost the opportunity to play on teams; some coaches who have condoned hazing have lost their jobs. Teaching respect and responsibility to athletes, modeling appropriate treatment of all teammates, and reinforcing how to respectfully welcome new teammates will prevent hazing.

Interscholastic sport participants represent their schools. For most athletes, this is a new level of responsibility they can learn about, accept, and fulfill. In the absence of concerted efforts on the part of coaches, and reinforced by parents, to help these young people understand how to follow team rules, treat opponents as honored guests, respect officials, play by the letter and spirit of the rules, and win and lose with grace, many of these athletes will model their behaviors after collegiate and professional athletes. This may lead to irresponsible actions, disrespectful behaviors, and violations of rules. Educational programs through which athletes understand their responsibilities as representatives of their schools and role models for younger athletes in their communities are important in helping to ensure interscholastic athletes behave in responsible ways. Whenever athletes help establish codes of conduct, they are more likely to internalize a commitment to behaving appropriately. Should coaches be held accountable for teaching athletes to play fair, show sportsmanship, and take pride in their ethical conduct?

Overemphasis on Winning

Many argue that as an extracurricular educational experience for adolescents, the primary purpose of interscholastic sport should not be winning. Many others disagree with this statement because they believe winning elevates the status or prestige of their schools, communities, coaches, athletes, and fans. The intense desire to claim "we're No. 1" is associated with some interscholastic sports, especially football and basketball. Driving into towns, it is not unusual to read a sign listing state championship teams. Should it be the responsibility of adolescents to enhance the identity or bragging rights for fans in a community? Many young people have learned, however, that they carry a heavy responsibility to win, as the book, movie, and television series *Friday Night Lights* about high school football in Odessa, Texas, described and illustrated dramatically. Winning football games for many has become more important than school work, athletes' physical and psychological well-being, and families. The pressures on adolescent athletes to maintain winning traditions or to win championships are intense and can be relentless as coaches, parents, and fans demand victories or else. This else can be abusive treatment, withholding of love, or loss of status.

Oftentimes, coaches pressure athletes to win because they believe their jobs depend on winning. These coaches demand year-round conditioning, specialization in one sport and position, and unquestioning compliance with coaches' directives. Coaches praise athletes who have adopted similar levels of drive, intensity, and commitment, with everything else in life secondary to sport. Some athletes are subjected by coaches to demeaning treatment, abusive punishments for failure to perform at expected levels, and vulgar language—that is, many coaches believe their positions entitle them to do anything and everything it takes to win, even if this means sacrificing the physical, psychological, or emotional well-being of athletes in the process. For these coaches, winning has become the only outcome acceptable.

Teaching Values in Interscholastic Sport

Rather than this overemphasis on winning, striving to win in sport does not have to be characterized by abusing athletes or ignoring moral values. If it is assumed interscholastic sport can help prepare adolescents for their adult lives, then life lessons, character, and moral values should be taught and reinforced through sport. Since for every sporting event there is at least one team or individual who does not win on the scoreboard, has the importance of winning gotten out of balance? Given there will be more nonwinners than winners, should the emphasis be on rewarding or reinforcing effort and how well the game is played? How can school administrators and members of boards of education temper their expectations of winning? Should they expect all coaches to develop athletes physically, psychologically, and ethically?

Intercollegiate Athletics

Mission statements of intercollegiate athletic programs usually state a commitment to the development of athletes academically, athletically, socially, and ethically. Intercollegiate athletics is typically dedicated to helping athletes achieve their potential in sports, enrich their educational experiences, and prepare for life. It is claimed that intercollegiate athletic programs, including coaches, players, and sport managers, comply with institutions' and intercollegiate athletic organizations' regulations, respect each individual, and promote integrity within the context of fiscal responsibility. Many who applaud the lofty aspirations of intercollegiate athletic programs do so to justify their status within institutions of higher education.

Problems and Controversies in Intercollegiate Sport

Intercollegiate athletes realize they compete at a much higher level than in high school with the expectations for winning increasing significantly. In many cases, they have received grants-in-aid as recruited athletes. In essence, their sports have become their jobs, with all the requisite demands on their time and effort. Pressures to win are associated with recruiting, academics, and commercialism along with the problems and controversies associated with each. An emphasis on winning is intertwined with recruiting, academics, and commercialism as recruiting the most highly skilled athletes, keeping athletes eligible, and maximizing revenues become a self-perpetuating and ever-growing cycle. In seeking to operate winning programs, sometimes developing character is not emphasized by coaches and sport managers.

Recruiting

The NCAA, NAIA, National Junior College Athletic Association (NJCAA), and other smaller athletic organizations govern intercollegiate athletics beginning with the recruitment of high school athletes. Hundreds of pages of rules and regulations specify what is and is not permissible as coaches and others try to entice adolescents to attend certain institutions. While some of these rules and regulations have been written to protect prospective intercollegiate athletes, most were established to control the actions of zealous coaches seeking to gain advantages in the cutthroat process of recruiting highly talented athletes. For example, there are limitations on the time of the year when coaches and recruiters can contact high school athletes, because otherwise some coaches would continually bombard these adolescents with letters, calls to their cell phones, and text messages. Impermissible contacts continue primarily because intercollegiate athletic organizations do not allocate the personnel and financial resources required to enforce their rules and regulations. Of course, this raises questions about whether coaches are morally obligated to follow the rules for recruiting, whether any actions in recruiting are justifiable as long as coaches are not caught, or if ethical recruiting can be legislated and enforced.

During the recruiting process, prospective college athletes are permitted to take a limited number of expense-paid trips to college campuses. During these visits, coaches attempt to convince the high school athletes to join their teams through tours of impressive athletic facilities, promises of stardom, and fun experiences. Sometimes these campus visits get out of hand, such as when hosts, who usually are intercollegiate athletes or attractive females, provide prospective recruits with alcohol and sexual encounters, as happened at the University of Colorado and University of Louisville.

Another approach used to get the most highly skilled athletes to attend a specific institution is to provide inducements or benefits to the athlete, family members, or friends. Extra benefits have been given even though this practice violates the rules and regulations of intercollegiate athletic organizations, because as amateurs, athletes are not permitted to receive these benefits and maintain their eligibility to compete. Although cash payments, cars, credit cards, clothing, and houses for athletes and their families are not openly provided, coaches and friends of athletic programs have used creative ways to get payments to athletes, as illustrated in movies such as *Blue Chips*. The NCAA banned Southern Methodist University from competing in football for one year because of repeated rule violations and especially for giving money to athletes. Some coaches have secured the signing of a prized recruit by hiring as a member of the coaching staff the athlete's father, the athlete's interscholastic or club coach, or another significant individual to this athlete. Many question whether such hires are unauthorized inducements, even though there are no specific rules prohibiting such hires.

The recruiting process is an intensely stressful time for coaches and prospects because coaches are limited in the number of recruits to whom grants-in-aid can be awarded, and prospects have one chance to commit in writing (through a national letter of intent) to an institution. If the coach is incorrect in assessing the potential contributions of a recruit, three possible outcomes are likely to occur. First, the coach can simply accept his or her incorrect assessment of talent and honor the grant-in-aid commitment annually. Second, the coach can pressure the athlete to renounce his or her grant-in-aid, which frees the coach to award a new grant-in-aid to some other athlete. Third, the coach can decide not to renew a grant-in-aid if it is claimed this athlete is not skilled enough, is not putting forth the required effort or training, or some other reason the coach can allege.

Once signed, the athlete also has three probable alternatives. First, if the athlete chooses to leave the team because of lack of skill, playing time, or interest, the grant-in-aid is not renewed the subsequent academic year. Second, the athlete can choose to remain on the team, if permitted by the coach, but typically without the grant-in-aid. Third, the athlete can transfer to another institution, although sitting out a year (i.e., not playing) is required if the transfer is at the same level of competition, such as from a NCAA Division I institution to another NCAA Division I institution. In analyzing these options, differing opinions may develop. One perspective is that since intercollegiate athletics is a business, athletes should know if they do not have the requisite skills, then whatever happens is just how the game is played. Others argue athletes have become disposable and replaceable commodities to be used to help a team win or, if not, be expendable.

Another vital aspect of the recruiting process is getting athletes admitted into colleges. Because of accusations of poorly qualified recruits who have enrolled in colleges just to play sports, the NCAA over the years has raised its requirements regarding minimal standards for admission relative to high school grades and admission test scores. Also, given institutions have varied in how effectively they monitored and enforced academic admission requirements, the NCAA, rather than institutions, qualifies through its Clearinghouse all athletes who compete through member institutions in NCAA Divisions I and II.

Once recruits meet the minimal academic requirements specified by intercollegiate athletic organizations, another hurdle exists at the institutional level. Admissions staffs, especially at institutions with selective admission standards, are expected to treat all applicants equitably and admit the class of students with the highest overall academic credentials and potential. Faculty members agree because they expect students who are admitted to have the academic preparation and abilities to succeed. But, coaches argue that once recruits, especially highly talented athletes with the potential to make significant contributions to help win, have met the minimal qualifying standards academically as specified by an intercollegiate athletic organization, they should be admitted, regardless of institutional requirements.

This conflict between admitting the most academically qualified class of students and individuals with special athletic skills has been resolved on most campuses in favor of coaches, as they are granted at least a certain number of preferred admissions. Coaches justify this unique admission status for some of the best athletes by saying these prospective students are essential for staying competitive within the conference or on the national level. They also argue these athletes are being treated the same way as outstanding musicians or others with special talents.

Many faculty members counter these arguments by emphasizing that students with outstanding musical and academic abilities and potential achieve at high levels in academic programs, while athletes only perform in an extracurricular activity. Preferred admissions are not unique to NCAA Division I institutions, as they occur at academically elite institutions as well as less academically elite institutions, and regional state universities (Shulman and Bowen 2001)—that is, having exceptional athletic talent greatly increases the likelihood of admission. However, once admitted, these students often fail to perform up to their potential academically and many do not earn degrees (Shulman and Bowen 2001).

An oft-heard argument from faculty is that an athletic coach should not be allowed to determine who some of the students admitted will be just so they can potentially win more games. In selective admission institutions, some faculty state admitting talented athletes through preferred admissions discriminates against more highly qualified applicants academically may have been denied admission. University administrators, athletic directors, and coaches counter by emphasizing the value of providing educational opportunities to athletes who would not be able to attend college, as well as the importance of the public relations and financial benefits associated with winning teams and championships.

Academics

The overriding academic issues for many intercollegiate athletes are whether they are primarily attending college to play sports and whether the current operation of intercollegiate athletics impedes the likelihood of athletes earning their degrees. Young adults who realistically evaluate their skills realize playing intercollegiate athletics is unlikely to lead to professional careers. As such, some of these athletes fail to take advantage of educational opportunities provided through grants-in-aid. Some athletes choose not to attend classes or complete their assignments, usually resulting in their doing poorly and even failing their courses. An apathetic attitude toward learning may have been reinforced earlier in their lives as athletes when they were allowed to not take their schoolwork seriously and were given grades to ensure eligibility.

Since intercollegiate athletes are adults, some question whether they should be forced by their coaches to attend classes. Mandatory class attendance occurs when coaches send class checkers around campus to monitor whether athletes go to and remain in their classes. Failure to attend classes usually results in punishments like early morning running or loss of playing time. Would it be more beneficial to help these young adults learn to appreciate their educational opportunities so they would choose to attend classes and learn?

Another issue regarding class attendance deals with the number of classes some athletes miss due to competitions and travel to competitions. Baseball and softball players play several games in the fall semester, begin up to a 56-game regular season schedule in February, and play on several days of the week, with games and travel precluding attending numerous days of classes. Basketball players (and student managers, cheerleaders, and student athletic trainers) miss numerous classes during the regular season, and if basketball teams continue to win in conference and other postseason tournaments, the days of missed classes mount rapidly. It was reported that members of one men's basketball team that won the NCAA Division I championship did not attend any classes during their postseason play for an entire month. Not surprisingly, most of these athletes dropped, failed, or did poorly in their classes that semester. Ignoring their academic work taught these athletes that basketball was much more important than their learning and making progress toward earning their degrees.

It could be argued the number of classes intercollegiate athletes miss is excessive because these students are denied opportunities to learn from their professors and classmates. Also questioned is whether it is fair to expect athletes to be serious students when their days and nights are filled with

competitions, travel, rehabilitation from injuries, and practices. The NCAA specifies athletes can spend only 20 hours
a week in coach-directed activities associated with their sports
(exclusive of travel time to games), but most athletes admit
they are involved with their sports many more hours than this
in-season and out-of-season. In the NCAA's GOALS Study of
the Student Athlete Experience Initial Summary of Findings
(2016) athletes reported they spent significantly more time
in-season on athletic activities. For example, football players
in the Football Bowl Subdivision (FBS) reported they spent
an average of 42 hours weekly, while players in the Football
Championship Subdivision (FCS) reported 40 hours or more.
The weekly average number of hours for Division I baseball
players was 40 or more and softball players reported 39.
Division I athletes averaged 34 hours weekly on their sports;
Division II athletes averaged 32 hours per week; Division III
athletes averaged 28.5 hours per week.

Intercollegiate sports are played every day of the week, and
often at times to meet the demands of ESPN or other television
outlets. It is hard for athletes to be prepared for and concentrate
in an early morning class after playing in an away game that
ended late the previous night. Are athletes being taught their
academic work is less important than their sports? Are athletes
in football, and more often in basketball, learning their academics are subservient to an institution making money from
the broadcasting of their games?

Many intercollegiate athletic programs provide academic
support services to athletes. The usual rationale for providing
staff to advise these athletes in enrolling for courses, which
most often occurs prior to courses being opened to other students, is so athletes do not have classes conflicting with team
and individual practices and conditioning times. Sometimes
the goal is to enroll athletes in easy courses with faculty who are
more likely to give athletes good grades.

Tutoring is provided to athletes to bridge the learning gap,
especially for those admitted preferentially because they had

not demonstrated the past academic achievement of admitted classmates. Tutors assist athletes in completing their academic work in the limited time available to them around their obligations as athletes, such as during study hall. One issue surrounding the provision by athletic departments of academic support services to athletes is whether there is oversight to ensure hired tutors and study hall monitors do not complete the academic work for athletes, such as writing papers or doing other assignments for them. Because of numerous academic abuses, such as at the Universities of Tennessee, Georgia, Minnesota, and North Carolina which led to distrust about the unethical conduct of some staff members hired by athletic departments, a few institutions have moved academic support services for athletes under faculty or chief academic officers.

Another issue in the academic sphere deals with whether or not first-year students should be allowed to compete immediately upon matriculation. First-year students enrolled in institutions that were members of the NCAA prior to the early 1970s were not eligible to play on varsity teams. Some stated this rule existed so athletes could acclimate to the academic rigors of collegiate study and engage with other students socially. Freshman eligibility changed all this, with intercollegiate athletes immediately immersed in the demands of conditioning, practicing, and competing while transitioning into college academically and socially. The 20, 30, 40, or more hours per week athletes dedicate to their sports leave limited time to succeed academically, make friends outside of their teams, work at a part-time job, and engage in other extracurricular activities. Many argue this sport-centric world unfairly restricts the learning opportunities and all-around development of athletes, precludes them from working so they can pay educational costs, especially since most college athletes do not receive full grants-in-aid, and isolates them socially.

Given the time demands on athletes and sometimes their marginal preparation for college study, many athletes struggle academically and fail to earn their degrees. In the past, many athletes were victimized by an overemphasis on maintaining their eligibility by taking a smorgasbord of easy courses. An egregious example occurred between 1993 and 2011 when the University of North Carolina at Chapel Hill allowed students, about half of whom were athletes, to receive grades for "paper classes" and independent study courses requiring no class attendance and no course work other than a single paper awarded a high grade to ensure athlete eligibility (Wainstein, Jay, and Kukowski 2014).

Intercollegiate athletic organizations in attempting to thwart athletes majoring in eligibility rather than earning legitimate degrees have strengthened eligibility requirements. For example, the NCAA requires athletes to make satisfactory progress toward earning their degrees by receiving minimal passing grades in a specified number of courses each year to remain eligible to play. Each athlete must declare a major that leads to a degree, and each year each athlete must complete a required portion of this program of study. In addition, the NCAA has implemented a measure called the Academic Progress Rate (APR) to monitor the success or failure of athletes in making progress toward graduation. Each team is required to achieve at or above a 50 percent graduation rate, exclusive of those athletes who left the institution early for nonacademic reasons or else face the loss of grants-in-aid that can be awarded and eligibility for postseason competitions. The APR will result in penalties to teams and institutions because some athletes have chosen to focus on their sports instead of emphasizing earning degrees.

The Knight Commission on Intercollegiate Athletics, The Drake Group, many faculty, and some in the general public increasingly question whether some groups or levels of intercollegiate athletics are threatening the academic integrity of higher education. Although numerous rules and regulations exist, issues such as preferred admissions, unearned grades given to maintain eligibility, missed classes, lack of progress toward degrees, and an overemphasis on athletics persist to the detriment of academics. The driving force behind this imbalance in most cases is the commercialized business model of intercollegiate athletics.

Commercialism and the Arms Race

A historical way to begin to explore commercialism in intercollegiate athletics is to examine the evolution of conferences. Intercollegiate athletic conferences began to be established over 100 years ago among institutions with similar enrollments, missions, and geographical proximity. The geographical basis for these conferences sought to reduce the number of missed classes, which the faculty supported, and reduce costs, which benefited the athletic department. This has changed dramatically over the years, especially at the highest level of competition in the NCAA.

The goal of the Power Five conferences—Atlantic Coast, Big Ten, Big 12, Pac-12, and Southeastern—is to obtain the widest feasible geographical reach, which enables them to extract higher rights fees from network and cable television because of the size of potential viewing audience. Conference commissioners and athletic directors actively pursue maximal revenues. Many faculty members are less supportive of conference expansion and realignments because athletes miss more classes due to travel time to and from distant institutions.

Television, radio, and the Internet exert considerable influence over intercollegiate athletics. Commercialism leads some athletic directors and coaches to schedule competitions almost anywhere and anytime if these contests yield greater revenues. Television has led to rule changes in sport, such as adding a number of television time-outs for broadcasting more commercials. This is important because advertising sales are the primary revenue sources for network and cable television companies, which pay conferences and athletic departments. Cable companies also receive subscription or carriage fees, with ESPN receiving the highest fees and dominating college football and basketball telecasts by outbidding competitors for games.

There is a fear television has become so dominant in intercollegiate athletics that institutions of higher education can no longer control its influence. For example, the current structure of the postseason football bowl games is controlled by television. Whether a specific bowl can deliver attractive teams, based on their conference affiliations and won–lost records, determines whether payouts to teams are in the thousands or millions of dollars. Commissioners of the Power Five conferences are the real powerbrokers who developed the College Football Playoff to expand their revenues without having to share these with institutions not playing at their competitive level.

Another issue in intercollegiate athletics is the arms race as institutions continually improve and expand the quantity and quality of their sport facilities for conditioning, practicing, and competing. Intercollegiate athletics is an increasingly expensive enterprise given the costs of uniforms, equipment, travel, and personnel. When institutions choose or are required by their intercollegiate athletic organizations or conferences to support a certain number of teams for male and female students, the revenues seldom cover the expenses. This problem grows when conference or national rivals build bigger and better facilities. So as not to fall behind in attracting the most talented athletes, other athletic departments add costly new sport facilities. While many times funds for these athletic facilities come from private donations, a concern for many institutions is these donations detract from fund-raising efforts to support academic programs. A related concern is state funding may be redirected into facilities used exclusively or primarily by a small percentage of athletes.

This arms race has been extended to salaries for football and basketball coaches. Claiming market factors, some athletic directors have negotiated multimillion-dollar contracts for high-profile coaches. These coaches are paid far in excess of the salaries paid to institutional presidents or outstanding faculty; plus, their salaries exceed those of many professional sport team coaches. Justifications for these salaries include these coaches are the most visible and successful public relations ambassadors for their institutions, they are analyzed and critiqued incessantly, and their teams win.

Because of the importance placed on winning, these coaches are usually able to command whatever extra benefits they request for their teams and financial packages, including television shows, summer sport camps, cars, and incentives and bonuses associated with winning. An ethical issue about the increasing salaries for high-profile coaches is why nonprofit educational institutions would pay coaches millions of dollars primarily because their teams win games. How are such salaries justified when other teams are being eliminated or funds, especially from state coffers and mandatory student fees, are being allocated to offset budgetary shortfalls in athletic departments? That is, even though NCAA Division I athletic departments have multimillion-dollar budgets, they spend every dollar they receive from ticket sales, television rights fees, donations, and merchandise sales. Almost all Division I institutions rely on institutional allocations and student fees, with FCS colleges and institutions not offering football teams depending on these funds for over 70 percent of their budgets.

Another commercial influence on intercollegiate athletics is corporate advertising and sponsorships. Almost everything, except for the institution's name and athletes' names, seems to have a price and can be bought by a corporation or local business. Corporate logos are visible throughout athletic facilities and on uniforms (e.g., Nike, Adidas, and Under Armour). Special events, courts and fields, facilities, and most everything else include or can include advertisements. Athletic directors justify this commercialization of intercollegiate athletics because of increased expenses. With the emphasis on winning, it is inevitable more money will be needed for grants-in-aid; travel accommodations commensurate with the level of the institutions' teams; and expanding personnel costs for administrative staffs, facilities, and coaches' salaries.

Another commercial feature in intercollegiate athletics is licensing and merchandise sales. Many athletic programs view

this as an underutilized source of revenue. Some athletic directors argue the sale of jerseys, sweatshirts, other clothing items,
and licensed merchandise is associated most often with athletics, so the athletics department should be the primary recipient of the revenues. Sometimes, such as at the University of
Kansas, control of institutional word marks, trademarks, and
mascot symbols has been transferred to athletic departments.
Does this mean that intercollegiate athletics is more visible and
more important than the institution?

It is agreed by most that intercollegiate athletics is a business and operates with an emphasis on profit maximization in
the selling of entertainment and licensed merchandise. Why
then, ask tax-paying businesses against whom they compete for
consumers, are intercollegiate athletic programs not required
to pay unrelated business income taxes? According to Internal
Revenue Service rules, because of their affiliation with not-for-
profit educational institutions, intercollegiate athletic programs
have been able to justify revenues from the sale of entertainment and licensed merchandise being used to directly fund
their athletic programs, while they have not had to pay income
taxes on their business transactions. Many question whether
multimillion-dollar salaries for coaches and expenditures for
large traveling parties during bowl trips directly benefit athletes
or divert funds to administrators or other supporters of commercialized intercollegiate athletics.

Another issue facing intercollegiate athletics is gambling.
Some athletes have shaved points, which occurs when gamblers promise payments to athletes for playing in ways to keep
the point spread within the range of the bets placed by the
gamblers. Since intercollegiate athletes are not permitted to
accept pay for their play, some are vulnerable to this entice-
ment, especially since they do not have to lose the game, just
help manipulate the point spread. In addition, the point spread
provided in newspapers and online makes gambling an ethical
issue for college students, including athletes.

Another area of concern affecting some intercollegiate athletes occurs when they sign with sports agents and receive impermissible benefits as college athletes. Intercollegiate athletic organizations require athletes to maintain their amateur status, which means athletes cannot receive benefits provided by sports agents who seek to represent these athletes in negotiating contracts with professional teams. Some athletes have lost their eligibility to compete because they received cash, cars, and other inducements from sports agents who anticipated making money from lucrative professional contracts the agents claimed they could negotiate for these athletes. Marcus Camby, an All-American basketball player at the University of Massachusetts, acknowledged taking thousands of dollars in cash and gifts while playing in college from sports agents John Lounsbury and Wesley Spears. Some athletes may be tempted to accept money to shave points or accept cash and other benefits from sports agents because they feel exploited—that is, these athletes realize athletic departments make millions of dollars because of their athletic performances. Yet, each athlete is limited to receiving a grant-in-aid.

Whether intercollegiate athletes should receive financial benefits in addition to the allowable tuition, fees, room, board, and books is a significant concern for some outstanding players. Huma and Staurowsky (2012) argued many athletes lived below the federal poverty line with an average football scholarship shortfall of $2,841. The need to pay the full cost of education led to NCAA Division I institutions to vote in 2015 to allow each institution to increase its grant-in-aid amount to cover the full cost of education. Thus far, most institutions have chosen not to increase their grants-in-aid to this permissible level.

Because of a related lawsuit settled out of court in 2008, the NCAA allocated millions of dollars that intercollegiate athletes could access to help them pay other educational expenses. Even with the availability of this assistance, some athletes claim they are being exploited. Economists agree the marginal revenue added by an outstanding intercollegiate football and basketball player was several hundred thousand dollars. For example, for the 2009–2010 season, the top football player's annual fair market value was worth between $345,000 and $514,000, and the top basketball player's annual fair market value was estimated between $620,000 and $1 million (Huma and Staurowsky 2012).

The issue of potentially paying football and basketball players is complex. First, where would the money come from to pay these athletes? Second, would only some football and basketball players be paid? Third, how much would each athlete be paid, and how would this amount be calculated? Fourth, would any other athletes be paid, and if so, how much? Fifth, if only male athletes were paid, would this violate Title IX of the 1972 Education Amendments? Sixth, would paying athletes make them employees of the institution and thus eligible for benefits such as worker's compensation?

For the millions who attend NCAA Division I football and basketball games, the growing revenues and expenses in intercollegiate athletics are usually perceived as necessary for entertaining fans. It is fun to tailgate, socialize, and party in support of favorite teams, and especially if these teams win. What many fans and most of the general public do not understand is that almost all athletic departments operate at a loss. In 2014, only 24 FBS athletic programs reported net positive generated revenues, with all of the other hundreds of athletic programs operating with deficits (Fulks 2015). As a result, millions of dollars from institutional resources were provided to athletic departments to subsidize a small percentage of students. Over the past five-year period, student fees, which accounted for over half of the subsidies provided to athletic programs to cover their expenses, were paid by students. For example, students at the College of William and Mary paid over $1,000 a year during 2014–2015; a full-time Georgia State University student paid $554 (Wolverton, Hallman, Shifflett, and Kambhampati

2015). Is this fair? If not, should this practice be allowed to continue?

Proposed Reforms and Teaching Values in Intercollegiate Athletics

The issues and controversies associated with intercollegiate athletics have led to calls for reform as individuals question whether the integrity of higher education is being jeopardized by an overemphasis on winning associated with recruiting, academics, and commercialism (Byers and Hammer 1995; The Drake Group 2016; Duderstadt 2000; Knight Commission on Intercollegiate Athletics 2001, 2010; Sperber 1990). The overarching suggestion has been for institutions and their presidents to reduce the commercialization of intercollegiate athletics that is interwoven with the emphasis on winning. To return to an emphasis on education first, is greater institutional oversight and control needed? Intercollegiate athletics, it is argued, should not compromise the well-being of athletes, the academic mission of the institution, or the good name of the institution to win or make money.

Some people advocate for the elimination of recruiting. Then, institutions would be admitting only those athletes who meet the academic standards for admission applying to all other students. Coaches could be expected to develop the skills of players who choose to attend each institution. (And, for those individuals who really are not interested in going to college, they could join developmental or minor leagues funded by the professional leagues, as happens in other countries.) Institutions could limit grants-in-aid to tuition, fees, and books, award them to athletes only on the basis of need, and guarantee them for four years. If these changes were to be enacted, intercollegiate athletics could again be described as extracurricular activities for students, rather than part-time to full-time jobs for recruited athletes, many of whom are not interested in earning a college degree.

One way to emphasize academics, and thereby reduce the emphasis on athletics and winning, could be to require one-year residency prior to competition for freshmen and transfer students. With this change, academic eligibility to participate would be based on a student's academic performance in college and not on a standardized test score or high school grades. Students who want to compete in athletics could be required to attain and maintain a minimum cumulative gradepoint average of 2.0 and make incremental progress toward earning a degree in four years. To keep athletics from replacing academics as the reason for attending college, the schedules of all teams could be shortened and restricted to one academic term. Maybe athletes could compete only one day per week while classes are in session. Athletes could be excused from classes no more than five days per academic year for travel and competition. With athletics no longer consuming the lives of athletes, academic support services for athletes could be the same as for other students. If these changes were to be enacted, intercollegiate athletics would be much less likely to replace academics in importance, and athletes would have the time and ability to focus on learning and earning degrees.

The commercialism of intercollegiate athletics could automatically lessen if these changes were to be implemented. For example, millions of dollars would be saved by eliminating some recruiting expenses, including fewer coaches for recruiting, reducing the amounts of grants-in-aid, eliminating athlete-only academic support services, and lowering salaries for coaches since they would no longer be expected to recruit as much. Athletic directors could be expected to constrain, not expand, their budgets, and place the welfare of athletes ahead of the demands of television or needs of professional sport teams. If these changes were to be enacted, personnel in athletic departments would be evaluated on the basis of developing athletes' sport skills, developing the character of athletes, and preparing athletes for careers other than in sports, not on how much money they brought in or number of games won.

Concluding Comments about Sport in the United States

Numerous problems plague youth, interscholastic, and inter-collegiate sport. The most significant culprit is the overemphasis on winning because of how it contributes directly to financial and ethical problems. Coaches and athletes cheat, engage in gamesmanship, and use, or condone the use of, performance-enhancing drugs to gain competitive advantages to help win. When fun and the other goals of young athletes are not achieved, it is usually because of adults focusing more on winning than on providing children with character-based lessons for life. When academic rules, eligibility regulations, and ethical expectations are violated in pursuit of victories, many interscholastic athletes are being taught winning is more important than showing respect and responsibility. When the most important outcome is winning, some coaches and athletes in intercollegiate athletics will break recruiting and academic regulations.

One reason sport is important in society is because it provides the opportunity to teach character at all levels of sport. Coaches and sport managers can teach sportsmanship, which includes playing fair, following the letter and spirit of the rules, respecting the judgments of officials, treating opponents with respect, shaking hands at the end of the game, never running up the score, never cheating, and never taunting. Since many lessons learned in sports will last a lifetime, coaches, parents, and sport managers have opportunities to ensure character development is emphasized and achieved.

When coaches and other adults teach, model, shape, and reinforce the development of character, athletes will become individuals who compete in morally responsible ways. The way to develop the values of athletes is through teaching moral values and moral reasoning and consistently reinforcing these. Athletes will follow the behaviors and actions of coaches and other adults who model moral courage and do the ethically right thing. Since people do what is measured and reinforced,

athletes will be more likely to reason morally and live principled lives whenever character and other moral values are
expected and rewarded.

Performance-Enhancing Drugs

The following section on the issue of performance-enhancing
drugs is included between the problem and controversies
impacting sports in the United States and international sport
because it impacts sport throughout the world. The steroid
era in MLB and the doping scandals in international cycling
and extensive drug testing from youth sport through intercollegiate athletics illustrate the use of performance-enhancing
drugs is more widespread among athletes than many imagine.
To some, the use of performance-enhancing drugs is strictly
a legal issue—that is, is the only question whether obtain-
ing these drugs violates federal law? To others, the use of
performance-enhancing drugs is a moral issue because the athletes who use them are intentionally gaining physical advantages in ways making a mockery of the best athletes versus each
other (not who has the best pharmacist).

Why have many elite athletes risked harming their bodies,
possibly permanently, to get stronger, faster, or more skillful? Is
it because of the associated financial rewards and ego benefits
of winning? Some athletes seem to want to win so intensely
or are driven by multimillion-dollar contracts, astronomical
endorsement deals, and celebrity status that they will do whatever it takes to attain these.

The use of performance-enhancing drugs has touched the
lives of youth, adolescent, and young adult athletes. The term
performance-enhancing reveals why athletes choose to use
these drugs—that is, they are seeking competitive advantages
to help them win (some athletes argue they take these drugs to
level the playing field because other athletes use them). While
the use of performance-enhancing drugs is not a recent phenomenon, the extent of the current use by athletes may not

yet fully be known. For example, MLB has been accused of ignoring the widespread use by its players of steroids, amphetamines, and other performance-enhancing drugs and did not adopt mandatory random drug testing until 2002. Only when evidence, including the 2007 "Report to the Commissioner of Baseball of an Independent Investigation into the Illegal Use of Steroids and Other Performance Enhancing Substances by Players in Major League Baseball" and congressional hearings in 2005 exposed what was happening did owners and players take action with expanded drug testing and stiffer penalties in 2014 for using banned drugs. It is unknown how many youth, interscholastic, and intercollegiate athletes have been influenced to use performance-enhancing drugs by record-setting performances, celebrity status, and multimillion-dollar contracts of drugged sport heroes and heroines.

Athletes can obtain performance-enhancing drugs from teammates, coaches, athletic trainers, personal trainers, doctors, and parents. Many athletes believe these drugs can help them quickly become bigger, stronger, and faster, which they believe will lead to greater success in sports. Naively, many athletes ignore the risks of the side effects associated with these drugs even though they may be jeopardizing not only their playing careers but also their lives. Has an overemphasis on winning clouded their judgment? For example, researcher Bob Goldman began asking elite athletes in the 1980s and biannually for the next decade whether they would take a drug that guaranteed winning a gold medal if this drug would kill them within five years. The results were verified again and again—about half of the athletes would take the drug (Reynolds 2010). Similar, in a 1995 survey, aspiring Olympic athletes revealed that well over half of them would take a performance-enhancing drug if it would guarantee winning every competition for five years, even though taking this drug would kill them (Longman 2001). Is this an example of winning at any cost?

Opposition to the use of performance-enhancing drugs is not universal. Some believe athletes have the right to do whatever they choose to do to win, and hence they would not condemn Olympic athletes who decide the money, notoriety, and other benefits outweigh any personal harm. Some claim taking performance-enhancing drugs is no different than taking vitamins, training intensely, or using various methods or drugs to rehabilitate from injuries. Others argue that taking performance-enhancing drugs is acceptable as long as athletes are smart enough not to get caught, especially if their competitors also are taking drugs. Still others emphasize that it is acceptable to take performance-enhancing drugs as long as there is no rule against it. (This is the position of some baseball players who claimed no rules of the game were violated when they used performance-enhancing drugs.)

Those who stress taking performance-enhancing drugs is wrong, dishonest, and unfair believe this practice destroys the integrity of sport. These individuals emphasize that sports should be competitions between athletes who have trained and worked hard in their skill development and physical and mental conditioning, not contests between pharmacists focused on the most effective drugs or the drugs that will not get detected in drug tests.

Drug testing is controversial because some athletes believe this practice singles them out as likely drug users and violates their constitutional rights. Specifically, they claim the Fourth and Fourteenth Amendments to the U.S. Constitution guarantee their rights against an unreasonable search, which they argue urinalysis is. Because so many athletes have found ways to avoid being caught using performance-enhancing drugs, such as through the substitution of the urine of others, urine samples in many cases are no longer obtained in private. This has raised the issue of drug testing as an invasion of privacy. Another issue with drug testing is that many claim it has failed to achieve the desired goal of eliminating drug use in sport—that is, new performance-enhancing drugs are being developed and used because they cannot be detected with existing tests or they require taking a blood sample, a more invasive and expensive procedure.

Despite these claims, for years the NCAA has required drug testing of college athletes at its championships and postseason football bowl games. In addition, intercollegiate athletic programs require their athletes to take drug tests during the season and off-season as a deterrent to the use of performance-enhancing drugs. Some states require drug testing of high school athletes. Even in youth sport at some championships, athletes must take drug tests, because some athletes at the youth level are using performance-enhancing drugs.

Lacking in most sport programs, however, are educational programs that potentially could help athletes decide not to use performance-enhancing drugs, rather than just reduce their use for fear of getting caught. Rather than requiring athletes to sign statements affirming they have not used performance-enhancing drugs to be eligible to play, and thereby possibly perjuring themselves, ethical behavior in sport emphasizes that athletes learn the morally right decision of choosing not to violate the letter and spirit of the rules. Many believe the use or nonuse of performance-enhancing drugs in sport rests upon athletes demonstrating honesty, responsibility, and integrity.

Worldwide Perspective

The Olympic Games provide a comprehensive backdrop for understanding political, national, cultural, and ethical pressures to win in international sport. Ethical breaches have occurred because the stakes have become so high, with huge financial rewards and benefits accruing to those who win. This section examines amateurism, nationalism, politics, racial and sexual discrimination, bidding scandals, unethical behaviors, and the use of performance-enhancing drugs and their impact on the values espoused by leaders of the Olympic Movement and in other international sport competitions. Numerous specific examples will provide the context for explaining that some athletes, officials, and others associated with sports have chosen to behave in unethical ways to gain competitive and personal advantages.

Doping scandals have threatened international cycling as some sponsors have chosen to no longer associate with this tainted sport. Racism, sexism, gamesmanship, cheating, and the fixing of competitive contests plague some international sports. Athletes and others associated with sports have attempted to rationalize or justify their unethical behaviors as the way the games must be played to win. Others view these same actions as unprincipled and immoral. In seeking to address unethical problems, several sport organizations have enacted drug testing, legislated codes of ethics and other rules governing behavior, and honored those who have served as exemplars of sportsmanship, integrity, and character in sport.

Amateurism in the Olympic Games

The English heritage of the word amateur carries the meaning of "lover of." An amateur describes a person who engages in an activity like sports without formal preparation and is used in contrast with the expert who possesses extensive knowledge, education, or ability. An amateur also is a person who engages in an activity like sport without receiving monetary benefits or making a living by engaging in this activity. For example, Bobby Jones has been praised for being an amateur and playing for the love of the game. Jones did not dedicate himself solely to golf or receive prize money when he won the U.S. Amateur, British Amateur, U.S. Open, and British Open championships in 1930.

The concept of amateurism in sports, which was modeled upon the nineteenth-century British Amateur Sport Ideal, became an essential feature of the modern Olympic Games from their beginning in 1896 through the 1970s. The myth or façade of amateurism was removed when higher levels of performance, possible only through extended physical training, were expected and significant financial benefits were accepted.

When Frenchman Pierre de Coubertin sought to reestablish the Olympic Games, he began by calling a conference in 1894 that led to the formation of the IOC. The IOC helped organize the first Olympic Games in the modern era, which were held in Athens, Greece, in 1896. One espoused goal was to provide friendly competitions among amateurs who competed for the love of their respective sports. Even as the world changed, the IOC through the Olympic Movement tried to preserve a nineteenth-century perspective of amateurism founded on elitist class distinctions and masculine dominance.

Amateurism as a participation requirement for athletes was an idealistic requirement for the Olympic Games for decades. If an amateur is narrowly defined as an individual who does not dedicate extensive amounts of time and effort to skill development and has not received pay or benefits because of his or her athletic abilities, athletes who competed in the early years of the Olympic Games were dishonest in claiming to be amateurs. However, given the IOC's rule for amateurism, many of the early Olympic athletes were upper-class individuals who enjoyed the leisure time to practice their skills, such as in private clubs, and the financial means to provide needed equipment.

As IOC president between 1952 and 1972, Avery Brundage attempted to vigorously enforce the amateurs-only requirement for athlete eligibility. To dramatically emphasize this in 1968, he led the IOC to disqualify Austrian skier Karl Schranz for receiving money from ski equipment companies. Even though most people wanted to believe the love of the game motivated athletes to spend endless hours training and honing their skills, in reality, this level of dedication was almost impossible without their receiving financial benefits because of their athletic abilities and successes.

Despite resistance from most IOC members, by the 1970s many Olympic athletes were receiving appearance fees and other under-the-table payments; several governments were supporting athletes, such as through military appointments with assignments to train and compete in their sports; and equipment and shoe companies also were subsidizing athletes. Inevitably, the ever-increasing quest to become "swifter, higher, stronger," as stated in the Olympic Motto, resulted in a dramatic change in eligibility rules of the Olympic Games from the myth of amateurism to the reality of elite athletes benefiting financially from their sport achievements.

Since the 1980s, each international sport federation determines the eligibility rules for athletes competing in the Olympic Games and other international competitions. For example, basketball players could be professionals starting in 1992, while the first professional boxers could participate in the Olympic Games starting in 2016. While some Olympic committees, like the United States Olympic Committee (USOC), pay athletes for winning gold, silver, and bronze medals, others do not, possibly due to financial limitations.

Most Olympic athletes, such as those who compete in judo, badminton, and rowing, receive limited media coverage, endorsement opportunities, and financial benefits as they pursue their dreams of being the best in their respective sports and events. Although a few publicized Olympic athletes, such as swimmer Michael Phelps in the 2008 Beijing, 2012 London, and 2016 Rio de Janeiro Olympic Games, are known, most people would never recognize the names of the hundreds of Olympic athletes who are not sponsored by sport equipment or apparel companies. Some athletes benefit from coaches provided by national Olympic committee or national training centers, while most athletes fund themselves or have family members help them financially. Each athlete's training and financial circumstances are individualized depending on the wealth, political context, and sport structure of his or her nation.

While many athletes continue to embody the amateur ideal of competing for the love of the game, a comparatively small number of Olympic athletes enjoy fame and fortune. Television, corporations willing to invest millions of dollars in sports for sponsorship and advertising purposes, an increasing number of professional athletes, and lucrative endorsement opportunities for winners of the most prestigious events have contributed to a swelling tide of commercialism associated with the Olympic Games.

Nationalism and Politics in the Olympic Games

The Olympic Charter states its competitions are between individuals, not nations. In reality, though, individuals are not permitted to enter the Olympic Games, only athletes who have been selected by national Olympic committees are. Athletes, dressed in team uniforms, enter the stadium during Opening Ceremonies behind their nations' flags. National anthems are played to honor the athletes who win gold medals. Nations winning the most medals or gold medals claim these symbolize the superiority of their political systems.

IOC members for years claimed the Olympic Games promoted international peace, friendship, and camaraderie among athletes. Yet, the IOC structured competitions, pageantry, and rewards based on national affiliation. Beginning in the 1956 Melbourne Olympic Games, athletes during the Closing Ceremonies were encouraged to enter the stadium intermingled with athletes of the world, not as representatives of their nations. Still, the rhetoric about friendship among nations seemed to ring hollow and ignore the reality that the Olympic Games were highly politicized. Many Olympic athletes realized they were sometimes used to achieve purposes far afield from friendship among nations. When the Soviet Union's athletes competed for the first time in 1952 Helsinki Olympic Games, they were housed separately from other competitors, as Soviet leaders alleged concerns about the safety of their athletes. This action did not seem to adhere to the spirit of friendship and internationalism among athletes.

Nationalism became a volatile ideological clash between nations within the context of the Olympic Games in the years following World War II. Since the beginning of the modern Olympic Games, the IOC stressed national Olympic committees should operate independent of politics and affiliations with governments. But, the IOC willingly ignored the governmental control over the Soviet Union's Olympic Committee because the IOC wanted to include athletes from this huge and increasingly powerful nation in the Olympic Movement.

Despite eligibility rules defining amateurs as athletes who did not receive financial support because of their talents and skills, the IOC in another deviation from stated policy allowed the Soviet Union to be represented in the Olympic Games by state-supported athletes. Previously, a few athletes who were in the militaries of other countries, including the United States, had spent considerable time training for the modern pentathlon in lieu of fulfilling other military duties. But, the Soviet Union was the first nation to be represented by many athletes whose military status appeared to be in name only as they dedicated themselves to sport training.

In another postwar situation, controversies raged about what nation should represent China and Germany in the Olympic Games. Did Nationalist China (renamed the Republic of China), the island nation home to the national Olympic committee, represent China? Or, was it Communist China (People's Republic of China) with its millions of people? Although athletes from the People's Republic of China competed in the 1952 Helsinki Olympic Games, the government refused to allow its athletes to compete in the 1956 Melbourne Olympic Games because the Republic of China was participating. This conflict disappeared for a while when the Communist nation withdrew from the Olympic Movement and the Republic of China or Taiwan became the only representative in 1956 Rome Olympic Games. The People's Republic of China did not return until the 1980 Lake Placid Winter Olympic Games.

Controversy also surrounded how to deal with Germany after that nation was divided into Communist and democratic sectors after World War II. In 1952, the Federal Republic of Germany (West Germany) competed, but the German Democratic Republic (East Germany) was not invited to send a team. In 1956 (Melbourne), 1960 (Rome), and 1964 (Tokyo), the IOC negotiated a unified team composed of athletes from both nations. IOC president Brundage claimed the Olympic Games had successfully brought the two German sectors together. This supposed harmony was short-lived as politics, as characterized the China issue, always won out over athletic competitions.

As the politically charged issues of Chinese and German representation were debated within the IOC, governments that did or did not recognize one or more of the participating nations used the Olympic Games to make their case. Respect for national heritage and the rights of athletes and responsible actions seemed not as important as using the Olympic Games to advocate that one political system was superior to another.

Boycotts of the Olympic Games have been used to make political and ideological statements for years. Given that the Olympic Games had become the most significant international sport festival, some nations and individuals chose to use them to advance a cause, communicate with people throughout the world about a human rights or equity issue, and express opposition to the actions of others. A boycott, which inevitably began with the threat of preventing athletes from competing in the Olympic Games, came to be viewed as a viable approach to attempt to force changes in behaviors or concessions from other nations. Whenever boycotts actually occurred, the denial of the opportunity to test one's athletic abilities against the top athletes of the world illustrated a loss of fairness and justice that most people believed should characterize all sports.

Boycotts in the Olympic Games began in 1956 when Spain, Switzerland, and the Netherlands withdrew in protest against the 1955 Soviet invasion of Hungary. Egypt, Lebanon, and Iraq refused to participate in the 1956 Melbourne Olympic Games to protest the intervention with the Suez Canal by France and Great Britain. Twenty-two African nations plus Guyana boycotted the 1976 Montreal Olympic Games. Even though their threat was successful in getting the IOC to ban South Africa and Rhodesia due to their practice of apartheid, these 23 nations still boycotted because the New Zealand team was allowed to participate. (The issue here was a New Zealand rugby, a non-Olympic sport at the time, team had competed in South Africa.) Due to the 1979 invasion of Afghanistan by

Soviet Union troops, the United States and 64 other nations boycotted the 1980 Moscow Olympic Games. The Soviet Union and 14 Eastern Bloc nations boycotted the 1984 Los Angeles Olympic Games, possibly in retaliation. Cuba, Ethiopia, Nicaragua, and North Korea for political reasons refused to send teams to the 1988 Seoul Olympic Games.

The deadliest use of politics occurred during the 1972 Munich Olympic Games when eight Black September terrorists of the Palestine Liberation Organization killed two Israelis and took nine hostages. Wrestling coach Moshe Weinberg and weightlifter Yossef Romano fought against the kidnappers, allowing one wrestler to escape, before they were killed. After hours of tense negotiations at the airport where the kidnappers and hostages had been transported, the other Israelis were killed (weightlifter David Berger, weightlifter Ze'ev Friedman, wrestling referee Yossef Gutfreund, wrestler Eliezer Halfin, track coach Amitzur Shapira, shooting coach Kehat Shorr, wrestler Mark Slavin, fencing coach Andre Spitzer, and weightlifting judge Yacov Springer).

The Olympic Games—and specifically these 11 victims—were used as political pawns as the terrorists sought the release of imprisoned sympathizers to their cause. IOC president Brundage suspended competitions for one day and at the Memorial Service in honor of those slain declared the Games must go on. Brundage, whose idealistic belief that the Olympic Games were more important than just about anything, advocated that even the death of Olympians would not be allowed to forestall this international sport festival.

Many historians of the Olympic Games have questioned Brundage's decision; others applauded it. No doubt, though, the ease with which the terrorists entered the Olympic Village where the athletes were living forever changed the Olympic Games. The scope and expense of security for the athletes since 1972 vividly shows the Olympic Games are no longer innocent sporting pastimes. The reality is the Olympic Games operate on a massive international and televised stage. So, the Olympic

Movement will likely suffer through subsequent political conflicts, such as those caused by boycotts, terrorism, and demonstrations, as the Olympic Games are used to protest and advance national and political agendas.

Racism and Human Rights in the Olympic Games

The international dimension of the Olympic Games provides it with unusual influence that at times governments have been unable or unwilling to wield in addressing human rights issues. For example, the Olympic Movement and IOC members at times have focused attention on discriminatory practices and the lack of human rights adversely affecting potential Olympians. Notable among these violations has been the South Africa's historical practice of apartheid and refusal to permit integrated sports.

South African apartheid eventually led the IOC to revoke recognition of the South African National Olympic Committee in 1970. Only after governmental changes in that nation led to the end of apartheid was South Africa readmitted into the Olympic Movement in 1991. A racially mixed team represented South Africa in the 1992 Barcelona Olympic Games.

When Germany was awarded the 1936 Berlin Olympic Games, Adolf Hitler's regime promised Jewish athletes would be allowed on its team. Nonetheless, the persecution of Jews and other groups persisted and worsened as history revealed. In 2001, evidence surfaced that Iraqi athletes had been tortured by Uday Hussein, who was president of the Iraqi National Olympic Committee. Thousands of individuals in Atlanta (1996), Beijing (2008), London (2012), and Rio de Janeiro (2016) were displaced from their homes to make way for construction of the sport venues for those games. Many individuals claimed they were not fairly compensated.

Since Beijing was awarded the 2008 Olympic Games, the host nation and the IOC have endured a firestorm of criticism because of perceptions that the People's Republic of China engaged in unjust human rights practices. Its commercial relationship with

Sudan, where hundreds of thousands died in Darfur, has helped fuel the allegation that the People's Republic of China emphasized economic advancement over human rights. It also has been alleged that children were abused in factories making souvenirs for the Olympic Games. Even though promises were made during the bidding process that human rights issues would be addressed, numerous protesters during the Olympic Torch Relay questioned whether these promises used to obtain the bid were kept.

Racism in International Sports

The United Nations (UN) General Assembly in 1977 adopted an International Declaration against Apartheid in Sports because racism denied athletes competitive opportunities. Since prejudice and discrimination continued to plague sports, in 1985, the UN held an International Convention against Apartheid in Sports, which called for the establishment of a Commission against Apartheid in Sports. The UN in its declaration of 2005 as the International Year of Sport and Physical Education continued to work to counter racism in sport through peaceful competitions and play. This yearlong initiative promoted the belief that the values potentially learned through sport are universal and advocated that sport could serve as a global language in the elimination of discrimination and racism.

To illustrate the adverse effects of racism, one overt situation involving Basil D'Oliveira, who was born in Cape Town, South Africa, will be provided. He was prohibited from playing first-class cricket in that nation because he was classified as colored due to apartheid. After playing nonwhite cricket in his homeland, he migrated to England and became a British citizen. After playing in international test matches for England, the Marylebone Cricket Club (MCC), which at the time governed cricket, was pressured by South African white political leaders not to select D'Oliveira to play in the 1968–1969 test matches against South Africa. A public outcry against this discriminatory decision led to the MCC adding him to England's team. As a result, South African representatives canceled the tour matches.

Racism has plagued international football, or soccer, as athletes of different colors, ethnicities, and religions have been subjected to the prejudice of athletes, coaches, officials, and spectators. The term hooliganism describes the unruly, rowdy, destructive, abusive, and sometimes racist behaviors of international soccer fans. Numerous incidents of racist taunts from fans have victimized black athletes when they have played internationally, especially in Brazil, Spain, Italy, Germany, and Eastern Europe. Even the renowned Brazilian star Pele had to endure racially based taunting and other discriminatory abuse. Based on prejudicial attitudes, some have claimed black soccer players were not as skilled as their white counterparts.

The International Federation of Association Football (FIFA), which has more members than either the IOC or the UN, governs international soccer, which is the most popular sport in the world. FIFA has clearly stated in its disciplinary code that players, coaches, and officials guilty of making disparaging, discriminatory, or denigrating statements, or engaging in actions directed toward another person's race, color, language, religion, or ethnic origin would be suspended and fined. Also, teams can be penalized if their fans engage in racist behaviors, and spectators can be banned. The FIFA's Code of Ethics specifically condemns racism.

In an attempt to address the issue of racism, in 1999 several associations and players' unions formed Football Against Racism in Europe (FARE). Through organizations in over 30 European countries, FARE seeks to eliminate racism among fans, players, coaches, and officials at grassroots, national, and transnational levels. It also combats far-right nationalism, sexism, homophobia, and other types of discrimination as it seeks to advance social cohesion and use of sport for social change.

In 2008, the Council of Europe of the International Sport and Culture Association, in support of the campaign for "All Different All Equal," held an international seminar that examined the issue of discrimination and racism in soccer. One outcome of that dialogue was to urge organizational leaders to establish and enforce policies to fight violence and racism in sport because of their cancerous effects on society in general and players in particular. The attendees advocated sport has the potential to serve as a powerful tool to facilitate the acceptance of all people, regardless of race, ethnicity, religion, sex, or ability.

Athletes in numerous sports have had to deal with overt and subtle racism. The following three examples illustrate this. Althea Gibson, who was from the United States, was excluded from tournaments throughout the world due to the bigotry of the white tennis establishment that controlled the exclusive country clubs at which these events were held. Not until 1951 did she become the first African American invited to the Wimbledon Championships in England, thus opening the door forever to tennis players of all races and ethnicities. Before Tiger Woods became the top golfer in the world, he had to endure racist comments from individuals who were reluctant to accept him into their exclusive, white-dominated clubs. The first African American auto racing driver in Formula One, Englishman Lewis Hamilton, had to endure insults, jeers, and other racial abuse while racing in Spain in 2008. Many athletes, coaches, and officials have experienced abuse due to racism and prejudice, including taunts, insults, and disparate treatment. They persevered and demonstrated the strength of character to display sportsmanship and respect, even though they were not the beneficiaries of similar treatment.

In response to racism in its sport, in 2006 the International Cricket Council adopted an antiracism code including a standard of conduct that sought to eliminate discriminatory behaviors from this sport. This code included a statement of the expectations for spectators and encouraged the use of clear wording on tickets and signs in venues to emphasize these expectations. This code also required the use of public announcements at international matches condemning racist chants and other abusive or offensive behaviors. Offenders of this code would be removed from the venues, banned from attending future matches, and subjected to prosecution. This code might serve as an international model for players, coaches, officials, and fans in their respectful and responsible treatment of athletes of all races, ethnicities, religions, and cultures.

Females in the Olympic Games

Pierre de Coubertin and other initial IOC members believed the Olympic Games should provide opportunities for highly skilled males to display their athletic prowess. They did not believe females should be competitive athletes. While females were excluded from the first modern Olympic Games in Athens in 1896, they were permitted to participate in the 1900 Paris Olympic Games. According to IOC records for these Games 22 females competed in two sports. These female Olympians competed in the individual, leisurely sports of golf and tennis while wearing Victorian-style clothing appropriate to their sex. Archery was the only sport for the six females in the 1904 St. Louis Olympic Games (International Olympic Committee 2014).

In the 1912 Stockholm Olympic Games, females began competing in swimming and diving. Not until the 1928 Amsterdam Olympic Games did the IOC add gymnastics and a few track-and-field events for females, with the 800 meters the longest distance run. Not until the 1972 Munich Olympic Games were females allowed to run a longer (1,500-meter) race. The women's marathon was added in the 1984 Los Angeles Olympic Games. The first team sport for women was volleyball in the 1964 Tokyo Olympic Games. Other team sports added for females were basketball and team handball in 1976 (Montreal), field hockey in 1980 (Moscow), softball (eliminated after 2008 and will return in 2020) and soccer in 1996 (Atlanta), and ice hockey in 1998 (Nagano). As these team sports and other individual sports and events were provided for females, their participation numbers increased. In the 2012 London Olympic Games, 44.2 percent (4,676) of the athletes were females compared with 5,892 males (International Olympic Committee 2012); in the 2014 Sochi Winter Olympic

Games, there were over 2,800 athletes with over 40 percent female athletes (International Olympic Committee 2015).

The resistance toward females in the Olympic Games and gradual expansion of sports and events were reflective of societal attitudes about the role of females—that is, numerous sports were perceived to be too aggressive or inappropriate for females. Or, this reluctance to grant full acceptance to females may have reflected prejudicial or sexist attitudes of the all-male IOC that females were not welcome in many Olympic sports. The male control over the Olympic Games has been accused of being discriminatory and unfair, unjust, and disrespectful toward females. Not until 1981 were the first women, Pirjo Haeggman of Finland and Flor Isava-Fonseca of Venezuela, selected for IOC membership. In 2016, 22 of the 93 members of the IOC were females (International Olympic Committee 2016).

Another historical issue regarding females in the Olympic Games raising ethical concerns dealt with sex testing, which was used to guarantee only females competed against females because of sex-specific physiological abilities. Stella Walsh (Stanislawa Walasiewicz), a Polish sprinter raised in the United States who won the gold medal in the 100-meters race for Poland in the 1932 Los Angeles Olympic Games, was later accused of being a male. Hermann Ratjen, a German high jumper who competed as a female in the 1936 Berlin Olympic Games, was revealed to be a male in 1955. Tamara Press and Irina Press, who won five track-and-field Olympic gold medals for the Soviet Union in 1960 (Rome) and 1964 (Tokyo), ended their careers when sex testing was introduced. It was alleged the Press sisters were male imposters.

Sex testing began in 1966 at the European Track and Field Championships in Budapest. Since female athletes were required to parade naked in front of physicians, five world-class athletes chose not to compete in these championships. In the 1968 Mexico City Olympic Games, sex testing was initiated in an attempt to prevent males with inherent physiological advantages from masquerading as females, and thus cheating to try to win. While preventing the deceit of male imposters, sex testing was viewed by many females in the Olympic Games as degrading, sexist, and an invasion of privacy.

One of the controversies surrounding sex testing was that some females were unfairly disqualified from the Olympic Games and other international competitions even though they were females. Misdiagnoses were associated with genetic conditions and an individual's chromosomes. According to physicians, there was compelling scientific evidence that chromosome-based sex testing could be functionally and ethically inconsistent. Because of these problems, as well as the fact that sex testing emotionally traumatized and socially stigmatized some female athletes, the IOC stopped sex testing for all female Olympians in 1999. As recently as the 2008 Beijing Olympic Games, though, if the sex of any female athlete was questioned, she has had to submit to a blood test to verify her eligibility.

Sexism in International Sports

Sexist treatment of females persists in many nations due to disparities in the number of sport opportunities and associated support structures, inadequacy of funding, stereotypical and cultural expectations about the roles of women, and lack of media coverage. Discriminatory practices against females begin at youth levels and continue to deter many females from reaching their potential in international sports. One contributing factor to these inequalities is that primarily males make sport policies by controlling governing organizations. Most broadcasters, reporters, directors, photographers, and other media personnel are males.

Islamic fundamentalists in some Muslim countries have barred females from sports, unless they are dressed in head-to-toe clothing leaving only their hands and faces uncovered. Muslim countries, such as Afghanistan, Algeria, Iran, Iraq, Kuwait, Pakistan, Qatar, Saudi Arabia, and the United Arab Emirates, historically prohibited or strongly discouraged females from sport competitions. Those Muslim female athletes who have chosen to train and compete often have been subjected to jeering, obscenities, and other abuse. In Indonesia, the most populous Muslim nation in the world, and other countries that are predominately Muslim in Asia, however, female athletes enjoy the freedom to compete in sports of their choice without clothing requirements.

The Council of Europe founded in 1949 seeks to promote human rights and democratic principles. In 1992 in its European Sports Charter, this council stated that each individual should be guaranteed opportunities in sports, and it advocated for the protection and development of the ethical basis of sport. Discrimination was specifically prohibited. While progress had been made, worldwide equality of opportunity for females in sport has not yet been achieved.

Bidding Scandals in the Olympic Games

Given the significant time and financial investment required to develop bids for hosting the Olympic Games, unsuccessful aspirants sometimes have hinted at the possibility that votes of IOC members who select the host cities may have been influenced by factors, such as money, other than the quality of the bids. Some people involved with Salt Lake City's previous unsuccessful bid process for the Winter Olympic Games seemed to believe the only way to be selected as the host city was to spend thousands of dollars in courting and entertaining IOC members to secure their votes. In 1998, bribery and corruption among individuals associated with the 2002 Salt Lake City Winter Olympic Games Organizing Committee were exposed. The resulting scandal revealed committee representatives had given cash, scholarships, lavish gifts, and other improper benefits to several members of the IOC and their families. In 1999, four IOC members resigned, one who had been implicated died, and the IOC voted to exclude six of its members for inappropriate conduct, including breaking the

Olympic Oath and harming the reputation of the Olympic Movement.

In the wake of this scandal, additional allegations were made and some evidence was provided that IOC members had accepted bribes for their votes during past bidding processes. The allegations broadened to include that vote buying had been a common practice in the successful bids of Atlanta (1996), Nagano (1998), Sydney (2000), and Salt Lake City (2002). Some critics accused the IOC of fostering a corrupt bidding process because IOC members were invited to prospective host cities and treated lavishly. Over the years, the IOC had done nothing to prevent the likelihood of unethical influence on IOC members' votes, possibly because members enjoying these benefits shifted their votes.

In attempting to overcome the smear to its image in the aftermath of the Salt Lake City fiasco, the IOC established tighter ethics rules, including barring members from visiting any of the bidding cities. The IOC restricted members from receiving gifts from bidding cities and added other reforms to the selection process. The IOC also changed the life terms of its members to eight-year renewable terms along with a mandatory retirement age of 70 and changed the nomination process for potential IOC members.

Most dramatic of the reforms may have been the change in the representational composition of the IOC. In the past, IOC members had been considered representatives of the IOC to countries of the world. While no incumbent IOC member would be excluded, over time the IOC will be composed of 115 members, including 15 Olympic athletes elected by their peers at the time of the Olympic Games, 15 representatives of national Olympic committees, 15 representatives of international sport federations, and 70 other members who would bring unique abilities and experiences. Through these reforms, the IOC hoped to regain its status as a principled group of sport leaders serving as guardians of the integrity of the premier international sport festival.

The Olympic Games have withstood dramatic societal changes throughout their more than 100-year history. Once obscure, the Olympic Games are now televised and viewed worldwide via the Internet and social media. Revenues from television and other media support the operations of the IOC, international sport federations, national Olympic committees, and the host cities' organizing committees, all of which are increasingly dependent on these funds. Females enjoy increasing opportunities to compete in more sports and events, rather than being relegated to the sidelines to cheer. The Olympic Games, once open to only amateurs, are primarily competitions among professional athletes. National Olympic committees pay athletes who win medals as they vie for bragging rights and associated political capital. Many athletes who win gold medals in the Olympic Games enjoy significant monetary rewards, including endorsements and celebrity status. Because of financial benefits, some competitors choose to do whatever it takes to win. Playing by the letter and spirit of the rules is sometimes ignored and violated while in pursuit of victories.

Unethical Behavior among Officials in the Olympic Games

Officials in the Olympic Games are selected by the international sport federations for each sport, such as the International Basketball Federation, International Swimming Federation, and International Skating Union. Officials are expected to adhere to the highest ethical standards, with a representative official repeating this commitment during the Opening Ceremonies. Despite these expectations, there have been numerous problems with perceived and actual cheating by officials in the Olympic Games. Whenever cheating occurred, athletes who trained for years and made huge financial and personal sacrifices were denied the right to receive the honor and recognition their performances merited.

The sports most affected by judging controversies and unethical behaviors have been those requiring considerable subjectivity, such as dealing with artistic merit in skating events or when points are added or subtracted in boxing and gymnastics. Sometimes Cold War politics or sentiments opposing an athlete's national origin have robbed rightful winners of the recognition of a gold medal or the self-esteem of being the best—that is, athletes were cheated by corrupt officials representing international sport federations who were behaving unethically. A few examples are provided to illustrate how athletes have been cheated by unethical officials.

The men's basketball gold medal game in the 1972 Munich Olympic Games ended in controversy surrounding the actions of officials on and off the court. After the team from the United States took a one-point lead on a free throw, the Soviet Union's team had only three seconds left in the game to attempt to score. Whether due to mistakes by the court officials, clock problems, or inappropriate interference by the secretary general of the International Basketball Federation, the Soviet team after two failed attempts successfully scored on the third try. The protest filed on behalf of the U.S. team was denied by the five-member Jury of Appeal, which voted along ideological lines between Communist and non-Communist countries. While the Soviet team members received gold medals, the U.S. team members refused to accept the silver medals because they believed they had been cheated.

In the 2002 Salt Lake City Winter Olympic Games, a French judge admitted to being pressured to vote for the Russian pair in ice skating, rather than the Canadian pair almost everyone else agreed had a superior performance. Initially, the International Skating Union (ISU) refused to take any action to rectify the injustice done to Jamie Salé and David Pelletier. Only after being pressured by IOC president Jacques Rogge were ISU officials willing to admit unethical behavior had cheated the Canadian pair, who then were awarded gold medals.

Numerous other examples of questionable judging in skating events have occurred, yet the ISU has continued to allow national sport federations to appoint judges. As a result, some of these officials became beholden to national organizations and were more likely to succumb to pressure from their leaders to assign certain ratings to selected skaters. While there have been some changes in the scoring systems in skating events, it could be argued that dropping high and low marks was dealing with the aftermath, rather than the source, of the problem of biased judges.

In gymnastics, Pound (2004) suggested the Soviets, through their control of the International Gymnastics Federation, were able to devise a scoring approach favoring their gymnasts over the Romania team. He argued this strategy enabled the Soviets to win the team competition in the 1976 Montreal Olympic Games, even though Romanian Nadia Comaneci and her teammates performed superbly.

Pound (2004) also described an example of unethical behavior in the 1988 Seoul Olympic Games, which he described as the most flagrant example of collusion and unethical behavior of boxing judges. He based this claim on evidence documenting the bribes some boxing judges were paid to unfairly deliver the gold medal to Korean Park Si-Hun, who was out-boxed in the finals of the light middleweight class by Roy Jones Jr. of the United States.

Conflict of interest threatens the integrity of the Olympic Games when officials in positions of authority over the outcome of competitions appear to favor athletes from their own countries (Pound 2004). In the 1992 Barcelona Olympic Games, Judith McGowan, who was the lead referee in synchronized swimming, was in the position to rectify an immediately acknowledged scoring mistake made by a judge. With the beneficiary of the mistake an athlete from the United States who received the gold medal, McGowan, also from the United States, alleged no conflict of interest in allowing an incorrect score to remain. In response to a protest from the Canadian delegation on behalf of the rightful winner, McGowan reviewed her own decision and again ruled in favor of her nation's athlete. Only after significant pressure was applied, including the threat of an appeal to the Court of Arbitration for Sport, did the International Swimming Federation finally acknowledge the injustice done to Sylvie Freechette. But, it took over a year to rectify the abuse of power and harm done to this athlete and finally award her a gold medal.

Numerous other examples could be provided to illustrate how officials entrusted with upholding the integrity of Olympic competitions have failed in their duties. Athletes' dreams have been shattered whenever arbitrary and capricious actions of officials cheated and stole from athletes their probable once-in-a-lifetime opportunity to stand atop the victory stand as the champions of the world. Through no fault of their own, these athletes were victimized by officials who for political reasons, financial influence, or other personal benefits acted dishonestly, disrespectfully, unfairly, and irresponsibly.

Use of Performance-Enhancing Drugs in the Olympic Games

The Olympic Oath specifies athletes must abide by the rules and show the spirit of sportsmanship. To publicly reinforce this commitment, an athlete from the host nation, on behalf of all athletes, recites the Olympic Oath during the Opening Ceremonies. Despite what the Olympic Oath states, many Olympic athletes have chosen to violate the rules in numerous ways to increase their chances of winning. Apparently, these athletes have convinced themselves their training and abilities do not give them the extra second, meter, or skill needed to excel over other competitors, so they need to enhance their performances through drugs and other rule-breaking methods. In addition to cheating in violation of the Olympic Oath, these athletes have stolen from their opponents an equitable opportunity to win.

Amphetamines, steroids, and other drugs and substances have been used by athletes to gain competitive advantages in the Olympic Games long before there were any written prohibitions. However, most athletes and others interested in the purity of sports emphasized the use of performance-enhancing drugs was cheating—that is, sports stopped being competitions among athletes with an equal opportunity to win, but, rather, gave unfair advantages to athletes who chose to artificially or chemically enhance their performances.

In 1928, the International Amateur Athletic Federation (IAAF), which governs athletics (track-and-field) competitions, banned the use of stimulating substances. Even as other international sport federations followed with similar bans, drug use continued in the absence of drug tests. In the 1960 Rome Olympic Games, Danish cyclist Knud Jensen, who had taken an overdose of amphetamines, collapsed during his race and died shortly thereafter. In response, the IOC established a medical commission and published its first list of prohibited substances. Drug tests were introduced at the 1968 Grenoble Winter Olympic Games and the 1968 Mexico City Summer Olympic Games.

Ethical questions surfaced, however, as some athletes argued drug tests were invasions of privacy and violated their rights. Others claimed submitting to drug tests characterized all athletes as cheats and, therefore, they were assumed to be tainted with drugs unless they could prove their innocence. Conversely, the IOC emphasized use by some athletes of performance-enhancing drugs had forced the IOC to implement drug tests to identify and penalize those athletes who compromised the integrity of the Games through doping.

A large number of athletes from the German Democratic Republic (GDR), especially females, became medalists beginning in the 1976 Montreal Olympic Games. Numerous questions were raised when this small nation's athletes won 40 gold medals and 11 out of 13 gold medals in women's swimming.

While steroid use in the Olympic Games had been banned since 1974, not until 1984 did the IOC begin requiring drug tests for steroids. (Testing for steroids began in 1983 at the Pan American Games.) After the fall of the Berlin Wall in 1989, it was learned that many of the GDR's athletes had been given performance-enhancing steroids without their knowledge or permission. In a noteworthy act of sportsmanship in 1998, one swimmer Carola Nitschke, who had been given steroids beginning at age 13, returned her medals and asked for the removal of her name from records of the Olympic Games. The IOC honored her request.

Canadian Ben Johnson's victory in world-record time in the 100-meter sprint in the 1988 Seoul Olympic Games was short-lived when he tested positive for use of an anabolic steroid. He was disgraced with the loss of his medal and world record, as well as banishment from international competition for two years. Johnson and many other track-and-field athletes have for years denied the use of performance-enhancing drugs, even after failing drug tests.

The Chinese swimming team used anabolic steroids and human growth hormones for years, which enabled it to become a world power in this sport. Positive drug tests in other championships and subsequent bans of more than 40 Chinese swimmers since 1990, however, decimated later Olympic teams. In the 1996 Atlanta Olympic Games, Michelle Smith representing Ireland won three gold medals and one bronze medal in swimming. Suspicions were raised, however, since her improvement as a swimmer had been too remarkable to believe possible without performance-enhancing drugs. After avoiding taking several drug tests, Smith was finally tested in 1998. When the test revealed a high alcohol level that was believed to have been used as a masking agent used to hide the presence of performance-enhancing drugs, she was suspended from competition for four years.

Blood doping has been a part of the rampant doping in and tainted image of cross-country skiing for years. In the 2002 Salt Lake City Winter Olympic Games, Austrian cross-country skiers Marc Mayer and Achim Walcher were disqualified for using blood transfusions, and two team officials who administered these transfusions were banned for the next two Winter Olympic Games. Spain's Johann Muehlegg and Russian medalists Olga Danilova and Larissa Lazutina also tested positive for a drug that boosted the production of red blood cells carrying oxygen to the muscles.

Marion Jones from the United States won three gold medals (100 meters; 200 meters; and 1,600-meter relay) and two bronze medals (long jump and 100-meter relay) in the 2000 Sydney Olympic Games, but she was stripped of these medals based on her guilty plea in lying to federal investigators about using steroids in the Bay Area Laboratory Co-Operative (BALCO) case. Asli Cakir Alptekin of Turkey surrendered her 1,500-meter gold medal won in the 2012 London Olympic Games for blood doping and was banned for eight years having previously served a two-year ban for use of anabolic steroids.

Despite these examples of disqualified athletes and forfeited medals, the extent of doping among Olympic athletes is not known. It has been suggested many top athletes are willing to risk their physical well-being and reputations to earn positions on their national teams and possibly win Olympic medals, even though they may get caught and punished for using performance-enhancing drugs.

In 1999, the IOC convened a World Conference on Doping in response to doping scandals in international sports. The Lausanne Declaration on Doping in Sport, which was developed at this conference, called for the establishment of an international organization to fight doping. The World Anti-Doping Agency (WADA), which was fully operational by the 2000 Sydney Olympic Games, has as its purpose to promote and enforce the fight against doping in sports. WADA developed and implemented the World Anti-Doping Code and rules for the international harmonization of antidoping policies, testing, therapeutic use exceptions, and a list of prohibited substances and methods. This code standardizes minimum and maximum sanctions for doping violations, with the first serious violation carrying a two-year suspension and a second serious violation a lifetime sanction.

Some athletes who have tested positive for banned substances have returned to compete in the Olympic Games and win medals. So in 2008, the IOC passed a rule that athletes would be banned for the following Olympic Games if they had been suspended for at least six months during the four years prior to the Games for testing positive for banned substances. The IOC enacted this new rule to strengthen its efforts to keep the use of performance-enhancing drugs out of the Olympic Games. This rule was applied for the first time in the 2010 Vancouver Winter Olympic Games.

Many people have stressed that athletes, along with their trainers and pharmacists, may be years ahead of the most sophisticated drug tests the World Anti-Doping Agency has implemented—that is, many athletes believe they can use performance-enhancing drugs to help them succeed with little risk of getting caught. Seemingly, for these athletes, competing is not about playing by the rules, but rather only about winning by doing whatever it takes chemically.

In December 2014, a German documentary entitled *Top Secret Doping: How Russia Makes Its Winners* exposed a widespread use of performance-enhancing drugs and blood doping by Russian track-and-field athletes. Although the IAAF suspended the Russian track-and-field federation indefinitely, investigative reports issued by WADA in 2015 and January 2016 detailed not only the state-sponsored doping program in Russia but also corruption of IAAF officials who attempted to cover up this doping scandal. Former IAAF president Lamine Diack who since 2009 knew about and failed to expose and punish Russian track-and-field athletes and coaches for the doping scandal led the embedded culture of IAAF corruption for 16 years. Russian track-and-field athletes were banned from international competition, a sanction that did not prevent their participation in the 2016 Rio de Janeiro Olympic Games. The IOC announced potential bans on Olympic athletes who had tested positive for banned substances in the 2008 Beijing and 2012 London Olympic Games through more advanced drug tests to retest doping samples in 2016.

As the Paralympic Games, elite sporting events for athletes from six disability groups, have risen in stature with an increased emphasis on winning, drug tests have revealed some of these athletes also have used performance-enhancing drugs. In the 1992 Barcelona Paralympic Games, five athletes tested positive for banned substances. That number increased to 14 athletes in the 2000 Sydney Games. In the 2002 Salt Lake City Winter Paralympic Games, Thomas Oelsner, a German Nordic skier, was stripped of his gold medal in the standing biathlon after testing positive for doping.

Individuals who win medals in the Olympic Games and Paralympic Games have reached the pinnacle of their sports. Their achievements have been the results of years of training and sacrifice. However, when they violated the rules or benefited from unethical behaviors to gain unfair advantages, they have cheated their opponents and sports. Their unprincipled actions resoundingly declared the only thing that matters is winning and self-advancement. Cheaters failed to display the integrity the leaders of the Olympic Movement believed should characterize the Olympic Games. Discriminatory practices, political and nationalistic ploys manipulating athletes, and the use of performance-enhancing drugs have no place within peaceful, friendly, respectful, and fair competitions among the best athletes of the world.

Doping Scandals in International Cycling

The use of performance-enhancing drugs and methods is not unique to the Olympic Games, as it now threatens the integrity of many sports. The World Conference on Doping was initiated by the IOC in 1999 partially in response to doping scandals in cycling. A triggering event occurred in 1998 when Willy Voet, an employee of the Festina racing team, was caught with a carload of performance-enhancing drugs, including erythropoietin (EPO), human growth hormones, testosterone, and amphetamines. The Tour de France expelled the Festina team from its race, with several of the Festina riders admitting to having used performance-enhancing drugs.

Doping has plagued the Tour de France almost since its beginning in 1903. In seeking an advantage or to cope with this grueling 21-stage race, riders, especially since the 1960s, have used alcohol, cocaine, and amphetamines. It was amphetamines that contributed to the death of England's Tom Simpson in the 1967 Tour. In more recent years, steroids, human growth hormones, and blood doping have been used by numerous cyclists.

Lance Armstrong, after surviving testicular cancer, won the Tour de France seven consecutive years between 1999 through 2005 before announcing his retirement. After returning to competition and the Tour de France, he retired again in 2011. Suspicions about Armstrong's use of performance-enhancing drugs were repeatedly raised during his historic run of victories and climaxed when his former U.S. Postal teammate Floyd Landis was stripped of his 2016 Tour de France victory because his level of testosterone exceeded the allowed limit and accused Armstrong of doping, too. After Armstrong disparaged numerous allegations from teammates and others about his extensive doping and based on a federal investigation, the United States Anti-Doping Agency (USADA) and International Cycling Union (cycling's governing body) stripped him of his seven Tour titles and banned him from competitive cycling for life. Not until 2013 in a televised interview did Armstrong admit to taking cortisone, testosterone, and EPO and using blood transfusions to boost his oxygen levels (Lance Armstrong Biography 2016).

On the day before the start of the 2006 Tour de France, news broke of the Operation Puerto drug bust that accused a Spanish physician, Eufemiano Fuentes, and others of administering performance-enhancing drugs to over 200 athletes, many of whom were cyclists. Tour favorites Jan Ullrich (who had won the 1997 Tour de France and a gold medal in the 2000 Sydney Olympic Games), Ivan Basso, and Oscar Sevilla were implicated in this scandal. These and other riders were suspended by their teams for allegations of using performance-enhancing drugs. Now retired, Ullrich has repeatedly denied doping, even though he paid a six-figure fine in hopes of clearing his name and reputation.

Many cyclists have used blood doping, which cannot be detected by any existing drug test, to gain advantages in international cycling. The process for blood doping involves athletes removing some of their own blood, which results in their bodies developing replacement red blood cells. Close in time to competitions, these athletes are reinfused with their own blood, thus increasing the blood's oxygen-carrying capacity and muscular endurance. Many retired cyclists, including Germany's Jorg Jaksche, have admitted to blood doping, even though it is not permitted in international cycling. The 2007 Tour de France had just begun when the prerace favorite, Alexandr Vinokourov of Kazakhstan, was found to have engaged in blood doping.

Some cyclists and other athletes who use performance-enhancing drugs also consume substances to hide their cheating. For example, in 2002, Italy's Stefano Garzelli tested positive for a diuretic used to mask the presence of other drugs. In 2007, Bjarne Riis, who won the 1996 Tour de France, admitted that he had used EPO regularly between 1993 and 1998. These and other doping scandals in the Tour de France and throughout professional cycling have so seriously undermined the credibility of this sport that numerous team and event sponsors have withdrawn financial support because they do not want to be associated with this tainted sport.

While most people rail against the use of performance-enhancing drugs in sports, not everyone categorizes their use as bad or unethical. Some people advocate that if an athlete chooses to use performance-enhancing drugs and accepts the penalties if caught for violating the rules, this athlete should be allowed to use these drugs. Another argument suggests knowing where to draw the line between therapeutic use of drugs and drugs used for performance enhancement has become increasingly blurred. It also has been proposed that instead of banning or penalizing the use of performance-enhancing drugs, drug use should be permitted and these drugs made available equally to all athletes. This, they argue, would be fairer than having competitions between athletes who have access to better pharmacists and those without performance-enhancing drugs.

Gamesmanship and Cheating in International Sports

Athletes who cheat do so intentionally and apparently do not feel bound by the same rules they expect others to follow. Following are a few examples of cheating, including one occurring in the 2000 Sydney Paralympic Games. The basketball team representing Spain in these Games was disqualified after winning the gold medal when it was discovered most of the players did not have the alleged disabilities that qualified them for these competitions.

The World Cup finals between the United States and China in 1999 was one of the most highly attended and significant women's sporting events ever. Those in attendance saw the U.S. goalkeeper Briana Scurry intentionally move forward in violation of the rules before the Chinese player Liu Ying contacted the ball on her penalty kick. The U.S. team's championship, won due to Ying's missed kick deflected by Scurry, was tarnished by cheating, with Scurry openly admitted she used this unfair strategy to gain an advantage.

More soccer players are faking injuries and rolling around on the ground supposedly in pain as they attempt to mislead officials to get them to stop or delay games. For example, in the 2002 World Cup, Brazilian player Rivaldo faked an injury so obvious he was fined for cheating. But, most athletes faking injuries are not penalized, which has led to an increase in this gamesmanship ploy. Another benefit derived from faking injuries is the unwritten rule in soccer that when a player is injured, the team in possession of the ball will kick it out-of-bounds. But, if the injury is deceptive, rather than real, it can result in a stoppage of play to the benefit of the team of the athlete faking the injury. In addition, when play is restarted, the ball is supposed to be passed back to the team that deliberately hit it out.

But, since there is no rule requiring this, it opens the door for players to take unfair advantage of those who previously showed good sportsmanship. Either of these tactics potentially can influence the outcomes of games.

The code of conduct of cricket is based on gentlemanly behavior and proper etiquette, as players are taught at an early age to display sportsmanship and civility toward competitors. In the midst of highly competitive matches where winning is paramount, however, players sometimes engage in sledging. This term is used to describe swearing at opponents or intentionally saying abusive and offensive words to competitors to negatively affect their play.

These are just a few examples of how athletes have chosen to use gamesmanship and have cheated to help them gain advantages. These choices seem to prioritize winning over playing fairly or displaying sportsmanship.

Gambling and Fixing Outcomes in International Sports

Gambling and fixing the outcomes of events threaten the integrity of sports. In 1915, a British football betting scandal occurred when Manchester United was trying to prevent relegation (forced movement to a lower level of competition because of a poor win-loss record). Its opponent was Liverpool, which was not in jeopardy of relegation or fighting for top honors. So, a Football League First Division match was fixed in Manchester United's favor, as players from both sides wagered on the result. Manchester United's Sandy Turnbull, Arthur Whalley, and Enoch West, and Liverpool's Jackie Sheldon (who was the plot's ringleader), Tom Miller, Bob Purcell, and Tom Fairfoul were banned from professional soccer for life. The bans of four men were lifted in 1919 in recognition of service to their country during World War I (except Turnbull, who was killed during the war; West, who claimed his innocence, was not reinstated until 1945).

In 1964, another British betting scandal in soccer involved eight professional players who subsequently were jailed for fixing matches. The instigator, Jimmy Gauld, approached other players to entice them to bet on the outcome of fixed matches. David Layne, Peter Swan, and Tony Kay bet against their side in a match in 1962. In 1964, Gauld sold his story to a British tabloid and incriminated these three players. His taped conversations subsequently were used to convict all four players. Six other players, Brian Philips, Sammy Chapman, Ronald Howells, Ken Thomson, Richard Beattie, and Jack Fountain, also received jail sentences for their involvement. All 10 of these players were banned from professional soccer for life.

In 1993, Marseille, which historically has been the most successful soccer club in France, won the title in that nation's top league and the United Europe Football Association (UEFA) Champions League. Because the Marseille chairman, Bernard Tapie, subsequently was found guilty of financial irregularities and match-fixing, the club was stripped of both titles and relegated from the top competitive league.

In 1994, Andres Escobar, a defender on the Colombian team, was murdered after he returned home from the FIFA World Cup. His own-goal (i.e., a player accidently causes the ball to go into the goal scoring a point for the opposing team) was responsible for the difference in a 2–1 loss to the U.S. team. There was speculation that members of the Medellin drug cartel had bet a significant amount of money on Colombia to win and blamed Escobar for the loss.

German soccer referee Robert Hoyzer in 2005 confessed to fixing the outcome of matches and was sentenced to prison for fraud. Hoyzer also received a lifetime ban from officiating by the German Football Association. Croatian gambler Ante Sapina, who operated the organized crime syndicate behind this massive scandal, was sentenced to prison as well. Although Hoyzer alleged other referees and some players had received money for their participation in this match-fixing scandal, only referee Dominik Marks, who denied involvement, received a suspended sentence. In 2009, about 200 soccer matches in Europe, including qualifying games in the Union of European

Football Associations (UEFA) Europa League and UEFA Champions League, had been fixed by gamblers.

Bookmaking (i.e., accepting bets and paying winnings depending on the outcome of the sporting event) in many European nations is regulated but not illegal. Many international tennis tournaments are played in nations where gambling is socially acceptable and part of the cultural fabric. Since only one player in a game where unforced errors occur regularly is needed to determine the outcome of a match, international tennis may be a likely victim for fixing outcomes and gambling manipulators. Proximal to events as prestigious as Wimbledon and the Davis Cup, anyone, even while matches are being played, can place a bet on the overall outcome, winner of each set, or result of a specific rally. In 2007 and 2008, Italian tennis players Alession di Mauro, Giorgio Galimberti, Potito Starace, and Daniele Bracciali were suspended and fined by the Association of Tennis Professionals (ATP) for betting on tennis matches (although they were not involved in any of the matches).

In 2007, the ATP developed anticorruption rules that seek to eliminate wagering from international tennis. These rules require players to report within 48 hours any attempts to influence the outcome of matches. Rule violations will lead to bans, disqualifications, and fines. These penalties could help dissuade players from tanking, through which they put forth minimal effort to lose the match. In 2016, widespread allegations were raised against unnamed tennis players that they had fixed matches along with betting syndicates and bookmakers, including matches at Wimbledon.

While other specific incidences of unethical behaviors in international sports could be provided, these are sufficient to illustrate the existence of the intentional rule-breaking and lack of sportsmanship and fair play displayed by some. Most individuals actively involved with sports want to preserve the integrity of their games. This may be because they believe in the potential of sport to develop character, understand the impact sport potentially can have on societal values, or at least do not wish to erode public confidence. Sport organizations have attempted to address threats to the integrity of sports through legislating expectations for ethical conduct.

Codes of Ethics

Many organizations in the United States and worldwide have established codes of ethics or conduct for players, coaches, and fans. These codes help set a standard that expects everyone to behave in morally responsible and sportsmanlike ways. Table 2.1 provides several examples. These codes reinforce that one important goal of sport at all levels is everyone involved will help make sporting experiences as positive and rewarding as possible. Guidance given in Table 2.2 can serve as a model for how to behave ethically in sports.

Table 2.1   Examples of and URLs for Codes of Ethics for Athletes, Fans, and Coaches

Sport Organization	Type of Code	URL
International Olympic Committee	Code of Ethics	http://www.olympic.org/ Documents/Commissions_PDFfiles/ Ethics/2016_ioc_code_of_ethics-en. pdf
National Basketball Association	NBA Fan Code of Conduct	http://www.nba.com/news/ nba-fan-code-of-conduct/
National Football League	Fan Code of Conduct	http://www.nfl.com/news/ story/09000d5d809c28f9/article/ nfl-teams-implement-fan-code-of-conduct
National Youth Sports Coaches Association	Code of Ethics	https://www.nays.org/coaches/ training/code-of-ethics/
SHAPE America	Coaches Code of Conduct	http://www.shapeamerica.org/ advocacy/positionstatements/sports/ loader.cfm?csModule=security/ getfile&pageid=4628
National Athletic Trainers' Association	Code of Ethics	http://www.nata.org/ membership/about-membership/ member-resources/code-of-ethics

(continued)

Table 2.1   (*continued*)

Sport Organization	Type of Code	URL
National Federation of State High School Associations	Coaches Code of Ethics	https://www.nfhs.org/nfhs-for-you/coaches/coaches-code-of-ethics/
United Nations Educational, Scientific and Cultural Organization	Code of Sports Ethics	http://portal.unesco.org/education/en/ev.php-URL_ID=2223&URL_DO=DO_TOPIC&URL_SECTION=201.html
United States Tennis Association	The Code	http://assets.usta.com/assets/1/15/2.%20The%20Code.4.pdf
United States Olympic Committee	Code of Conduct	https://www.teamunify.com/lscnes/UserFiles/File/USOC%20Code%20of%20Conduct.pdf
USA Gymnastics	Code of Ethical Conduct	https://usagym.org/pages/aboutus/pages/code_of_ethics.html

Table 2.2   Code of Ethics for Athletes, Coaches, Parents, and Fans in Sports

As an athlete. . .

1. I will show respect to opponents, officials, coaches, and teammates.
2. I will try my hardest to improve my skills and fitness so that I can be a contributing member of my team.
3. I will praise and positively reinforce the play of my teammates and enjoy having them as teammates.
4. I will play by the rules of the game as well as the spirit of the game.
5. I will take responsibility for my behavior at all times, play fair, and show sportsmanship.
6. I will put forth my best effort, realizing that this determines whether I win or lose.

As a coach, parent, and fan. . .

1. I will be supportive of and positive toward all players and their efforts to do their best.
2. I will model respectful behavior toward officials, coaches, and all athletes and act responsibly at all times.
3. I will keep winning in perspective and always demonstrate sportsmanship.

In 1999, the IOC Ethics Commission was created as Rule 22 of the Olympic Charter. This commission was charged with guarding the ethical principles of the Olympic Movement, as described in the Olympic Charter and Code of Ethics. To help encourage greater autonomy, no more than four of the nine members of the IOC Ethics Commission may be IOC members. This Code of Ethics governs the ethical behaviors of IOC members, international sport federations, national Olympic committees, organizing committees of host cities, athletes, and others associated with the Olympic Games, such as officials and delegation leaders. It was the Code of Ethics IOC members violated by accepting financial benefits in exchange for votes for cities bidding to host the Olympic Games. It is the Code of Ethics, as well as the World Anti-Doping Code, Olympic athletes violate when they choose to use performance-enhancing drugs. The IOC Ethics Commission has the authority to issue sanctions, including permanent or temporary ineligibility and disqualification, for noncompliance with this code.

In 2004, FIFA approved a Code of Ethics, developed by its Commission for Ethics and Fair Play. This code, which seeks to safeguard the integrity and reputation of soccer throughout the world, governs the behaviors of athletes, coaches, officials, and others associated with soccer. Revised in 2006, this code called for the establishment of an independent ethics committee to investigate immoral and unethical methods and practices like illegal betting, match fixing, bribery, and conflicts of interest. Based on the FIFA Code of Ethics, FIFA in 2015 banned FIFA president Sepp Blatter and UEFA president Michel Platini from all football-related activities for six years for bribery and corruption. FIFA representatives have emphasized that rigorous enforcement and exclusion of offending athletes, players' agents, coaches, officials, and administrators were needed. Discrimination on the basis of culture, ethnicity, sex, race, politics, or language is specifically banned, as is gambling.

In 1998, the International Tennis Federation developed a Code of Ethics for Coaches in response to coaches in several countries who had acted unethically toward the players they were coaching. This code, developed in conjunction with male and female professional players, provides for reporting mechanisms and disciplinary action against offenders.

The IAAF promotes ethical values among track-and-field athletes and officials including an emphasis on integrity in its strategic plan. Its Code of Ethics specifically emphasizes equality, dignity, fair play, antidoping, and friendly and loyal cooperation and understanding among everyone associated with the IAAF and its operations.

These examples of the codes of ethics developed and enforced by international sport organizations have responded to an increase in unprincipled actions by athletes and others associated with these sports. The need to specify expectations and sanctions for unprincipled actions in sports indicates the cultures in many sports have changed. While around-the-clock televised and online coverage of sports has contributed to the notoriety of unethical actions, the media are not causing these problems. For many individuals, cheating has replaced sportsmanship as the accepted norm in sports. A mentality of win at any cost could describe those athletes, coaches, and trainers who espouse the idea "if you are not cheating to win, you are not trying hard enough."

Examples of Sportsmanship in the Olympic Games

This chapter will conclude with three examples drawn from the Olympic Games. In the midst of the highest level of sport competition, these athletes put aside their goals of winning because they chose to do what they believed was right. While not seeking fame or fortune as they displayed the epitome of the true spirit of sportsmanship during the Olympic Games, each one subsequently was awarded the Pierre de Coubertin medal by the IOC.

The first recipient of this medal was German Lutz Long who suggested to Jesse Owens in the 1936 Berlin Olympic Games to begin his leap in the long jump farther back to prevent the likelihood of disqualifying himself by fouling a third time. Long, in helping his chief competitor who went on to defeat him for the gold medal, risked the ire of Adolf Hitler but won the admiration of Owens and others.

At the 1964 Innsbruck Winter Olympic Games, Italian Eugenio Monti and his teammate were expected to win the gold medal in the two-man bobsled. They were in first place with the fastest time when Monti learned the British team of Tony Nash Jr. and Robin Dixon discovered a broken axle bolt just prior to their final run. In a remarkable display of sportsmanship, Monti removed the axle bolt from his sled and gave it to Nash and Dixon, who had an outstanding run and won the gold medal. When asked about his action, Monti replied the axle bolt had not won the gold medal, but rather the skill and performance of Nash and Dixon had. Monti truly respected the spirit of competition more than winning.

In the 1988 Seoul Olympic Games, Canadian Finn class sailor Lawrence Lemieux was sailing in second place in the fifth of the seven-event race when, due to dangerous winds, the Singapore team of Joseph Cahn and Shaw Her Siew sailing in the 470 class were thrown into the water. With the capsized and injured men in peril, Lemieux immediately left his race and sailed to rescue them. Lemieux was honored for his sportsmanship, self-sacrifice, and courage.

Concluding Comments about Worldwide Sport

Ethical challenges face athletes, coaches, officials, and fans throughout the world. With an emphasis on winning in the Olympic Games, issues of amateurism, nationalism and politics, racism, sexism, bribery, use of performance-enhancing drugs, cheating, gambling, and other unethical behaviors have negatively impacted sport competitions. When winning at any costs overshadows playing by the letter and spirit of the rules, everyone loses. Rather than honest champions who through their diligent training demonstrate their superior athletic performances, the sanctity of sport is eroded when individuals care only about winning. Codes of ethics, enforcement of rules, and sportsmanship offer hope that unethical behaviors will not destroy the beauty and magnificence of the human body in motion in sports.

References

Byers, W., with C. Hammer. 1995. *Unsportsmanlike Conduct: Exploiting College Athletes*. Ann Arbor: University of Michigan Press.

Drake Group, The 2016. Available at: http://thedrakegroup. org/about/.

Duderstadt, J. J. 2000. *Intercollegiate Athletics and the American University*. Ann Arbor: University of Michigan Press.

Fulks, D. L. 2015. "Revenues and Expenses 2004–2014, NCAA Division I Intercollegiate Athletics Programs Report." Available at: https://www.ncaa.org/sites/default/files/2015%20Division%20I%20RE%20report.pdf.

Huma, R., and E. J. Staurowsky. 2012. "The Price of Poverty in Big Time College Sport. National College Players Association." Available at: www.ncpanow.org/research/body/The-Price-of-Poverty-in-Big-Time-College-Sport.pdf, 33 pp.

International Olympic Committee. 2012. "Factsheet. London 2012 Facts and Figures." Available at: www.olympic.org/Documents/Reference_documents_Factsheets/London_2012_Facts_and_Figures-eng.pdf.

International Olympic Committee. 2014. "Factsheet. Women in the Olympic Movement." Available at: www.olympic.org/Documents/Reference_documents_Factsheets/Women_in_Olympic_Movement.pdf.

International Olympic Committee. 2015. "Factsheet. Sochi 2014 Facts and Figures." Available at: www.olympic.org/Documents/Games_Sochi_2014/Sochi_2014_Facts_and_Figures.pdf.

International Olympic Committee. 2016. "IOC Members." Available at: www.olympic.org/ioc-members-list.

Knight Commission on Intercollegiate Athletics. 2001. "A Call to Action: Reconnecting College Sports and Higher

Education." Available at: www.knightcommission.org/images/pdfs/2001_knight_report.pdf.

Knight Commission on Intercollegiate Athletics. 2010. "Restoring the Balance Dollars, Values, and the Future of College Sports." Available at: http://knightcommission.org/images/restoringbalance/KCIA_Report_F.pdf.

Lance Armstrong Biography. 2016. Available at: www.biography.com/people/lance-armstrong-9188901.

Longman, J. 2001. "Pushing the Limits—A Special Report: Someday Soon, Athletic Edge May Be from Altered Genes." Available at: http:// www.nytimes.com/2001/05/11/sports/pushing-limits-special-report-someday-soon-athletic-edge-may-be-altered-genes.html?pagewanted=all.

National Collegiate Athletic Association. 2016. "NCAA's GOALS Study of the Student Athlete Experience Initial Summary of Findings." Available at: www.ncaa.org/sites/default/files/GOALS_2015_summary_jan2016_final.pdf.

National Federation of State High School Associations. 2016. "The Case for High School Activities." Available at: www.nfhs.org/articles/the-case-for-high-school-activities/.

Pound, R. W. 2004. *Inside the Olympics: A Behind-the-Scenes Look at the Politics, the Scandals, and the Glory of the Games.* Etobicoke, Canada: J. Wiley and Sons.

Reynolds, G. 2010. "Phys Ed: Will Olympic Athletes Dope if They Know It Might Kill Them?" Available at: http://well.blogs.nytimes.com/2010/01/20/phys-ed-will-olympic-athletes-dope-if-they-know-it-might-kill-them/?_r=0.

Shulman, J. L., and W. G. Bowen. 2001. *The Game of Life: College Sports and Educational Values.* Princeton, NJ: Princeton University Press.

Sperber, M. 1990. *College Sports, Inc.: The Athletic Department vs. the University.* New York: Henry Holt.

Wainstein, K. J., A. J. Jay, III, and C. D. Kukowski. 2014. "Investigation of Irregular Classes in the Department of

African and Afro-American Studies at the University of
North Carolina at Chapel Hill." Available at: http://3q
h929iorux3fdpl532k03kg.wpengine.netdna-cdn.com/
wp-content/uploads/2014/10/UNC-FINAL-REPORT.pdf.

Wolverton, B., B. Hallman, S. Shifflett, and S. Kambhampati.
2015. "Sports at Any Cost: How College Students Are
Bankrolling the Athletics Arms Race." Available at: http://
projects.huffingtonpost.com/ncaa/sports-at-any-cost.

While the other chapters reflect the research and opinions of the author, this unique chapter offers ethical perspectives through nine essays written by 11 other authors. Each lead author, individually or with a coauthor, was invited to choose an important ethical issue facing competitive sports. In each short essay, a real, controversial issue was supported or opposed using a reasoned ethical argument. The reader is challenged to thoughtfully assess whether there is agreement or disagreement with the conclusion of each essay.

The Ethics of Parents Choosing an Early Specialization vs. Early Sampling Pathway for Their Children in U.S. Youth Sports
Michael Sagas and Pete Paciorek

The most recent national data available from the NCAA (Wimmer Schwarb 2016) provided the most comprehensive insights into the developmental pathways used by elite youth athletes in the United States. Specifically, this research found a majority of NCAA college athletes competing during the 2014–2015 season chose to compete in a single sport as a youth athlete.

Phoenix Suns' center Marcin Gortat, left, falls backward to the floor next to Washington Wizards' center JaVale McGee, right, deceiving the referee into calling a charge in the third quarter of an NBA basketball game in Phoenix in 2012. The NBA has since penalized "flopping," defined by the league as "any physical act that appears to have been intended to cause the referees to call a foul on another player." (AP Photo/Paul Connors)

These findings are quite alarming given that at the highest levels of professional sport, the majority of players have chosen to continue to follow a multisport pathway through their youth and high school playing years. For example, a vast majority of athletes drafted in the 2016 NFL draft (88.5 percent) were multiple sport athletes through high school (Branstad 2016). Similar findings have been noted for Minor League Baseball players and in studies of Olympic athletes (Gibbons, Hill, McConnell, Forster, and Moore 2002; Ginsburg, Danforth, Ceranoglu, Durant, Robin, Smith, and Masek 2014).

The decision to specialize is likely made jointly by those who influence the talent development process of youth athletes most attentively—youth sport coaches, athletes, and parents of athletes (Holt and Neely 2011). To our knowledge, the motivations of parents to enable a single sport pathway through the current U.S. "pay for play" youth sport model have not been subject to any scientific study. However, experiential data from media reporting on the subject suggest early specialization is often pursued by parents as a means to provide their child a distinct competitive advantage over peers (Fletcher 2015). Further, from our personal experiences as researchers in youth sports, we can say without a doubt that the biggest change in the youth sports over the past decade has been the push toward early and single sport specialization.

Indeed, parents may be emphasizing early sport specialization as a result of ignorance or lack of competence needed to make optimal positive development decisions for young athletes. Alternatively, they may be committed to early specialization as a pathway to allow their child to have early career sport success, and the belief that these achievements predict future sport excellence. Regardless of the motivation or rationale used in the decision making of parents, we question the ethical judgments of parents choosing an early specialization pathway as opposed to an early sampling pathway for their children. As is evident in the brief review of the literature surrounding both the early sampling and early specialization pathways, parents are clearly failing to make the developmentally correct decisions for their children when they choose an early specialization developmental path.

Early sampling can be defined as giving children between ages 6 and 12 the opportunity to sample various sports and high levels of play activities. Early specialization can be characterized as the inverse of early sampling relative to the number of sports an athlete participates in and the amount of play involved (Côté, Lidor, and Hackfort 2009). An early specialization pathway demands children choose only one sport, is characterized by high levels of deliberate and focused practice (rather than play) and often focuses on performance and winning at early ages (Burgess and Naughton 2010; Côté, Lidor, and Hackfort 2009).

The research literature provides some support for the early specialization pathway. The strongest support is found in sports in which peak performance occurs in adolescence or early adulthood (e.g., women's gymnastics). It also is safe to suggest that early specialization is likely the best path for athletes looking to achieve early age-group success. Another potential benefit of the early specialization pathway involves the environmental and psychological domains of development. Scholars have shown that "early significant incidents" during development can have an important effect on an athlete's attitudes and perceived competence (Burgess and Naughton 2010). These experiences can be very beneficial to the motivation of a young athlete while also excluding the late bloomer or underserved athlete who is not playing in the correct leagues or tournaments to get identified and selected (Horton 2012).

Beyond the few benefits or specific contexts outlined, the majority of the literature suggests early specialization can actually have significant negative consequences on the development of an athlete. For example, studies have shown that an early specialization pathway can lead to increased injury, burnout, and drop out from sport (Gould and Udry 1997), less enjoyment and higher rates of injury (Fraser-Thomas and Côté 2008; Jayanthi 2015), social isolation (Wiersma 2000); physiological imbalances (Dalton 1992); shortened careers (Côté, Lidor, and Hackfort 2009), and a limited range of motor skills (Wiersma 2000). As is evident in a recent consensus statement of more than a dozen scholars and experts (LaPrade et al. 2016), the research on this topic is quite clear; the early specialization pathway fails to consider many of the physical, psychological, and social costs to young participants, especially when considering the development of an athlete through adolescence.

Youth and amateur sport, if facilitated appropriately by coaches, administrators, and parents, has the potential to teach life skills to positively influence and prepare youth for future success (Broh 2002; Camiré, Trudel, and Bernard 2013). Unfortunately, given the findings demonstrating an increase in early specialization pathways of current NCAA and youth sport athletes, we contend youth sport parents of today likely adhere and promote ethical egoism. This ethical frame is a normative theory that posits how one ought to act or behave. Ethical egoism subscribes to the belief that there is only one ultimate way to act, and in one's own self-interests. Acting solely out of one's own best interest is the only way to truly know and promote one's self (Rachels 2012). This ethical mind-set is one likely leading to the incessant quest for immediate personal accolades, awards, and the belief these behaviors will lead to the ultimate prize, a college athletic scholarship (Farrey 2008). Subsequently, the actions resulting from the self-interests of parents are unfortunately pushing deliberate play and early sampling to the sidelines.

References

Branstad, M. 2016. "88.5% of 2016 NFL Draft Picks Played Multiple Sports in High School."

Tracking Football. Available at https://www. trackingfootball.com/blog/88–5–2016-nfl-draft-pick s-played-multiple-sports-high-school/.

Broh, B. 2002. "Linking Extracurricular Programming to Academic Achievement: Who Benefits and Why?" *Sociology of Education 75* (1): 69–95.

Burgess, D. J., and G. A. Naughton. 2010. "Talent Development in Adolescent Team Sports: A Review." *International Journal of Sports Physiology and Performance 5* (1): 103–116.

Camiré, M., P. Trudel, and D. Bernard. 2013. "A Case Study of a High School Sport Program Designed to Teach Athletes Life Skills and Values." *Sport Psychologist 27* (2): 188–200.

Côté, J., R. Lidor, and D. Hackfort. 2009. "ISSP Position Stand: To Sample or to Specialize?: Seven Postulates about Youth Sport Activities That Lead to Continued Participation and Elite Performance." *International Journal of Sport and Exercise Psychology 7* (1): 7–17.

Dalton, S. 1992. "Overuse Injuries in Adolescent Athletes." *Sports Medicine 13* (1): 58–70.

Farrey, T. 2008. *Game On: The All-American Race to Make Champions of Our Children.* New York: ESPN.

Fletcher, M. 2015. "The Case for the Multi-Sport Athlete: How Youth Sport Lost Its Way." *Molly Fletcher.com.* Available at https://mollyfletcher.com/the-case-for-th e-multi-sport-athlete-how-youth-sports-lost-its-way/.

Fraser-Thomas, E., and J. Côté. 2008. "Structured Sports and Physical Activities: Their Critical Role." *Physical and Health Education Journal 74* (1): 27–29.

Gibbons, T., R. Hill, A. McConnell, T. Forster, and J. Moore. 2002. "The Path to Excellence: A Comprehensive View of Development of U.S. Olympians Who Competed from 1984–1998." United States Olympic Committee.

Ginsburg, R. D., N. Danforth, T. A. Ceranoglu, S. A. Durant, L. Robin, S. R. Smith, and B. Masek. 2014. "Patterns of Specialization in Professional Baseball Players." *Journal of Clinical Sport Psychology 8* (3): 261–275.

Gould, D., and E. Udry. 1997. "Coping with Season-Ending Injuries." *Sport Psychologist 11* (4): 379.

Holt, N. L., and K. C. Neely. 2011. "Positive Youth Development through Sport: A Review." *Revista Iberoamericana de Psicología del Ejercicio y el Deporte, 6* (2): 299–316.

Horton, S. 2012. "Environmental Influences on Early Development in Sport Experts." In *Talent Identification and Development in Sport: International Perspectives*, edited by J. Baker, S. Cobley, and J. Schorer, 39–50. New York: Routledge.

Jayanthi, N. 2015. "Sports-Specialized Intensive Training and the Risk of Injury in Young Athletes." *Schweizerische Zeitschrift Für Sportmedizin and Sporttraumatologie, 63* (3): 54–55.

LaPrade, Robert F., et al. 2016. "AOSSM Early Sport Specialization Consensus Statement." *Orthopaedic Journal of Sports Medicine 4:* 1–8.

Rachels, J. 2012. "Ethical Egoism." *Ethical Theory: An Anthology 14*: 193.

Wiersma, L. D. 2000. "Risks and Benefits of Youth Sport Specialization: Perspectives and Recommendations." *Pediatric Exercise Science 12* (1): 13.

Wimmer Schwarb, A. 2016. "After School Specialized." *NCAA Champion Magazine 9* (2): 11.

Michael Sagas is current professor and chair of the Department of Tourism, Recreation and Sport Management at the University of Florida. His research focuses on youth and college athletics.

Pete Paciorek is the founder of a nonprofit called "Character Loves Company," and an author of a coaching guidebook with the same title as his nonprofit. After a professional baseball career, he has been a college and high school head coach and teacher for the past 15 years. His passion is character development in youth through the vehicle of sports. Pete also runs a youth development company in SoCal with his family called "BAT100."

The Ethics of Flopping
R. Scott Kretchmar

In sports like basketball and soccer we often see players "flopping" or "diving." The widespread use of such tactics may suggest they are morally acceptable, but some wonder if they are. After all, it was once common practice to own slaves, bind women's feet, and settle disputes by holding duels. But nobody today would argue that common practice made these behaviors right.

Thus, we need to examine the practice of flopping, as popular as it is, to determine its moral credentials. Flopping can be described as any attempt to deceive an official by exaggerating the appearance of illegal contact when, in fact, little or no contact occurred. This "play acting" typically involves flailing one's arms, thrusting the head back, falling dramatically, and often vocalizing in protest when the supposed contact occurs.

Flopping, thusly understood, is at least in part a skill. As with other skills in the game, those who are better at it are rewarded. Those who are not often put themselves at an unnecessary disadvantage. We have all seen the unsuccessful flop in basketball that leaves the play actor on the floor and the offensive player with an easy basket. This, in fact, is one of the common defenses of this practice. Like all skills it can be done well or poorly. Like all strategies, it can work beautifully or backfire. Furthermore, because other teams employ the flopping tactic, fair play suggests one's own team be allowed to use it, too. Even if the rulebook discourages flopping, it is clearly part of the game, part of the ethos of the game. And finally, in a game like basketball, where multiple fouls are called, it is unlikely these occasional deceptions will have any significant impact on the game. After all, if flopping truly threatened the integrity of basketball or soccer, rule makers could impose and enforce extreme penalties like automatic ejection for anyone caught using such deceptions. The fact they have not lends support to the claim that intentional deceptions of officials are either an acceptable part of the game or, at minimum, relatively harmless.

These points notwithstanding, several arguments can be raised to question the ethics of flopping. For purposes of gaining ethical clarity, I will use one argument from each of the three major ethical systems commonly employed today: [1] deontological, utilitarian, and virtue ethics.

Deontologists take the rights of individuals seriously and argue that we should be able to universalize a behavior if it is to pass muster. Deontologists might identify flopping as a form of lying—specifically, lying nonverbally to an official with the intent to deceive. Lying to officials in pursuit of victory treats them as means to an end, makes their already-difficult job even harder, and fails to respect them and their rights. In addition, lying cannot be universalized. Athletes cannot honestly recommend that everyone else flops regularly because doing so would eliminate their advantage. After all, lying works because most people, most of the time, tell the truth. The same is true for flopping. Flopping works because most athletes, most of the time, do not flop. Thus, for both reasons—disrespecting officials and the inability to universalize the action—deontologists can argue flopping is wrong. Even though flopping can aid in the quest for victory, the ends do not justify the means.

---

1 One easy-to-read book that focuses on these three ethical systems is M. Sandel, 2009, *Justice: What's the Right Thing to Do?* New York: Farrar, Straus, and Giroux.

Utilitarians are not so much concerned about people's rights as with promoting the good and diminishing harm. In other words, for utilitarians, the ends (e.g., maximizing pleasure) do justify the means. They might argue flopping diminishes the pleasure both players and spectators receive from the game by substituting less interesting skills (falling to the field or floor in dramatic ways) for more challenging and demanding skills (shooting, dribbling, controlling the ball, maintaining good defensive position, displaying excellent teamwork). Also, the penalties assessed for successful flopping (e.g., free throws in basketball or free kicks in soccer) are less interesting for spectators to watch and players to execute than the full game. For both reasons, flopping diminishes the game. Flopping reduces pleasure from watching and playing the game and, for that reason, is not morally acceptable.

Virtue ethicists take yet another approach when attempting to solve such dilemmas. They argue the right (appropriate behavior) cannot be separated from the good (things valuable in themselves). Ethics begins then by identifying the good. Accordingly, basketball and soccer can be described as practices that embody any number of goods or excellences—motor excellences like accurate passing, strategic excellences like knowing when to make a certain move, and excellences of character like resilience and determination. Virtues are behavioral traits that allow athletes to realize these excellences. Honesty might be one such virtue. The honest athlete refuses to take shortcuts (like flopping) in his or her effort to realize the unique excellences required by basketball or soccer. Nobody ever has made (or will make) the Hall of Fame in either sport by flopping because athletes who rely on this tactic to win games dishonor the excellences those games embody. The virtue of honesty in respecting the game shows flopping is wrong.

Other arguments could be used to raise questions about the ethics of flopping. It is likely that none of the brief vignettes presented here is conclusive. In fact, some argue sport is dominated today by instrumental ethics, a questionable brand of morality that marches to the drummer of pragmatics and necessity. It suggests that it is morally acceptable for athletes and teams "do what they have to do" to win. If the rules are silent on a matter, if officials cannot effectively monitor a rule, if a penalty is less costly than the advantage gained by breaking a rule, if "working an official" will increase chances of getting the next call, if "testing" an opponent who is known to be injured will enhance chances for a "W"—the smart thing to do is to take advantage of these opportunities. On this account, a well-timed and beautifully enacted strategic flop—particularly one that turns defeat into victory—is perfectly acceptable. What do you think?

R. Scott Kretchmar is professor emeritus of exercise and sport science at Penn State University. He is a founding member of the International Association for the Philosophy of Sport and served as its president. He has been editor of the Journal of the Philosophy of Sport, *is a Fellow in the American Academy of Kinesiology and Physical Education, and has authored a popular text in the philosophy of sport. He has published over 80 refereed articles and more than 35 book chapters on such topics as ethics, the nature of sport, and the operation of human intelligence in physical activity.*

Assessing the Morality of NCAA Commercialism through Utilitarian Moral Theory
Robert C. Schneider

NCAA commercialism reached new heights when it agreed in 2016 on an $8.8 billion contract extension with Turner Broadcasting and CBS Sports to broadcast the March Madness national championship games through 2032 (Pallotta 2016). Financially bountiful, broadcasting this tournament accounts for 90 percent of the NCAA's annual revenue (McNeely 2013). Similarly, the NCAA's major college football programs' commercialistic efforts also generate tremendous sums of money with the Ohio State University (OSU) football program near the top. In 2015 OSU generated $167,166,065, most of which came from ticket sales ($63,149,938) and broadcasting rights and licensing agreements ($57,144,221) (NCAA Finances 2016).

Keeping in mind commercialism's goal is to grow both consumer demand and commercial revenues (Kraak and Pelletier 1998), there is little question the NCAA makes a concerted, ongoing effort to increase fan interest for the purpose of generating revenue, particularly in men's basketball and football at major universities. The question, therefore, begs whether or not the characteristics associated with NCAA and institutional commercialism are congruent with values inherent to higher education. More generally, the question whether such large-scale NCAA commercialism is an endeavor of morality within the higher education context is worth examining. Such an examination also will shed light on the moral standing of the NCAA as a governing body.

Utilitarian moral theory can help reveal a perspective relative to the morality of the commercialism of men's basketball and football and more generally on the NCAA as a governing body. Two classical utilitarian moral theorists, Jeremy Bentham and John Stuart Mill, provided the fundamentals of utilitarianism that can be used to help determine NCAA moral status based on its commercialistic behaviors. Utilitarianism bases moral judgments on the amount of happiness or unhappiness felt by persons as the result of particular actions, in this case, NCAA commercialistic actions. Moral good exists when the most possible amount of happiness is realized by the most possible number of people directly or indirectly related to the matter or entity at hand. Mill (1863/1969) generalized the utilitarian process with his Greatest Happiness Principle, which speaks to actions being "right" as they elicit happiness and "wrong" as they bring about unhappiness.

From a Bentham and Mill (1961) utilitarian standpoint, part of the process in determining the morality of the commercialistic-based NCAA Division I men's basketball championship or OSU's football program includes identifying the sporting community and determining the extent to which they are affected positively and negatively by commercialism. The sporting community, broadly defined by Schneider (2010) as persons involved in sport, including players, family and friends of players, coaches, fans, athletic directors, and general managers, largely decides whether sport policies are moral. The process of determining happiness and unhappiness resulting from the NCAA's commercialistic efforts can be fastidiously complex or holistically simple.

Utilitarian analysis can take place through Bentham's hedonic calculus, which is complex and, arguably, impractical. Mill's predecessor, Bentham (1961), identified 14 pleasures, ranging from wealth to skill to expectations; 12 pains, ranging from awkwardness to an ill name to memory; and 7 circumstances, including the intensity and duration of the pleasures and pains resulting from particular actions. If assessed via Bentham's hedonic calculus, the positive and negative effects of commercialism must be determined across all segments and persons within the sporting community, then calculated to determine the total pleasures on one side and the total pains on the other side.

A more simplistic holistic approach, however, as opposed to a literal application of Bentham's hedonic calculus, is recommended for the common person when attempting to determine the totality of all happiness and unhappiness felt by the sporting community as a result of NCAA commercialism of men's basketball and football. If the summation results in more overall short- and long-term happiness to the sporting community, the commercialistic behaviors will tend to be considered moral as opposed to immoral if the summation is weighted more heavily with unhappiness. If the overall happiness caused by commercialism across the sporting community outweighs the unhappiness, one can legitimately argue that the extensive commercialism present in college sports today supports the NCAA as a governing body that is moral. On the other hand, if commercialism's widespread effect on college sports, particularly major college men's basketball and football, results in more unhappiness than happiness, the case of the NCAA being immoral is strengthened.

I wish you luck in your moral analysis of the NCAA from a utilitarian moral theory standpoint. As for me, now that we all have gained an understanding of utilitarian moral theory, happiness, and the commercialism of major college sports, please excuse me while I submit my application to enter the OSU versus Michigan football ticket lottery. As an OSU alum, I will be quite happy if my name is selected as one of the few provided the opportunity to pay $195 for a single ticket to the game against our arch rival. If and when I attend the game, I will be even happier.

References

Bentham, J. 1961. *The Utilitarians: An Introduction to the Principles of Morals and Legislation* and Mill, J.S. 1961. *Utilitarianism and on Liberty.* New York: Doubleday.

Kraak, V., and D.L. Pelletier. 1998. "The Influence of Commercialism on the Food Purchasing Behavior of Children and Teenage Youth." *Family Economics and Nutrition Review 11* (3): 15.

McNeeley, K. 2013, October 15. "The NCAA Budget: Where the Money Goes." *NCAA.Org*. Available at: http://www.ncaa.org/health-and-safety/sport-science-institute/ncaa-budget-where-money-goes.

Mill, J.S. 1863/1969. "Utilitarianism." In *Mill's Utilitarianism*, edited by J.M. Smith and E. Sosa, 31–88. Belmont, CA: Wadsworth.

"NCAA Finances: 2014–15 Finances." 2016, April 18. *USA Today*. Available at http://sports.usatoday.com/ncaa/finances.

Pallotta, F. 2016, April 12. "NCAA Extends March Madness TV Deal with Turner, CBS until 2032."

Available at http://money.cnn.com/2016/04/12/media/
ncaa-march-madness-turner-cbs/index.html.

Schneider, R. C. 2010. "Developing Moral Sport Policies
through Act-Utilitarianism Based on Bentham's Hedonic
Calculus." *Sport Management International Journal* 6 (2):
95–106.

*Robert C. Schneider is the director of the sport management
program at the College at Brockport in the State University of
New York (SUNY) higher education system. Robert's research
interests include but are not limited to ethics of sport management and organizational sport leadership. An avid basketball fan
and former college coach, Dr. Schneider is the sole author of two
research-oriented textbooks:* Ethics of Sport: Theory, Practice,
and Application *(2009) and* Basketball for All Levels *(2008).
He is also co-editor of a third entitled* Entrepreneurship in the
Balkans: Diversity, Support and Prospects. *A fourth textbook,*
Organizational Management and Leadership of Sport, *is sched-
uled for publication in 2016. He is the author or coauthor of
over 80 peer-reviewed national or international academic journal
articles, and 130 presentations worldwide spanning beyond 20
countries.*

Laremy Tunsil: Criminal? Rule-Breaker? or Morally Righteous Guy?
Ellen J. Staurowsky

Is it possible for an image to define a person? In the case of
Laremy Tunsil, a former football player at the University of
Mississippi (Ole Miss) projected to be a top pick in the 2016
NFL draft, the answer to that question may be yes. On what
was expected to be a night of celebration for Tunsil, his prospects quickly fell as a video of him smoking marijuana went
viral, allegedly the result of a spurned advisor of Tunsil's hacking his social media account. Initially unrecognizable in the

clip because his head was encased in a black gas mask with a bong attached, his identity was revealed seconds later as he lifted the mask away and a cloud of smoke encircling his head drifted off. The video by itself was damaging but would soon be accompanied by an old e-mail exchange between Tunsil and his Ole Miss assistant coach documenting what appears to have been improper payments to Tunsil for his rent and his mother's electric bill, a situation Tunsil confirmed when asked about it during a press conference.

Poised on the threshold of his professional career, Tunsil's value in the draft dropped by more than $10 million and his disgrace played out across multiple media platforms for millions to see and comment on. The event itself became a projection screen for contemplation of wrongdoing and accountability. On the surface, there is an appearance Tunsil is to blame for his actions, that he is a criminal, a rule-breaker, and someone of low character with a faulty moral compass.

New Jersey governor Chris Christie, a guest host on the WFAN show *Boomer and Carlton*, commented upon viewing the video that as a former prosecutor he would have arrested Tunsil (Giglio 2016). The NFL in turn framed its response within its player disciplinary system requiring Tunsil to be examined by clinical professionals to determine if he will be required to participate in the NFL's drug program, a program that could potentially lead to his suspension. And Ole Miss, already in the midst of responding to a NCAA investigation that included concerns about other improper benefits Tunsil may have received as a player, vowed to "aggressively investigate" while cooperating fully with the NCAA and Southeastern Conference.

But is Tunsil a criminal? The state of Mississippi has some of the most progressive marijuana laws in the United States, decriminalizing its use in 1978. For those possessing 30 grams or less, the penalty is akin to a traffic ticket (Hall 2014). Thus, an argument can be made that Tunsil is not a criminal or certainly not viewed as one in Mississippi.

So is he a rule-breaker? According to the NCAA, yes. During the summer of 2015, Ole Miss prevented Tunsil from playing at the start of the season as both the University and NCAA investigated allegations that Tunsil received improper benefits not available to other athletes and students and outside the NCAA's rules regarding player compensation. After determining Tunsil had received loaner vehicles he did not pay for, a four-month, no-interest loan payment to buy a car, and other financial assistance, he served a seven-game suspension, was required to pay a charity the amount of the purported benefits he received, and performed community service. He also was required to personally make the down payment on the automobile.

Is it Tunsil, however, whose moral compass is broken? Or is it possible Tunsil is acting in accordance with the mores he understands exist within a morally comprised system? Sport lawyer and former NFL executive, Andrew Brandt (2016), pointed out in his analysis that NFL draft prospects of Tunsil's caliber are subjected to months of microscopic review from scouting staffs. The investment in players is so great that it would be highly unlikely anyone in the system was unaware of Tunsil's foray into marijuana use and given the level of investigation that goes on around player conduct, the news would not have been shocking. Tunsil remained a top draft pick despite his drop in value. And so, what was the league responding to? Was it Tunsil's conduct, which was likely known before the draft or was it the optics (how the incident looked to the public)? And if it was the optics of the moment, what does that suggest about their objections?

And what of the college sport officials sitting in judgment of Tunsil? They levied significant penalties against Tunsil when he sought financial assistance for himself and his family beyond the amount set by the NCAA, an amount that either did not allow him to respond to his family's needs without asking for more and/or simply were lower than what he thought his contributions to Ole Miss warranted. If we accept that the NCAA's system of economic distribution is ethically defensible, then the NCAA is justified in its punishment.

However, what if the rules governing Tunsil's life and the lives of other college athletes are not ethically defensible? Players, after all, are not members of the NCAA. The rules imposed on them are largely unilaterally determined by coaches, athletic administrators, and higher education officials. And so, were Tunsil's efforts to realize his value and provide for his family immoral?

An underground economy or black market where players and other individuals like Tunsil's previous advisor engage in transactions outside the official system has existed in college sport for well over a hundred years. The vibrancy and duration of that market over such a long span of time offers evidence of an imbalance of power favoring those most in a position to profit (i.e., college sport officials) and incentivized to suppress the value of players. The fact this system of compensation operates underground creates vulnerabilities for players ripe for manipulation and extortion (Staurowsky 2015).

Sally Jenkins (2016), a *Washington Post* reporter, wrote that the most damaging part of this subterranean economy is the way the modest efforts players make to realize some portion of their value is criminalized. In Tunsil's case, faced with the need to help his mother pay her bills, he was vulnerable to appeals from people who may not have had his best interests at heart.

And so, what in the end will define Laremy Tunsil, and who are the wrongdoers in this scenario? Is it possible Tunsil, who appears to be the criminal and the rule-breaker, may have the strongest moral compass?

References

Brandt, A. 2016, May 5. "Last Thoughts on the Draft." *MMQB.SI.com*. Available at http://mmqb.si.com/ mmqb/2016/05/05/themmqb-business-of-football-andrew-brandt-laremy-tunsil-dolphins-sam-bradford-eagles-paxton-lynch-broncos.

Giglio, J. 2016, May 2. "Chris Christie on Laremy Tunsil: 'I Would've Cuffed This Guy.'" *NJ.com.* Available at http://www.nj.com/sports/index.ssf/2016/05/chris_christie_laremy_tunsil_nfl_draft_wfan.html.

Hall, S. 2014, July 28. "Miss. among 14 States with Progressive Marijuana Laws." *The Clarion-Ledger.* Available at http://www.clarionledger.com/story/dailyledes/2014/07/28/mississippi-marijuana-laws/13268245/.

Jenkins, S. 2016, May 5. "NCAA Created Culture That Drove Laremy Tunsil toward Low-Lifes." *Washington Post.* Available at https://www.washingtonpost.com/sports/colleges/its-the-ncaas-fault-that-laremy-tunsil-was-drive n-toward-low-lifes/2016/05/05/20.

Staurowsky, E. J. 2015. "Northwestern Football, Unionization Efforts, and the NLRB's Decision Not to Exercise Jurisdiction." Presented at the American Bar Association Labor Law Section Conference, Philadelphia, PA.

Dr. Staurowsky is a professor in the Department of Sport Management and interim associate director for the Center of Hospitality and Sport Management at Drexel University. She is internationally recognized as an expert on social justice issues in sport including college athletes' rights and the exploitation of college athletes, gender equity, and Title IX, and the misappropriation of American Indian imagery in sport. She is coauthor of the book College Athletes for Hire: The Evolution and Legacy of the NCAA Amateur Myth, *editor of the forthcoming* Women in Sport: Continuing a Journey of Liberation and Celebration, *and she is working on a book entitled* Big Time Athletes, Labor, and the Academy. *Dr. Staurowsky served as a witness on behalf of the plaintiff in* O'Bannon v. NCAA. *She is lead author on the Women's Sports Foundation's 2015 report* Her Life Depends on It III: Sport and Physical Activity in the Lives of American Girls and Women *and coauthor on a forthcoming report from the WSF on workplace climate for women working in college sport.*

The College Sports Wasteland
Gerald Gurney and Donna Lopiano

The NCAA's most-wealthy conferences, known as the Power Five conferences (Atlantic Coast, Big Ten, Big 12, PAC-12, and Southeastern) successfully implemented autonomous authority to legislate in their own self-interest in a NCAA governance power grab that has ushered in a new era of spending in big-time college sports. Privately, however, many athletic directors inside and outside the Power Five expressed angst about how to fund this collegiate makeover and wonder about their programs' sustainability in this new era of spending (Schroeder 2015). The 65 richest athletic programs in the NCAA were given the autonomy by using the threat of leaving the NCAA to obtain this benefit.

It is not difficult to imagine this new era in the collegiate basketball and football arms race will explode in the headlong pursuit of winning. Only 20 NCAA athletic programs are currently generating more revenues than operating expenses (not including capital construction debt) (Fulks 2014). The remainder are heavily subsidized by student fees, general institutional funds, and private donations made possible by federal tax preferences. The moral quandary is whether higher education should exercise fiscal restraint and fiduciary discipline over extravagant athletic program excesses, especially in an era of declining state government support for higher education? Why do so few voices express concern over million-dollar coaches' salaries or the wasteful spending on extravagant facility and travel expenses regularly practiced by Division I athletic programs?

Acquiring and retaining successful coaches is an irrepressible marketplace. In June 2014, University of Kentucky coach John Calipari signed a seven-year, $52.5 million contract, increasing his annual salary from $7 million to $8 million for the final three years of his extension (Uthman 2014). *Newsday* reported an annual salary of $3.85 million for the 25 highest-paid college football coaches at public universities in 2014. The average

FBS football coach salary is $1.8 million at public institutions reflecting a 75 percent increase over the past seven years (Baumbach 2014). In contrast, when university faculty work for low salaries, it seems unreasonable, and questionable morally, for coaches to demand the outrageous salaries in the same nonprofit marketplace.

Extravagant spending and waste have run amuck. A glimpse into the future was portrayed in an investigative January 15, 2015, story in the *Louisville Courier-Journal* about a Bahamas trip hiatus organized for the University of Kentucky, young but NBA-ready, men's basketball team to prepare for the upcoming year of competition. Expense reports revealed the cost of the trip to be nearly $800,000, quadruple the amount spent by the University of North Carolina on a similar trip one year before. Included was an eight-night stay for Calipari in a $1,550 per night Atlantis hotel suite and a $23,855 reception dinner that included a band and an open bar attended by the teams. In addition to Kentucky's expenses, the school paid the expenses of the three professional national teams for the exhibition. It is believed paying professional team expenses for a foreign exhibition series was a first.

According to Calipari, the reason for this extraordinary foray was to season his players by hardening them for the challenges of competition by pitting his team against professional athletes. In other words, money is no object if it contributes to winning. Kentucky officials further explained expenses were partially offset by 57 boosters who tagged along for the boondoggle and donated $6,000 each.

The University of Kentucky isn't alone in this exercise of excess. Clemson University now boasts plans for a lavish $55 million operations center for its football players that includes laser tag, sand volleyball, and a nine-hole golf course, bowling lanes, a barber shop, and other amenities (Editorial Board 2015). At the University of Oregon (UO), an exclusive barber shop is adorned with a chair with a UO logo, durable Corian casework and wall finishes, a full-mirror wall with an integrated wall-mounted television, solid walnut flooring, and barber tools hand selected from Italy. Nike owner and most prominent booster Phil Knight donated the UO football building and barbershop (The House and Barber Shop That Nike Built 2014).

Louisiana State University (LSU) is raising funds for its Tiger Athletic Nutrition Center that will house a full-time chef and nutritionists to provide individualized, nutritional meals for athletes at LSU. Alternatively, maybe institutions of higher education should educate their athletes about good nutrition and then give athletes a meal card at the student center where food choices are available to all students.

Donations by boosters to college sport programs are generally eligible for an 80 percent tax break. Higher education is sending the message that tax-deductible booster contributions to cover athletic expenses related to education are always welcome regardless of how inappropriate they may be. Nonprofit educational leaders and governmental officials should question extravagances that reek of abuse of tax-exempt funds and poor stewardship, competitive advantage or not.

In college sports, players do not get paid. Nothing justifies athletic administrators and coaches enjoying the riches of commercialized college sport made possible by limiting athlete labor costs. These highly paid athletic officials enter into a clear conflict of interest when they are responsible for forming rules limiting what is spent on and given to athletes and not limiting what they spend on themselves.

If the public, state, and federal stewards of higher education do not start questioning these practices, the autonomy movement will continue to breed a wasteland of excess unjustified by any explanation. The standards of ethical conduct of nonprofit organizations are clear. There is an obligation to ensure prudent use of resources.

References

Baumbach, J. 2014, October 4. "Special Report: College Football Coaches' Salaries and Perks Are Soaring." *Newsday*,

Available at http://www.newsday.com/sports/college/
college-football/fbs-college-football-coaches-salaries-
are-perks-are-soaring-newsday-special-report-1.9461669.

Editorial Board. 2015, December 26. "Misplaced
Priorities in College Sports." *The Washington Post.*
Available at https://www.washingtonpost.com/opinions/
misplaced-priorities-in-college-sports/2015/12/26/4
57528c2-a9a1–11e5–9b92-dea7cd4b1a4d_story.html.

Fulks, D. L. 2014. "NCAA Division I Intercollegiate Athletics
Programs Report: Revenues and Expenses." Indianapolis,
IN: National Collegiate Athletic Association.

"The House and Barber Shop That Nike Built: The University
of Oregon." 2014, June 4. Available at http://www.
gentlemensavenue.com/howardsbarbershop/.

Schroeder, G. 2015, January 20. "NCAA Heads Down
Unchartered Path Where 'Real Work Begins.'" *USA
Today.* Available at http://www.usatoday.com/story/sports/
college/2015/01/17/ncaa-convention-cost-of-attendance-
autonomy-legislation-power-five/21941515/.

Uthman, D. 2014, June 5. "John Calipari, Kentucky
Agree to $52 Million Contract Extension." *USA Today.*
Available at http://www.usatoday.com/story/sports/ncaab/
sec/2014/06/05/univeristy-of-kentucky-john-calipari-
contract-extension-seven-years-52-million/10038673/.

*Gerald Gurney is an assistant professor of Adult and Higher Edu-
cation at the University of Oklahoma, where he teaches in the
subject areas of athletics in higher education, athletics academic
reform, and ethics in athletics. He is a former senior-level athletics administrator with 31 years of experience. He does research,
writes, and is a regular commentary contributor in a number of
national media sources.*

*Donna A. Lopiano, Ph.D., is the president of Sports Manage-
ment Resources, a consulting firm that brings the knowledge of*

*experienced former sport directors and sports management experts
to assist colleges and universities in athletics program strategic
planning, gender equity, growth and development challenges. She
is also an adjunct faculty member, teaching in the sports management program at Southern Connecticut State University. She
formerly served as the University of Texas at Austin Director of
Women's Athletics for 18 years and CEO of the Women's Sports
Foundation for 15 years. With Connee Zotos, she authored the*
Athletic Director's Desk Reference, *a comprehensive policy com-
pilation and handbook, among numerous other publications and
resources. She is nationally recognized for her gender equity expertise, often called upon to testify in court and before Congress, and
present at conferences.*

Role of the President in Intercollegiate Fund-Raising
Jody A. Brylinsky

There is no doubt the changing financial landscape of higher
education has dramatically influenced the financial stewardship
role of the president of an institution. While costs continue to
rise and state allocations decrease, there is a growing realization
that students can bear only so much financial burden. Institutions must have effective fund-raising efforts. While all institutions have a designated advancement or development office
or officer, the key to successful fund-raising relies on skilled
involvement of the president, especially in the areas of major
gifts. Many presidents see the tasks of seeking external funds as
an important way to operationalize their vision for the institution. Presidential fund-raising not only creates a personal legacy but also may become a comparative metric of satisfactory
performance.

Fund-raising is about relationships, connecting the passion
and interest of external donors with the needs of the university.
Who is better than the president to tell the institution's story,
conveying the importance of donating and the resultant impact
the prospective donor will have on the lives of students and

faculty? The president also has the opportunity to set priorities, establish themes for capital campaigns, and allocate resources to the fund-raising enterprise. Alumni and stakeholder giving is especially tied to the bonds, perceived satisfaction, and ongoing identification with the university. For many alumni, that lifelong connection is strengthened through high-profile athletics. The "Flutie Factor," a belief that highly successful athletic programs will have a positive impact on student applications and philanthropic giving, motivates many presidents to engage in fund-raising to support athletics specifically while indirectly bolstering the university's brand. Increased visibility provided by television contracts and revenue generated through licensed merchandise are expected to increase alumni support and donations. The success and high visibility of athletics are believed to be important in advertising the institution's perceived value to potential students, especially those outside a regional geographic area, and in turn generate alumni support. Whether the focus is on academic reputation or athletic dominance, there is increased evidence the growing dependence on non-tuition dollars and reduced state funding has increased the president's responsibility for marketing, increasing visibility, and fund-raising.

Despite the obvious benefits of having the president communicate fund-raising goals and be personally involved in the fund-raising process, there are some potential drawbacks. Many presidents have little to no formal training in philanthropic development or the ethics of fund-raising. In addition, many presidents cannot afford to spend the recommended 50 percent of their time in such endeavors. One might ask if 50 percent of the president's time should be spent in pursuit of donations rather than leadership and management of the university.

Another drawback involves a sense of obligation a president may feel to the respective donor. Resource dependence theory (Pfeffer and Salancik 1978) suggests organizations will place emphasis on developing or prioritizing activities that generate revenue, and in return will be subject to the demands of external sources providing those resources. State and federal funding for higher education has tried to leverage available resources through performance-based funding. To get their fair share of revenue allocations, public institutions must pay attention to student achievement and operational cost efficiency, reduce spending on non-instructional initiatives, and report efficiencies and outcome measures to stakeholders. However, revenues from large athletic and conference television contracts have equally, if not more so, motivated institutions to prioritize revenue-generating sports or seek membership in athletic conferences that might result in large media rights fees. In some cases, this prioritized alignment with generation of revenue conflicts with stakeholder interest. Changes in day and time of events, travel schedules and power rankings, and expenditure tiers creating prioritized and lesser sport teams within an institution are oftentimes criticized outcomes of the increased corporatization of sport. To what extent will presidential decisions be swayed by external sources to receive much-needed financial support? The president plays a critical role in responding to external pressures to accommodate special interests. Whether to go after million-dollar scoreboards or needed investments in sports medicine is often decided before dollars are raised through restricted giving. The president can play a role in helping donors see the need for fewer restrictions and more institutional control to determine the best use of funds. The Knight Commission on Intercollegiate Athletics (1991, 2001, 2010) has repeatedly requested greater presidential oversight of intercollegiate athletics, but can a president play a key role in fund-raising and provide impartial oversight?

Presidents justify their athletic fund-raising by calling athletics the "front porch of the university," providing unlimited opportunities to raise awareness and promote a marketable image of academia. Regardless of size, mission, or geographic location, universities are spending a larger portion of their available resources for athletics to position their institutions in the best possible market. Critics of presidential involvement have characterized the increased commercialization and spending trend as an "arms race." Interestingly most presidents believe the spiraling cost of intercollegiate athletics is not sustainable. The widening gap between per student athletic expenditures and academic spending has put increasing pressure on what to prioritize in fund-raising.

Again while most, if not all, presidents understand the critical role they play in securing additional resources, they also are faced with the possible conflicting message by actively seeking larger pieces of the potential revenue pot for athletics over academics. Numerous studies have poked holes in the Flutie Factor questioning whether it actually raises quality and quantity of admissions. Quality of intercollegiate athletics is relatively a low priority in attendance decisions, but may eventually impact student engagement (Peterson-Horner and Eckstein 2015). There appears to be a short-term bump in applications, but often by students who are not really going to pursue admission or may not be the best candidates. No doubt, athletics play a significant role in increased admitted students' engagement and alumni connections.

Given the importance of the president's direct involvement in the success of fund-raising, the question is not whether presidents should be involved but rather what is the opportunity cost of such commitment? Should the president prioritize time outside the office for donations to athletics or in generating revenue to support the primary academic mission of the university?

References

Knight Commission on Intercollegiate Athletics. 1991. "Keeping Faith with the Student Athlete." Available at http://www.knightcommission.org/images/pdfs/1991-93_kcia_report.pdf.

Knight Commission on Intercollegiate Athletics. 2001. "A Call to Action: Reconnecting College Sports and Higher Education." Available at http://www.knightcommission.org/images/pdfs/2001_knight_report.pdf.

Knight Commission on Intercollegiate Athletics. 2010. "Restoring the Balance: Dollars, Values, and the Future of College Sports." Available at http://knightcommission.org/images/restoringbalance/KCIA_Report_F.pdf.

Knight Commission on Intercollegiate Athletics. 2014. "Presidential Control and Leadership." Available at http://www.knightcommission.org/presidential-control-a-leadership/background37.

Peterson-Horner, E., and R. Eckstein. 2014. "Challenging the 'Flutie Factor': Intercollegiate Sports, Undergraduate Enrollments, and the Neoliberal University." *Humanity and Society 39* (1): 64–85.

Pfeffer J., and G. Salancik. 1978. *The External Control of Organizations: A Resource Dependence Perspective.* New York: Harper and Row.

Jody Brylinsky is the associate provost for institutional effectiveness at Western Michigan University but for the past 21 years, she has been a professor and coordinator of the Master of Arts in Coaching Sport Performance program in the Department of Human Performance and Health Education. Serving as the president of the National Association for Sport and Physical Education, Brylinsky was instrumental in the development and implementation of the National Standards for Coaching Education. Her current duties focus on facilitating the implementation and evaluation of the University Strategic Plan, assisting with program-specific accreditation processes and acting as the university liaison officer with the Higher Learning Commission.

An Ethical Analysis of Distractions in Sport
Danny Rosenberg

Distractions are pervasive in competitive sport. Young athletes are easily distracted by teammates and opponents, coaches, parents, fans, officials, the scoreboard, playing equipment and the environment. Players may be distracted by physical, cognitive, or emotional factors. Playing with an injury, worrying about a homework deadline, or becoming anxious over a serious personal issue may be distractions impinging on athletic performance. Some distractions are self-induced by athletes during the course of a contest. There are moments when lapses occur due to fatigue, frustration, and fear of choking set in, or because poor decisions are made, athletic execution falls short, and success appears elusive. As athletes become more skilled and proficient in sport, they sometimes try to distract opponents to seek a strategic competitive advantage. For instance, hockey players will set up outside the crease to distract the opposing goalie when a shot on goal is taken. Experienced athletes also are expected to learn to ignore or cope with certain distractions. For example, experienced free throw shooters must be focused and not be thrown off by fans behind the basket making a huge commotion. This short analysis will examine two cases of distractions in sport and comment on their ethical implications.

The first involves the barking dog play which typically occurs in middle school basketball games. Picture this. There are two seconds left in a basketball game and a team is down by one point. The team has an in-bounds pass to make under the basket. The team runs a play whereby four players set up in the key. As soon as the referee hands the ball to the in-bounds passer, a teammate sprints to the corner of the court, gets on all fours and starts barking loudly like a dog. The opposition is distracted and frozen long enough for the in-bounds pass to be made followed by an easy lay-up and the end of the game which results in a victory ("Barking Dog Basketball Play" n.d.).

Some might respond to this play by saying it is ingenious and ethical. The play is a clever ruse, and it is an option available to both teams; it involves no rule-breaking, which means it is not an instance of cheating and quite legitimate. But if one probes further, perhaps there are points making the barking dog play questionable. For example, are coaches deliberately devising such plays? How many times are they practiced? Are there tryouts to determine who has the best barking dog skills? Is it ethical to use or are there limits to using non-sport-specific skills to create distractions during competition? Are the parents of the barking dog player proud of their child who in effect won the game for the team?

In brief, one could argue the barking dog and similar plays are unethical and should be abandoned for the following reasons. First, if coaches devise plays they should incorporate sport-specific skills to create distractions. In basketball, a defender is often jumping up and down in front of an in-bounds passer to create a distraction. Effective and timely jumping is certainly needed in basketball, and this move is acceptable. One could also ask, why not create and use more bizarre plays as distractions? Second, practicing and being successful at running the barking dog play rests on at least one important assumption. The play basically exploits the inherent weaknesses of games and participants. In this case, we are speaking about relatively novice, less-accomplished athletes who are prone to being distracted. Moreover, just because rules are not broken and no cheating may be involved, the value and meaning of games are diminished by relying on such unexpected non-sport-specific tactics. Some coaches may refuse to conduct such plays on principle; therefore, it may not be an equally available option to opponents. Also, if these plays were used extensively in a game, they would make a mockery of sport. Third, the barking dog player is really fulfilling a demeaning and perhaps harmful role for the *good* of the team. It is unconscionable for a coach to ask a young player to bark like a dog in a contest because it diminishes the integrity of that person, even if that individual is an athlete. According to Kantian ethics, it is wrong to treat a person as a mere means. Parents who take pride in their child barking like a dog in a game contribute to this debasement. Finally, the barking dog play exemplifies a winning at all cost attitude. Teams that resort to the barking dog and similar plays are primarily driven to win in whatever way they can within the rules. These tactics ignore the fact that fair play in sport must require respectful, non-exploitive, sport-specific skilled behavior between opponents. Anything less, like the barking dog play, cheapens the value of human beings and sport.

The second distraction case involves former New York Yankee Alex Rodriguez (A-Rod) in a May 30, 2007, game against the Toronto Blue Jays. With two out in the ninth inning and the Yankees leading 10–5, a high, infield pop-up was hit by Yankee Jorge Posada. As A-Rod ran between second and third base, he yelled something like "ha, I got it" or "mine." Jays' third baseman Howie Clark, who was about to make the catch, thought he was being called off by shortstop John McDonald, so he stepped aside, the ball dropped, and a run scored. The two Jays' players were livid, the third base umpire scolded A-Rod, and the Jays' manager complained to the umpires. A-Rod only admitted he said "ha" but nothing else. There are no clear baseball rules to address this type of verbal distraction, which is prohibited by unwritten rules and standards of fair play. After the game, the Jays' manager called the play "bush league" ("A-Rod Yells 'Ha, I Got It'" 2007).

This description refers to the idea that shouting to distract fielders goes beyond competitive expectations even in professional sport, and professional athletes who resort to such tactics are basically scoundrels with no scruples. Such distractions may be successful, but they also tarnish the quality of play in elite sport and diminish the stature of individual athletes. Some may argue professionals must be alert for any and all unexpected occurrences in sport and this justifies A-Rod's behavior. However, this "blame the victim" viewpoint ignores the fact that much of sport is based on typical events and conduct and tacit agreements about how sport is practiced outside of the rulebook. Many of the criticisms of the barking dog basketball play apply to this case, even though the first was premeditated and involved a power imbalance between an adult coach and less-experienced younger players. A-Rod's yell was spontaneous and initiated by his own volition. Despite the differences, these types of exploitive, non-sport-specific, and degrading distractions in athletic contests do not showcase sport at its best.

References

"A-Rod Yells 'Ha, I Got It.'" 2007, May 30. Available at https://www.youtube.com/watch?v=x9NSSCzrnRw; http://www.thestar.com/sports/2007/05/31/arod_infuriates_jays_as_yanks_avoid_sweep.html.

"Barking Dog Basketball Play." Available at https://www.youtube.com/watch?v=4OGdkoeqG0Q.

Danny Rosenberg, Ph.D., is an associate professor in the Department of Kinesiology at Brock University in St. Catharines, Ontario, Canada. His primary teaching and scholarly interests are in the areas of sport philosophy and ethics. He has published articles in the Journal of the Philosophy of Sport; Sport, Ethics and Philosophy; Sport in Society; Olympika; Journal of Sport History; *as well as essays in several anthologies. He and Joy DeSensi are coauthors of the third edition book,* Ethics and Morality in Sport Management, *and he is a past president of the International Association for the Philosophy of Sport.*

Why Deflate-Gate Matters . . . Moral Controversy in the Present World of Gaining Advantage
Sharon Kay Stoll

It is not wrong to want to win. Games are played; score is kept; and unless the rules permit a tie, there is usually a winner and a loser. To win, coaches/athletes use specific strategies to gain advantage. The goal is to reduce the *chance* of losing and improve the *chance* of winning through better fitness levels, training, motor skills, coaching, and strategies. Gaining advantage is not in and of itself unethical and in fact is valued in the competitive arena; however, tension arises when gaining advantage becomes gamesmanship: using clever ploys outside of specific rules to enhance the chance of winning.

Historically many examples exist of great coaches practicing gamesmanship. Paul Brown of the Cleveland Browns began his coaching career around 1927 at Massillon, Ohio, and was a master strategist of the game. In those early years, no rules existed about the construction of a uniform but only required a number sewn on the jersey back. Brown had a slow backfield that year and an abysmal-throwing quarterback. Brown read the rulebook and concocted a novel idea within the rules. He cut footballs in lengthwise halves and sewed one half on the front of all the backfield players' jerseys. When the untalented quarterback handed off, the backfield cradled their half footballs. The ruse was beautiful—it worked for wins in a game or two. It was clever and within the rules of the game. The rule changed within a year, and today no footballs are permitted sewn on jerseys.

Many would argue Brown's ruse was against the spirit of the game and rules; others would argue no rule existed, thus it was fair. Rules have very specific purposes constituting what the game is and how the game is to be played. Rules exist to offer a level-playing field—a fair opportunity—though that field is seldom fair. Players are not born genetically equal—some are taller and some are shorter; some people have more red blood cells or white blood cells. Some have genetic markers conducive for the sport—the 300 plus pound Samoan football lineman and the 4'10" pixie ice skater, dancer, or gymnast. Others have genetic-cultural advantages (e.g., the Masa of Kenya, the world's best long-distance runners). In each case, the advantage is just that, an advantage. However, there is something wholly different in Brown's case, the action may appear fair—but it definitely was not good. Good practice has a conditional effect on who we are as people. Just because no rules exist against a practice and thus permit a practice does not mean it is the good thing to do; we should be very concerned about if it is *good* practice. Every deceptive action intentionally done outside the rules has an effect on our moral being. Just as every action of service to others and every action of doing *good* for others has a positive effect, every action to deceive, fool, or hurt another has a negative effect. The moral brain has this miraculous gift of neuroplasticity to grow throughout one's lifetime. The healthy brain can continue to develop by laying down cells, if the individual is involved in reflection (meditation), serves others, and lives in a supportive community. Unfortunately, the reverse also appears to be true; deceitfulness, intentional harm, uselessness, and segregation from others also affect growth negatively. Research is rather clear on this subject. *Good* does matter, and it matters very much.

Whereas Brown's case was about violating the spirit of a rule, there is another sort of gamesmanship more sinister: cheating to gain advantage.

A case in point: Deflate-gate. Deflate-gate refers to the 2015 American Football Conference Championship Game Football Tampering Scandal, in which the New England Patriots deflated footballs. Less pressure, especially in the inclement conditions—wet, stormy, and cold—supposedly gave Tom Brady, the New England quarterback, an advantage: softer ball to gain a better grip. During the game, a player on the Indianapolis Colts intercepted a Brady pass. The officials measured the pounds per square inch (psi) of the Patriots' balls and found them deflated. Within days the NFL tapped Ted Wells, an investigative attorney, to review the case. Within four months, the 243-page Wells's report concluded, using scientific analysis, that the loss of air pressure was not related to any set of environmental or physical factors, but happened through human intervention. Brady was suspended by the NFL without pay for four games for the 2015 season, the Patriots were fined $1 million, and the team lost a first-round pick in the 2016 draft and a fourth-round pick in 2017. In August, the NFL Players Association and Brady met with the NFL in the U.S. district court to discuss a possible settlement. None was reached; in September,

Judge Berman threw out Brady's suspension citing unfair due process. The NFL appealed, while Tom Brady played with no four-game suspension. The Patriots denied culpability but paid the fine. Team owner Robert Kraft stated emphatically that nothing was wrong with those balls—the atmospheric pressure was the reason—even though the pressure problem was apparently only on one side of the field. In April, 2016, a U.S. appeals court found the NFL had authority to suspend Brady for four games in 2016.

This gamesmanship example is blatant and intentional cheating. Sadly, the Patriots' coach has often stated his job is to win games by doing whatever is necessary; it is the officials' job to catch him.

One of the most essential moral qualities of sport is that players and coaches "cooperate" if the game is to be good. Rules include an implied or explicit *playing promise*, whereby competitors *promise* to play by the rules. Scheming, plotting, and planning how to outwit the opponent and officials is not promise keeping. Promise keeping is important, and it, too, matters very much.

Sharon Kay Stoll, Ph.D., is the director of the Center for ETHICS*, University of Idaho, the first center to be focused on measuring moral reasoning and moral development of athlete populations. Dr. Stoll is a former athlete and coach at high school and collegiate levels. She is a consultant for numerous institutions and agencies, which have ethics as a mission statement.

Lance Armstrong and the Tour de France
A. J. Schneider

The Tour de France is the ultimate endurance race, covering well over 2,200 miles in 21 stages. Riders are on their bikes daily for four or five hours at an average of 25 miles per hour making the physical demands enormous (International Cycling Union 2001). What makes stage racing different from other endurance sports is those daily demands are sustained over 23 days

(International Cycling Union 2001). The doping stigmatization, and similar problems cycling has, is directly related to the fact this kind of racing may well be the hardest sport competition that exists today (Schneider 2009). Daily efforts like this would require approximately 48 hours to recover and the maximum time these riders can get is 16 hours (Albert 1999). Although, there are well known, nonmedically invasive, steps (e.g., carbohydrates, protein, and fluids) that can be taken, many believe to make up for the missing 32 hours of recovery time, medical treatment is required (Lucia et al. 2001). Historically, on a symbolic and a psychological level only "death" is the proof for the riders that one has fought to one's maximum—fascination of going beyond one's capacity, to test one's strength (Schneider 2009).

Road cyclists can believe there are no limits to human effort: it represents the ultimate motivation to achieve, where the road cyclist is the only true hero in the sports world—pure willpower (International Cycling Union 2001). Those values are, indeed, the key to understanding the Tour de France, its appeal, and its connection to doping (Schneider 2009). Given the types of values honored in long-distance road cycling, it is of little surprise there has been a culture of doping (Kaplan 2001). The history of the Tour makes it clear, for example, public opinion about doping does not always conform to the prohibitionist line that is publicly embraced by many officials, and this in itself is a matter of real social significance (Palmer 2001). This tacit acceptance of certain kinds of doping by ordinary people would certainly help to account for the problem (Lhomme 2000). However, cycling is seen by many as a transparent sport, where the effort and will to win are made manifest (International Cycling Union 2001). There is no room to hide during the event, and, generally, little room to cheat. Doping threatens because it allows cheating to be hidden and to takes place off the road and out of sight, as was documented in the Lance Armstrong case. Doping presents a real challenge to the otherwise-transparent nature of the sport of cycling (Weiting 2000). Thus, when the Tour de France came under attack during the 1998 Festina doping scandal, its organizers, team managers, and athletes reacted to the political and media assault as a community bent on defending its autonomy, values, and, not least, survival (Schneider 2009).

In the past, it would seem the solidarity of the professional cycling fraternity has accommodated the semi-concealed consumption of illicit drugs (Voet 2001). Solidarity of this kind raises a number of questions about the sources and resiliency of the group's cohesion, which the Lance Armstrong case clearly tested and broke. There is an important question as to the nature of solidarity among professional athletes that seems to have been built in a culture with evidence of a shared allegiance to covert drug use (Watson 1990). It was a community that seemed to have inspired loyalty and self-sacrifice, and then it became viewed by many as essentially an aggregation of individual entrepreneurs who consented to maintain a mutually advantageous arrangement. Some former professional cyclists have tried to explain they think doping is inherent in the psychology required for the sport and is seen by certain riders as a permissible strategy consistent with the practice of bluffing the opponent (Woodland 1990).

There was a shift away from stimulants as the drug of choice toward EPO (Schneider 2009). The dissonance of accusation, indignation, and disappointment following the Lance Armstrong scandal struck at the heart of the idea that the cycling world constituted a coherent community built on shared ideals. The cycling community has been criticized that it is not a community based on cooperation, the shared acceptance of principles, and an ethos of restraint on behalf of shared goals. Rather, it has been claimed it is essentially an arrangement that allows its members to pursue individual goals in a self-interested way that may well be compatible with community coherence in a functional sense (e.g., the Tour de France as a profitable enterprise).

Armstrong's case, which began riding the wave created with the 1998 Festina doping scandal, became a tsunami of its own, cresting in January 2013 with his admission of guilt to Oprah Winfrey on prime-time television after years of repeated denial. Before his use of drugs was exposed, Armstrong was credited with having won the Tour de France seven times in a row, from 1999 to 2005.

A doping culture that sustains performance while destroying the body and which operates through peer pressure and secrecy is inherently unsustainable. The logical inconsistency regarding health leads many to question whether professional cycling essentially abandons true medical or health interests by virtue of what it does—leaving riders to fend for themselves. It has been argued in a situation like this that silence can take on the appearance of solidarity, but a refusal to inform on one's peers is not an adequate basis for group cohesion. For change to really occur the organizers and riders must come to really believe that if doping is the answer—we are asking the wrong questions. Should we confront the "inhuman" stress that requires drug use? Can the current physiological demands of the Tour de France giving rise to the doping culture be defended? Can the "special medical requirements" be defended, on principle, against outside criticism?

References

Albert, E. 1999. "Dealing with Danger: The Normalization of Risk in Cycling." *International Review for the Sociology of Sport 34* (2): 157–171.

International Cycling Union. 2001. "Forty Years of Fighting Against Doping." Lausanne, Switzerland: International Cycling Union.

Kaplan, J. E. 2001, June. "Tour de Lance." *Europe 407*: 47.

Lhomme, Fabien. 2000. *Le Procès Du Tour. Dopage: Les Secrets De L'enquête*. Paris: Éditions Denoël.

Lucia, A., J. Hoyos, and J. L. Chicharro. 2001. "Physiology of Professional Road Cycling." [Review]. *Sports Medicine 31* (5): 325–337.

Palmer, C. 2001. "Outside the Imagined Community: Basque Terrorism, Political Activism, and the Tour de France." *Sociology of Sport Journal 18* (2): 143–161.

Schneider, A. J. "Cultural Nuances: Doping, Cycling and the Tour de France." *Journal of Sport in Society 9* (2): 223–236.

Voet, W. 2001. *Breaking the Chain. Drugs and Cycling: The True Story.* London: Yellow Jersey.

Watson, G. 1990. *The Tour de France and Its Heroes: A Celebration of the Greatest Race in the World.* London: Stanley Paul and Co. Ltd.

Wieting, S. G. 2000. "Twilight of the Hero in the Tour de France." *International Review for the Sociology of Sport 35* (3): 348–363.

Woodland, L. 2000. *The Unknown Tour De France: The Many Faces of the Tour de France.* San Francisco: Van Der Plas Publications.

Angela J. Schneider received her Ph.D. in philosophy (ethics), writing her thesis on Doping in Sport in 1993, which formed the Ethical Rationale for Drug-Free Sport for the Canadian Centre for Drug-Free Sport (CCDS) established in Canada after the 1998 Ben Johnson doping scandal. She was the first woman director (ethics and education) at the World Anti-Doping Agency (WADA) when it formed (2002) and was assigned to follow and research the Tour de France as well as genetic doping for WADA. She was also assistant dean, Ethics and Equity, and co-director of the International Centre for Olympic Studies in the Faculty of Health Sciences at the University of Western Ontario. Dr. Schneider teaches and researches on ethics in sport, doping, and gender issues in sport in the School of Kinesiology. Her publications include numerous scholarly articles on ethical and gender issues in sport and the Olympic Games. She was the president of the International Association of the Philosophy of Sport and also chair of the Ethics Committee for Women's Sport International. Dr. Schneider has also been the chair of the Expert Advisory Committee on Education of the Canadian Centre for Ethics in Sport and a member of the Canadian Olympic Committee's Education Committee. Angela competed in the 1984 Olympics (Rowing) for Canada, winning an Olympic silver medal.

*This chapter provides profiles of some of the outstanding indi-
viduals who have helped shape the ethical culture of sport. These
athletes, coaches, sport administrators, and educators have modeled sportsmanship, fair play, and moral values. These individuals
demonstrated that sport can teach character, athletes can behave
ethically and be successful while keeping winning in perspective,
and "how the game is played" is much more important than the
outcome on the scoreboard.*

People

Henry (Hank) Louis Aaron (February 5, 1934–)

Hank Aaron was born to Herbert Aaron Sr. and Estella in
Mobile, Alabama, during the Depression and in the midst of
the segregated South. In 1951 he quit school and began playing
with the Indianapolis Clowns in the Negro American League.
After being recruited by the Milwaukee Braves and earning
Rookie of the Year honors with the Eau Claire Bears in the
Northern League, Aaron debuted in MLB in right field with
the Milwaukee Braves in 1954. By 1957, he was the National
League's MVP after hitting 44 home runs, knocking in 132
runs, and batting .322 while leading the Braves to their first

---

Rebekah Walker, 11, swings a golf club during an event marking the 10th
anniversary of The First Tee in Little Rock, Arkansas, on May 27, 2011.
The golf swing can be adapted starting at a young age. (AP Photo/Danny
Johnston)

World Series Championship since 1914. He surpassed Babe Ruth's iconic home run record when he hit his 715th in the first game of the 1974 season. After playing with the Milwaukee Brewers the following two seasons, he retired with 755 home runs and joined the front office of the Atlanta Braves. He was elected into the National Baseball Hall of Fame in 1982 as one of the most iconic and respected players ever. In addition to his remarkable baseball achievements, Aaron's championing the cause of minority hiring in baseball along with his humility and grace led to his receipt of the Presidential Medal of Freedom in 2002.

Arthur Robert Ashe Jr. (July 10, 1943–February 6, 1993)

Ashe was born to Arthur Sr. and Mattie Ashe in Richmond, Virginia, where Ashe learned tennis as a young boy in the segregated South. After graduating first in his class at Sumner High School in St. Louis, Ashe graduated from University of California, Los Angeles (UCLA) in 1966 with a degree in business administration. In 1963, he became the first African American on the U.S. Davis Cup team, his first of 10 teams. In 1965, Ashe won the NCAA singles tennis title and helped UCLA win the NCAA team championship. He won three major tournament singles titles—the U.S. Open (1968), Australian Open (1970), and Wimbledon (1975)—and was inducted into the International Tennis Hall of Fame in 1985. In 1969, Ashe cofounded the National Junior Tennis League, which focused on teaching children tennis while emphasizing academics, self-discipline, and learning life skills. Repeatedly denied a visa to travel to South Africa (finally granted in 1973), Ashe became an activist against apartheid. Due to a heart attack in 1979 and two heart surgeries, Ashe retired from competitive tennis but did not slow down. He captained five U.S. Davis Cup teams; his teams won in 1981 and 1982. Through a blood transfusion in 1983, Ashe contracted the human immunodeficiency virus. In 1988, Ashe published a three-volume book, *A Hard Road to Glory*, which detailed the history of African Americans in sports, to fill a void in the literature. In his memoir, *Days of Grace*, Ashe discussed how his contracting acquired immune deficiency syndrome (AIDS) provided him the opportunity to establish the Arthur Ashe Foundation for the Defeat of AIDS. Ashe's sportsmanship, professional courtesy, and graciousness on and off the court; dedication to equity and humanitarian causes; and boundless spirit left a remarkable legacy. In 1993 Ashe posthumously was awarded the Presidential Medal of Freedom.

Ernie Banks (January 31, 1931–January 23, 2015)

Banks was born in Dallas, Texas, to Eddie and Essie, the second of 12 children. After playing semi-professional baseball, as did his father, Banks served in Germany during the Korean War. After playing part-time with the Harlem Globetrotters while in the U.S. Army, Banks joined the Kansas City Monarchs in the Negro American League. Late in 1953 Banks debuted in MLB with the Chicago Cubs as the team's first African American player. A two-time MVP in 1958 and 1959 and 11-time All Star, Banks hit 512 home runs. In 1967, Banks won the Lou Gehrig Memorial Award for his character and integrity on and off the field. Banks, who was nicknamed "Mr. Cub," was beloved for being a warm and sincere person while being a pioneer African American superstar over his 19-year career. His optimism and passion for baseball was infectious as he became one of MLB's greatest ambassadors. Banks was inducted into the Baseball Hall of Fame in 1977 and received the Presidential Medal of Freedom in 2013.

Margaret Ann (Peggy) Kirk Bell (October 28, 1921–)

Bell, the daughter of Bob and Grace Kirk, attended Sargent College in Boston and graduated from Rollins College with a degree in physical education. At age 17, Bell, who was an all-around athlete growing up in Findlay, Ohio, started playing golf. As an amateur golfer, she won three Ohio Amateurs, the North and South Women's Amateur Golf Championship and the Titleholders in 1949, and was a member of the U.S. Curtis Cup team in 1950. Also in 1950, Bell became a charter member of the Ladies Professional Golf Association (LPGA). She and her husband bought (with others), expanded, and operated Pine Needles Lodge and Golf Club in Southern Pines, North Carolina, which hosted the U.S. Women's Open in 1996, 2001, and 2007. Bell wrote two instructional books, *Golf Magazine's Winning Pointers from the Pros*, with Gene Sarazen, and *A Woman's Way to Better Golf*, as well as an autobiography, *The Gift of Golf: My Life with a Wonderful Game*, with Lee Pace. A gracious person with an engaging personality, Bell made each one of her thousands of students feel special. Bell received the LPGA Teacher of the Year Award in 1961, in part because of her demonstration of professionalism throughout her career, and was the first woman inducted into the World Golf Teachers Hall of Fame (2004). In 1990, she received the Bob Jones Award from the United States Golf Association in recognition of her distinguished sportsmanship in golf. A pioneer in the development of the golf school and a tireless promoter of the game she loves, Bell received the 2007 Professional Golf Association First Lady of Golf Award.

Lorenzo Pietro/Lawrence Peter "Yogi" Berra (May 12, 1925–September 22, 2015)

Yogi, a native of the Italian "Hill" in St. Louis, Missouri, and born to Pietro and Paolina Berra, was captivated by baseball as he played alongside his friend and competitor Joe Garagiola. Spurned by his hometown Cardinals, Berra signed with the New York Yankees, but World War II intervened. A gunner's mate in the U.S. Navy, Berra landed on Omaha Beach during the D-Day invasion. After Newark Bears' coach Bill Dickey mentored him, Berra debuted late in 1946 before staying in the majors in 1948 with the Yankees. He was a 15-time All-Star, 10-time World Series champion, and 3-time Most

Valuable Player. He coached the New York Yankees and New York Mets to the World Series. Known for his "Yogi-isms," or malapropisms and unintentional witticisms, he was adored for his humor and wisdom. After his death in 2015, he received the Presidential Medal of Freedom for living his life with pride, humility, and an original, open mind welcoming all players to his beloved game.

William (Bill) Warren Bradley (July 28, 1943–)

Bradley was born in Crystal City, Missouri, to Warren and Susie Bradley. He was an Eagle Scout and later received the Distinguished Eagle Scout Award from the Boy Scouts of America. An outstanding student academically and All-American basketball player at Crystal City High School, Bradley spurned numerous grant-in-aid offers to attend Princeton University. Bradley was a three-time All-American, the 1965 National Player of the Year, and captain of the gold-medal basketball team in the 1964 Tokyo Olympic Games. In 1965, he was the first basketball player chosen to receive the Sullivan Award presented by the Amateur Athletic Union to the top amateur athlete in the United States. After completing his studies as a Rhodes Scholar at Oxford University, Bradley joined the New York Knicks. During his 10-year career, the Knicks won NBA Championships in 1970 and 1973. He was inducted into the Naismith Memorial Basketball Hall of Fame in 1983. In 1979, Bradley began his first of three terms as a U.S. senator from New Jersey, known for policy reforms, such as in child support, children's health, campaign finance, and federal budget cuts. After choosing not to run for reelection in 1996, Bradley became an unsuccessful presidential candidate for the Democratic nomination in 2000. In his 2000 best-selling book, *Values of the Game*, Bradley described the values he holds dear, including respect, responsibility, courage, discipline, passion, resilience, and teamwork. While Bradley explained the role of these values to basketball in this book, more importantly, he emphasized their application to life. Even though Bradley played basketball during a different era, his principles and values remain timeless.

Walter Byers (March 13, 1922–May 26, 2015)

Byers, who was born in Kansas City, Missouri, became the first executive director of the NCAA in 1951 and served until his retirement in 1987. Through leadership, integrity, dedication, energy, and vision, he built the NCAA into a formidable organization. His tenure as executive director spanned from the point-shaving scandal at the University of Kentucky to the death penalty assessed against Southern Methodist University for paying football players and other violations. When the NCAA changed its rules to permit giving financial aid based on athletic skill in 1956, Byers insisted on the use of the term student-athlete in an attempt to focus on a balance between academics and sports. He was expected to prevent people and institutions from violating NCAA recruiting, academic, and operational rules (and penalizing those who did through a new enforcement process), while generating millions of dollars annually for member institutions. Byers saw coaches' salaries increase from a few thousand to millions of dollars. He discussed in his book, *Unsportsmanlike Conduct: Exploiting College Athletes*, that players who were responsible for bringing in the ticket and television revenues should receive some pay, not be limited to the NCAA-allowed grant of tuition, fees, room, and board. Depending on who is asked, Byers either eagerly welcomed female athletes into the NCAA fold in the early 1980s or wrested control from the Association for Intercollegiate Athletics for Women. The NCAA under Byers lost control over televised football in 1984 in an antitrust lawsuit as the major football-playing conferences and teams were no longer willing to share the revenues. He led the NCAA in trying to reign in academic abuses by increasing standards and requirements, such as requiring minimum grade-point averages and standardized admission test scores. Byers's impact was significant as he shaped the growth of intercollegiate athletics from an extracurricular activity for college males to a commercialized business involving recruited male and female athletes.

Ken Carter (February 13, 1959–)

Carter, who was born in Fernwood, Mississippi, was a record-setting basketball player at Richmond (California) High School in the 1970s. He attended George Fox University in Oregon on a scholarship but did not graduate. After returning to coach at his high school alma mater, he sent a firm message to his team in 1999 that academic achievement was much more important than winning basketball games. When 15 out of 45 of the freshmen, junior varsity, and varsity players failed to honor their contracts to attend class, sit in the front row, turn in their assignments, and earn minimum grades, he locked them out of the gymnasium. Despite the varsity's 13–0 record, Carter forfeited two games and would not allow his players to return to the gym until, by spending their former practice and playing time studying, they got more serious about their academic work. Carter was undeterred by the criticism he received from parents and others because he wanted the boys to learn that unrealistic dreams of playing professional basketball, prison, and death were their likely fates without an education. The boys must have learned what Carter was trying to teach them since all varsity players attended college. The story of this team is retold in the movie *Coach Carter*. Carter believed sport could teach how to compete on the court and also how to become productive citizens throughout life. Carter wanted to be sure this lesson was learned by the boys on his team.

Roberto Clemente (August 18, 1934–December 31, 1972)

Clemente was born in Carolina, Puerto Rico, to Melchor and Luisa Clemente. He graduated from Vizcarondo High School, while playing baseball on local teams. Between 1955 and 1972 as a Pittsburgh Pirate, Clemente was a 12-time All-Star, won

12 Gold Gloves for his stellar play and strong arm in right field, won four batting titles, amassed 3,000 hits, was the National League's MVP in 1966, and helped the Pirates win the 1960 and 1971 World Series. In 1973 (posthumously), he was inducted into the National Baseball Hall of Fame, the first Latin American to be selected. Clemente's humanitarianism was greatly admired as he was actively involved with charity work, such as delivering food and baseball equipment to Latin American countries. Clemente's life ended in an airplane crash while attempting to deliver aid to earthquake victims in Nicaragua. MLB honors the player who best demonstrates Clemente's sportsmanship and service with the Roberto Clemente Award. Clemente became a baseball legend, hero throughout Latin America, and cultural icon through his drive and character. Posthumously, he was awarded the Congressional Gold Medal (1973) and Presidential Medal of Freedom (2003). Other players have honored him by calling him a great human being on and off the field.

Anita Luceete DeFrantz (October 4, 1952–)

Born in Philadelphia, Pennsylvania, DeFrantz is the daughter of Anita and Robert DeFrantz. While attending Connecticut College on an academic scholarship, DeFrantz was introduced to rowing. Three years later, she won a bronze medal in the women's eight at the 1976 Montreal Olympic Games. After receiving a bachelor's degree in philosophy from Connecticut College, DeFrantz continued rowing while earning a law degree from the University of Pennsylvania. She was a plaintiff in a lawsuit challenging President Jimmy Carter's decision that the United States would boycott the 1980 Moscow Olympic Games. While serving as vice president of the 1984 Los Angeles Games Organizing Committee, she helped convince 43 African nations not to boycott. She was the chief administrator of the Olympic Village. She served as founding president in 1984 and member of the board of directors of the Amateur Athletic

Foundation in Los Angeles (now the LA84 Foundation) until her retirement in 2016. Formed to manage Southern California's multimillion-dollar share of the surplus from the Los Angeles Olympic Games, this foundation awards grants to youth sport organizations and manages a sport resource center and library. In 1985, DeFrantz was the fifth woman appointed to the International Olympic Committee, as well as the first African American and American woman. She was the IOC's first female vice president between 1997 and 2001. Through her service with several organizations, DeFrantz continues to be a passionate advocate for athletes, children, women, and minorities.

Jean Driscoll (November 18, 1966–)

Born in Milwaukee, Wisconsin, Driscoll is the daughter of James and Angela, a utility worker and a nurse, respectively. She was born with spina bifida, a birth defect characterized by an incomplete closure of the spine, but Driscoll did not let that limit her even when she became confined to a wheelchair as a teenager. Recruited to play wheelchair basketball at the University of Illinois, she began to compete in track races while earning a bachelor's degree in speech communication. She later received a master's degree in rehabilitation administration from the University of Illinois. Driscoll became an eight-time winner of the Boston Marathon as a wheelchair racer and won 12 track medals in the 1988, 1992, 1996, and 2000 Paralympic Games. Driscoll has been a global advocate for Wheels for the World, which restores wheelchairs and provides them to potential athletes in third-world countries. She has worked with the American Association of Adapted Sports Programs to provide sport opportunities to school students with physical and visual challenges. The Women's Sports Foundation named her Sportswoman of the Year in 1991 and awarded her the Wilma Rudolph Courage Award in 2006. Driscoll's autobiography, *Determined to Win*, describes her dedicated efforts to overcome physical limitations and succeed in life.

Joe Dumars III (May 24, 1963–)

Dumars was born to Ophelia and Joe in Shreveport, Louisiana. He attended Natchitoches Central High School and McNeese State University. Dumars played guard for 14 years with the Detroit Pistons (1985–1999). He made the All-Defensive First Team in 1989, 1990, 1992, and 1993, was a six-time NBA All-Star, and won two NBA Championships (1989 and 1990), earning the Finals' MVP in 1989. In 1999, Dumars returned to the Pistons as vice president of Player Personnel. Then, when he was president of Basketball Operations, he built the team that won the 2004 NBA Championship. Dumars received the J. Walter Kennedy Citizenship Award for exemplary community service in 1994 and was inducted into the Naismith Memorial Basketball Hall of Fame in 2006. Despite starring on a team known as the "Bad Boys," Dumars exemplified ethical behavior, fair play, and integrity. In 1996, he won the first NBA Sportsmanship Award, which was later named in his honor because of his class, character, sportsmanship, and leadership.

Anthony (Tony) Kevin Dungy (October 6, 1955–)

Born in Jackson, Michigan, the son of Wilbur and CleoMae, Dungy was encouraged to emphasize academics since both of his parents were teachers. Dungy graduated from Parkside High School and the University of Minnesota, starring as quarterback. He played for the Pittsburgh Steelers as a defensive back in 1977 and 1978, helping to win the 1978 Super Bowl, and the San Francisco 49ers in 1979. After 16 years as an assistant coach with the University of Minnesota, Pittsburgh Steelers, Kansas City Chiefs, and Minnesota Vikings, Dungy got his first head coaching position with the Tampa Bay Buccaneers in 1996. Dungy brought his successful Tampa 2 defense to the Indianapolis Colts in 2002. In seven seasons, he led the Colts to an 85–27 regular-season record, five American Football Conference South titles, and a 29–17 victory over the Chicago Bears in the 2007 Super Bowl, becoming the first African American head coach to win the Super Bowl. Dungy has been an active contributor to community organizations and projects that benefit children and families. In 2007, Dungy was appointed to the President's Council on Service and Civic Participation, a representative group that seeks to promote the spirit of service. Dungy believes that coaches are teachers who prioritize faith and family ahead of football and who do not scream at or demean their players. His coaching philosophy resonates throughout his 2007 best-selling book, *Quiet Strength*, in which Dungy describes how football coaches can be successful without having to be vulgar and verbally abusive. Dungy stresses that every member of the team, from the highest paid to the least skilled player, is important to the team, so he is dedicated to the development and importance of each player. Parents of seven, Dungy and his wife, Lauren, in 2011 coauthored a children's book *You Can Be a Friend*, which teaches the importance of being a good friend.

Fred Engh (August 13, 1935–)

Engh is the son of Lynn and Rosealma and was born in Johnstown, Pennsylvania. Engh, who holds a bachelor's degree in physical education from the University of Maryland Eastern Shore, in 1981 founded and currently serves as president of the Board of Directors of the National Alliance for Youth Sports (NAYS). This organization offers educational programs for volunteer coaches, parents, and administrators to enhance youth sport programs. The services provided by the NAYS include Recommendations for Communities, which were developed through the National Summit on Raising Community Standards in Children's Sports, National Standards for Youth Sports, and associations for coaches, parents, youth sport administrators, and officials so they can work collaboratively for the benefit of youth. In 1999 Engh wrote *Why Johnny Hates Sports: Why Organized Youth Sports Are Failing Our Children and What We Can Do about It*. In it, Engh wrote about the moral and ethical misbehaviors that have led to the dropout of youth from sports and argued that instead of harming children, youth sports should teach character and sportsmanship and ensure youth have fun playing sports.

Henry Louis (Lou) Gehrig (June 19, 1903–June 2, 1941)

Gehrig, born in New York City, was the son of German immigrants Christina and Heinrich Gehrig. To honor his mother's wishes, he enrolled at Columbia University (on a football grant) to pursue a degree in engineering. His impressive hitting talents diverted him to the New York Yankees in 1923. After Gehrig replaced Wally Pipp at first base in 1925, he played 2,130 consecutive games, earning him the nickname the "Iron Horse." Gehrig hit 493 home runs (including 23 grand slams), had 2,721 hits, averaged 147 RBIs (runs batted in) a season, and achieved a lifetime batting average of .340. He set an American League record 184 RBIs in 1931, won the 1934 Triple Crown (meaning he led the league in home runs, RBIs, and batting average), and was the 1936 American League MVP. His .361 batting average in seven World Series helped lead the Yankees to six World Series titles. After Gehrig was afflicted with amyotrophic lateral sclerosis, a progressive neurological disease that came to be known as Lou Gehrig's disease, his consecutive game streak and career ended in 1939. When honored by the New York Yankees on Lou Gehrig Appreciation Day on July 4, 1939, Gehrig said he considered himself the luckiest man on the face of the earth. Gehrig was inducted into the National Baseball Hall of Fame later that year. A consummate gentleman, who never complained that teammate Babe Ruth sought out and received most of the publicity, Gehrig became an authentic American hero. He became legendary in baseball because of his reserved personality, humility, kind heart, winning attitude, honesty, and overall character. MBL annually honors him through the Lou Gehrig Memorial Award given to the player who exhibits the character and integrity of Gehrig on and off the field.

Grant Henry Hill (October 5, 1972–)

Hill, the son of Janet and Calvin Hill, was born in Dallas, Texas, where his father starred as a running back for the Dallas Cowboys. Hill was a 1990 All-American at South Lakes High School in Reston, Virginia. A graduate of Duke University, Hill helped Duke win the NCAA men's basketball championships in 1991 and 1992 and advance to the finals in 1994. He won a gold medal in the 1996 Atlanta Olympic Games as a member of the U.S. basketball team. An exceptional offensive and defensive player, Hill has played for the Detroit Pistons (1994–2000), where he earned the NBA Rookie of the Year Award (along with Jason Kidd), Orlando Magic (2000–2007), Phoenix Suns (2007–2012), and Los Angeles Clippers (2012–2013) in the NBA. Despite career-threatening injuries, each time Hill successfully returned to the court through diligent effort. In 2005, 2008, and 2010 he received the NBA Sportsmanship Award in recognition of his ethical behavior, fair play, integrity, and distinguished contributions. An All-Star in six seasons, Hill's talents in scoring, rebounding, and assists were impressive. Maybe more impressive has been his strong work ethic, humble and gracious personality, and outstanding sportsmanship. Hill embraces being a role model for academic achievement, emphasis on family, high moral code, and philanthropic contributions. Influenced strongly by his parents, he has established himself as a person of integrity, character, grace, and leadership.

Michael Terrence (Terry) Holland (April 2, 1942–)

Born in Clinton, North Carolina, Holland played basketball at Davidson College under Coach Charles "Lefty" Driesell and graduated with a degree in economics in 1964. After serving as an assistant coach for five seasons, Holland succeeded Driesell as head coach in 1969. In 1974, Holland became the men's basketball coach at the University of Virginia and in 24 seasons led his teams to a record of 326–173. He served as athletic director at Davidson College (1990–1995), the University of Virginia (1995–2001), and East Carolina University

(2004–2013). Holland's legacy as a coach and administrator has been to win with class. As a coach and Southern gentleman, Holland had a reputation for integrity, honesty, and reliability, as he emphasized academics, held his players to high standards, and mentored young professionals. Politely, he spoke his mind as an athletic administrator, including about reforms needed in intercollegiate athletics. Holland proposed changing game times to reduce missed class time for athletes, recruiting only athletes who could meet institutional academic requirements, and making freshmen ineligible to help them get established academically.

Robert (Bobby) Tyre Jones Jr. (March 17, 1902–December 18, 1971)

Bobby Jones was born in Atlanta, Georgia, the only son of Robert and Clara. In 1922, he earned a mechanical engineering degree from Georgia Institute of Technology, where he played on the golf team, followed by a degree in English literature from Harvard University in 1924. After one year in law school at Emory University, Jones passed the bar exam. Jones played golf on a part-time basis, retired from competition at the age of 28, and yet was one of the greatest golfers ever. After winning the Georgia State Amateur Championship at age 14, Jones played exhibition matches during World War I to raise money for war relief. After winning his first of four U.S. Opens in 1923, he captured a total of 13 major championships out of 21 attempts. In 1930, Jones became the only golfer ever to win the U.S. Open, US Amateur, the British Open, and the British Amateur in the same year. In five Walker Cup competitions representing the United States, Jones won nine of ten matches. In 1930, he received the first Sullivan Award given by the AAU to the outstanding amateur athlete in the United States. Jones exemplified sportsmanship and fair play. In the 1925 U.S. Open, for example, he called a penalty stroke on himself for slightly moving the ball prior to his shot. The United States Golf Association's sportsmanship award is named the

Bob Jones Award. Although a lawyer, and never a professional player, Jones made instructional films and wrote instructional books about golf. He also wrote three biographical books: *Golf Is My Game*, *Bobby Jones on Golf*, and *Down the Fairway: The Golf Life and Play of Robert T. Jones, Jr.* He helped develop the first set of matched golf clubs, codesigned the Augusta National Golf Course, and founded and popularized the Masters Tournament. Jones, who was respected for his humility, talent as a player, writer, teacher, and golf course designer, and for being a gentleman, was inducted into the inaugural class of the World Golf Hall of Fame in 1974.

Johann Olav Koss (October 29, 1968–)

Born in Drammen, Norway, Koss won gold and silver medals in the 1992 Albertville Winter Olympic Games and three gold medals in the 1,500-meter, 5,000-meter, and 10,000-meter speed skating events in the 1994 Lillehammer Winter Olympic Games. Skating in his native Norway, Koss set new world records in winning all three of these events. After his retirement from competition, Koss completed undergraduate medical training at the University of Queensland in Australia and an executive Master of Business Administration at the University of Toronto, Canada. In 1994, he was named a United Nations Children's Fund International Goodwill Ambassador, and from 1998 to 2002 he served as a member of the Athlete's Commission of the IOC. Koss founded Right to Play (formerly Olympic Aid), which uses sports and play to develop children and youth in more than 20 underprivileged and disadvantaged countries. Right to Play seeks to make a difference through sport in the lives of children by teaching commitment, communication, conflict resolution, fair play, integrity, respect, self-esteem, and teamwork.

Michael (Mike) William Krzyzewski (February 13, 1947–)

Mike was born in Chicago, Illinois, to Polish immigrants William and Emily Krzyzewski. He attended Weber High School and in 1969 graduated from the United States Military Academy (USMA). After completing his five-year military commitment, he served as a graduate assistant to his former college coach, Bobby Knight, at Indiana University. After serving as head coach at USMA (1975–1980), Krzyzewski moved to Duke University. Through the 2015–2016 season, his Duke teams recorded a 970–262 record and won five NCAA National Championships. He was inducted into the Naismith Memorial Basketball Hall of Fame in 2001. As the national basketball coach, Krzyzewski coached the U.S. men's team to gold medals at the 2008 Beijing, 2012 London, and 2016 Rio de Janeiro Olympic Games. He established the Emily Krzyzewski Family LIFE Center, a community center that serves economically disadvantaged children and their families. In addition to his service activities, Krzyzewski demonstrates a commitment to high academic standards and is recognized for the academic achievement of his players, with almost every player earning his degree. Krzyzewski has shared his coaching philosophy, strategies for teaching and motivating players, and especially his emphasis on leadership and application of principles for life in several books, including *Leading with the Heart: Coach K's Successful Strategies for Basketball, Business, and Life*, *Beyond Basketball: Coach K's Keywords for Success*, and *The Gold Standard: Building a World-Class Team*. Among these key words or concepts for Krzyzewski are commitment, integrity, respect, and selflessness, which he has modeled for his players.

Richard Lapchick (July 16, 1945–)

Richard Lapchick is the son of Bobbie and Joe, a former center for the Original Celtics and legendary coach for St. John's University and the New York Knicks. Lapchick serves as director of the Institute for Diversity and Ethics in Sport and DeVos Sport Business Management Program at the University of Central Florida. Lapchick, who was born in Yonkers, New York, earned a BA from St. John's University and Ph.D. from the University of Denver. Lapchick, an activist for human rights and racial equality, for many years has published the "Racial and Gender Report Cards," which are studies of racial and sex hiring practices and trends of major professional and college sport organizations in the United States through The Institute for Diversity and Ethics in Sports. Lapchick founded and serves as president of the National Consortium for Academics and Sport. Through this consortium, over 33,900 athletes have returned to college and earned their degrees while providing community service to millions of youth in the areas of race relations, violence prevention, conflict resolution skills, prevention of sexual violence, and avoidance of drugs and alcohol. Lapchick, an international scholar in social issues in sport, has written 16 books, including *Rules of the Game: Ethics in College Sport, New Game Plan for College Sport, Smashing Barriers: Race and Sport in the New Millennium*, and *Politics of Race and International Sport: The Case of South Africa*.

Dale Bryan Murphy (March 12, 1956–)

Dale Murphy, who was born in Portland, Oregon, graduated from Woodrow Wilson High School and attended Brigham Young University. He was drafted by the Atlanta Braves, with whom he debuted in 1976 as a catcher. He moved to the outfield, where he won five consecutive Gold Gloves from 1982 to 1986. He appeared in seven All-Star Games and won consecutive National League MVP awards in 1982 and 1983. He concluded his 18-year professional career with the Philadelphia Phillies and then Colorado Rockies in 1993. One of the "Athletes Who Care" named by *Sports Illustrated* as one of the Sportsmen and Sportswomen of the Year in 1987, Murphy has worked with the Make-a-Wish Foundation, March of Dimes, American Heart Association, and Operation Kids. His book *The Scouting Report on Professional Athletics* discusses how a professional athlete should balance his playing career, family, and giving to others. *The Scouting Report for Youth Athletes* provides information for young athletes, coaches, and parents with an emphasis on using sport to teach honesty, dedication, and sportsmanship. Murphy established the I Won't Cheat Foundation to promote ethical behavior among young athletes, with a special emphasis on not using performance-enhancing drugs in sports. Little League International in 2008 launched an IWC program to help youth athletes make the choice not to cheat. Murphy's honors include the Lou Gehrig Memorial Award (1985) and Roberto Clemente Award (1988).

Dikembe Mutombo (June 25, 1966–)

Dikembe Mutombo Mpolondo Mukamba Jean-Jacques Wamutombo was born to Biamba Marie Mutombo in Kinshasa in the Democratic Republic of the Congo. Mutombo came to Georgetown University on a United States Agency for International Development scholarship planning to become a doctor, even though at the time he spoke little English. Coach John Thompson recruited the seven-foot-two-inch Mutombo to play basketball and helped him become a superlative shot blocker. During his 19 seasons in the NBA, Mutombo played with the Denver Nuggets (1991–1996), Atlanta Hawks (1996–2001), Philadelphia 76ers (2001–2002), New Jersey Nets (2002–2003), New York Knicks (2003–2004), Chicago Bulls (off-season only), and Houston Rockets (2004–2009), was an eight-time All-Star, and won the NBA Defensive Player of the Year Award four times (1995, 1997, 1998, 2001). A well-known humanitarian, he established the Dikembe Mutombo Foundation in 1997 to improve living conditions in the Democratic Republic of the Congo. Personally and through his foundation, Mutombo donated millions of dollars to the construction of the first modern hospital in Kinshasa in nearly 40 years, which opened in 2007. In 1999, he was selected as one of the 20 recipients of the President's Service Award, the nation's highest honor for volunteer service. Mutombo has won numerous awards for his humanitarian service, including the only two-time (2001 and 2009) recipient of the J. Walter Kennedy Award given by the NBA for his outstanding service and dedication to the community.

James Naismith (November 6, 1861–November 28, 1939)

James was the son of Scottish immigrants Margaret and John Naismith in Almonte, Ontario, Canada. He lost his parents to typhoid fever at the age of nine and was raised by his uncle from whom he learned lessons in honesty, initiative, reliability, and self-reliance. Naismith graduated from Almonte High School in 1883, but only after dropping out and working for four years. He earned a bachelor's degree in physical education from McGill University in Montreal, a theology degree from Presbyterian College of Theology, and a medical degree from Gross Medical College in Denver. While teaching at the YMCA Training School in Springfield, Massachusetts, in 1891, Naismith developed basketball. Naismith in his book, *Basketball: Its Origin and Development*, which was published posthumously in 1941, explained that basketball developed initiative, cooperation, self-confidence, self-control, and sportsmanship. Amos Alonzo Stagg, the famous University of Chicago football coach and a friend from the YMCA Training School, recommended Naismith to the University of Kansas as an all-around athlete, medical doctor, and Presbyterian minister who did not smoke, drink, or cuss. For 39 years beginning in 1898, Naismith served as director of Physical Education and campus chaplain, started intramurals, and established a basketball team (he believed people played basketball, not coached it). Naismith used sports to develop men morally, spiritually, and physically. Naismith used his ministerial preparation to teach moral lessons; his medical education to measure, heal, and care for students' bodies; and his physical education expertise to teach sports and emphasize sportsmanship. Naismith tossed up the ceremonial first ball for the inaugural game of basketball in the 1936 Berlin Olympic Games. In 1959, he was the first inductee into the Naismith Memorial Basketball Hall of Fame.

Alan Cedric Page (August 7, 1945–)

Page was born in Canton, Ohio, the son of Georgiana and Howard. He was a star in several sports, especially football, at Central Catholic High School. Page graduated as an Academic All-American from the University of Notre Dame in 1967, was a member of the 1966 national championship team, and was named an All-American. Page earned his JD in 1978 from the University of Minnesota while playing professional football for the Minnesota Vikings (1967–1979) and Chicago Bears (1979–1981). A six-time All-Pro, in 1971, Page was the NFL Defensive Player of the Year and NFL Most Valuable Player. After his retirement, he practiced law before being elected as an associate justice of the Minnesota Supreme Court, where he served between 1993 and 2015. His numerous honors have included induction into the College Football Hall of Fame (1993) and Professional Football Hall of Fame (1988) and receipt of the Theodore Roosevelt Award (2004), given by the NCAA for his outstanding citizenship, achievements, and contributions. Motivated partially by having NFL teammates who could not read, Page became an advocate of education and stressed academic preparation was more important than sports. Page has emphasized athletics can and should teach life lessons, including hard work, dealing with success and failure, and sportsmanship. The Page Education Foundation, established in 1988, has provided grants to more than 6,500 ethnic minority students to help them attend college. In exchange for this financial assistance, the Page Scholars have provided over 420,000 hours of community service as role models and mentors for children.

Oscar Palmer Roberson (November 24, 1938–)

Oscar Robertson, who was born in poverty in Charlotte, Tennessee, grew up in segregated Indianapolis, Indiana. As a sophomore, his Crispus Attucks High School team lost in the state quarterfinals to the eventual state champions, Milan, which was the basis for the classic movie *Hoosiers*. He led his team to state championships in 1955 and 1956, the first for any all-black school in the United States. As a 6'5" point guard, Roberson became a three-time Associated Press All-American and winner of the national scoring title at the University of Cincinnati with an incredible 33.8 scoring average. He was the National Player of the Year in 1960. The United States Basketball Writers Association College Player of the Year Award was named the Oscar Robertson Trophy in his honor in 1998. He served as co-captain (with Jerry West) and won a goal medal with the men's basketball team at the 1960 Rome Olympic Games, a team inducted into the Naismith Memorial Basketball Hall of Fame in the 2010. Drafted as the first pick in 1960 by NBA's Cincinnati Royals, Robertson played 10 years with the Royals followed by four seasons with the Milwaukee Bucks. Robertson was the 1961 Rookie of the Year, a 12-time NBA All-Star, and MVP in 1964; he was inducted into the Naismith Memorial Basketball Hall of Fame in 1990. As president of the National Basketball Players Association in 1970, he filed a class-action antitrust lawsuit against the NBA and its teams. In attempting to halt a merger between the NBA and American Basketball Association that would restrict player salaries, the resultant settlement became known as the "Oscar Robertson Rule." This elimination of the reserve clause in player contracts that had discriminated against players by binding them to one team for life led to unrestricted free agency in the NBA. This enabled the predominant African American players in the NBA to receive more equitable financial compensation from the team owners who were all white. A successful small business owner and advocate for minority business owners, Robertson also has served as an international ambassador for basketball as a speaker, teacher, and clinician.

Frank Robinson (August 31, 1935–)

Born in Beaumont, Texas, to Frank Sr. and Ruth Robinson, he grew up in Oakland, California, and was mentored by George Powles in American Legion baseball. After experiencing racism in the minor leagues, in 1956 Robinson was named Rookie of the Year as an outfielder for the Cincinnati Reds and in 1961 earned MVP honors. After being traded to the Baltimore

Orioles, Robinson won the Triple Crown in 1966 batting .316, hitting 49 home runs, and driving in 122 runs. That year he also was the American League MVP and World Series MVP in leading his team to the championship. A second World Series title with the Orioles in 1970 was followed by seasons with the Los Angeles Dodgers, California Angels, and Cleveland Indians. Robinson became the first African American manager in MLB in both the American and National Leagues: Cleveland Indians (1975). San Francisco Giants (1981), Baltimore Orioles, and Montreal Expos. Robinson was induced into the National Baseball Hall of Fame in 1982 and received the Presidential Medal of Freedom in 2005. Robinson was highly regarded for being an exceptional example of character who battled through racial discrimination during his playing and managing careers. His leadership abilities and integrity contributed to his success in several roles in the MLB front office.

Jack (Jackie) Roosevelt Robinson (January 31, 1919–October 24, 1972)

Robinson was born in Cairo, Georgia, to Mallie and Jerry, and after his sharecropper father left, his mother moved her family to Pasadena, California. Robinson was a football, basketball, track, and baseball star while attending Muir Technical High School, Pasadena Junior College, and UCLA. After serving in a segregated U.S. Army during World War II, Robinson played for the Kansas City Monarchs in the Negro American League. He was scouted by the Brooklyn Dodgers because General Manager Branch Rickey was looking for an African American with exceptional courage, character, and self-control whom he wanted to give the opportunity to break the color barrier in MLB. Rickey, in signing Robinson, required Robinson to endure racial slurs, vindictive epithets, attempts to injure him, and death threats without retaliation. On April 15, 1947, Robinson became the first African American MLB player in the modern era as he withstood merciless attacks without fighting back to help ensure the acceptance of African Americans in

MLB. In tribute to his accomplishments on and off the field, on the 50th anniversary of his debut, MLB retired Robinson's number 42. His baseball achievements include the Rookie of the Year Award in 1947; National League MVP in 1949; member of six World Series teams, including winning the World Series in 1955; and induction into the National Baseball Hall of Fame in 1962. He also received (posthumously) the Presidential Medal of Freedom in 1984 and Congressional Gold Medal in 2003. The MLB Rookie of the Year Award is named the Jackie Robinson Award in his honor.

Arthur (Art) Joseph Rooney Sr. (January 27, 1901–August 25, 1988)

Rooney was born the son of Irish immigrants Daniel and Margaret in Coulterville, a suburb of Pittsburgh. He graduated from Duquesne Prep and attended Duquesne University. Rooney purchased a NFL franchise and founded the Pittsburgh Pirates in 1933 (he changed the team's name to Steelers in 1940). The Steelers had perennial losing records until the 1970s when his team won Super Bowls in 1975, 1976, 1979, and 1980. Rooney showed respect for every person as he became Pittsburgh's most beloved figure—people talked almost reverentially about Rooney and what he did for the city. Many described Rooney as a man with class who made people feel important by genuinely caring about each person. For more than 40 years, Rooney served as a guiding light in the NFL, became one of the league's leaders, and was highly respected by other owners for his wisdom and professionalism. Among his many honors was induction into the Professional Football Hall of Fame in 1964.

Wilma Glodean Rudolph (June 23, 1940–November 12, 1994)

Rudolph was born in Clarksville, Tennessee, to Ed, a railroad porter and handyman, and Blanche, who did cooking, laundry, and housecleaning for wealthy white families. In addition to having to overcome the prejudice of limited educational and financial opportunities in the segregated South, Rudolph was born prematurely weighing only 4.5 pounds, experienced several childhood illnesses, including double pneumonia and scarlet fever, and suffered from polio. Her mother and several older siblings provided physical therapy exercises in nursing Rudolph's left leg so she could walk with and eventually without a brace. While playing basketball in high school, Rudolph came to the attention of Ed Temple, the track-and-field coach at Tennessee State University, who invited her to attend a summer sport camp. Making the most of this opportunity, Rudolph become an Olympian at age 16 and won a bronze medal in the 4 × 100-meter relay in the 1956 Melbourne Olympic Games. While still in high school, Rudolph had her first child. After joining the Tennessee State track team, Rudolph won gold medals in the 100 meters, 200 meters, and 4 × 100-meter relay in the 1960 Rome Olympic Games, thus becoming the first female to win three gold medals in track and field in a single Olympic Games. After earning her bachelor's degree in elementary education, Rudolph was a teacher and track coach at DePauw University. The Wilma Rudolph Courage Award is presented annually by the Women's Sports Foundation to a female athlete who courageously overcomes adversity and serves as an inspirational model for others. In addition to the many honors and halls of fame inductions she received for her athletic achievements, Rudolph won the Sullivan Award in 1961 for her leadership, character, and sportsmanship.

Bill Russell (February 12, 1934–)

Bill Russell was born to Charles and Kate in West Monroe, Louisiana, where the family struggled with racism. To escape the segregated South, the family moved to Oakland, California, where they faced poverty during the Depression. Russell led the University of San Francisco to two consecutive NCAA championships in 1955 and 1956 and won a gold medal as captain of the U.S.'s gold medal team in the 1956 Rome Olympic Games. During his 13-year career with the Boston Celtics, his outstanding defense and shot-blocking helped his teams win 11 NBA championships; he was named MVP five times and an All-Star 12 times. Russell was inducted into the Naismith Memorial Basketball Hall of Fame in 1975. Russell was the first African American to coach in the NBA as a player-coach for the Celtics for his last three years; he also coached the Seattle SuperSonics in 1973–1977 and Sacramento Kings in 1987–1988. Russell advocated for human rights and equality with a passion, which helped earn him the Presidential Medal of Freedom in 2011. Russel was selected as a member of the founding class for the National Collegiate Basketball Hall of Fame in 2006 along with James Naismith, Oscar Robertson, Dean Smith, and John Wooden.

Dean Edwards Smith (February 28, 1931–February 7, 2015)

Born in Emporia, Kansas, Smith was the son of Alfred, a teacher and coach, and Vesta, also a teacher. At Topeka High School, Smith was a football quarterback, baseball catcher, and all-state basketball player. While attending the University of Kansas on an academic scholarship, Smith played on Coach Forrest "Phog" Allen's basketball team that won the NCAA championship in 1952. After serving as an assistant coach at the University of Kansas, United States Air Force Academy, and the University of North Carolina at Chapel Hill, Smith became North Carolina's head coach in 1961. When he retired in 1997, his teams had won 879 games and the NCAA men's basketball championships in 1982 and 1993. Smith coached the U.S.'s men's basketball team to a gold medal in the 1976 Montreal Olympic Games. The Naismith Memorial Basketball Hall of Fame inducted him in 1982, and the National Collegiate Basketball Hall of Fame recognized him in its founding class in 2006. Smith emphasized integrity and character and expected his players to behave appropriately on and off the court. He was respected for complying with NCAA, conference, and institutional rules, and for emphasizing education, with almost all of his players earning their degrees. His recruitment of Charlie Scott, as North Carolina's first African American grant-in-aid basketball player, helped promote desegregation and equal treatment in local businesses and on campus. Smith's coaching approach could be summed up with "Playing Hard, Playing Together, and Playing Smart" as he described in his book, *The Carolina Way: Leadership Lessons from a Life in Coaching*. While his teams won consistently, Smith was regarded as a coach who did not cheat to win. He stressed positive lessons learned in basketball would prepare the young men who played on his teams for making significant contributions later in their lives. He was awarded the Presidential Medal of Freedom in 2013.

Dawn Michelle Staley (May 4, 1970–)

Born in Philadelphia, Pennsylvania, and raised by her mother Estelle, Staley was *USA Today*'s National Player of the Year as a senior in high school. She became a three-time All-American and two-time National Player of the Year at the University of Virginia. Staley played professionally for two seasons in Europe, three seasons in the former American Basketball League, and eight seasons in the WNBA. Staley was a five-time WNBA All-Star and two-time winner of the WNBA's Kim Perrot Sportsmanship Award. In 1996, she established the Dawn Staley Foundation dedicated to working with at-risk youth and serving charitable and community causes. In 2007, the WNBA created the Dawn Staley Community Leadership Award in her honor because of her dedication to giving to the community and her spirit of generosity and character. Staley helped lead the U.S.'s women's basketball team to gold medals in the 1996 Atlanta, 2000 Sydney, and 2004 Athens Olympic Games and was chosen as the flag bearer for the United States in the Opening Ceremonies in 2004. After eight successful years coaching at Temple University, Staley became the women's basketball coach at the University of South Carolina in 2008. In 2013 she was enshrined in the Naismith Memorial Basketball Hall of Fame.

Sharon Kay Stoll (December 16, 1946–)

Stoll was born in Wadsworth, Ohio, to Carl and Hazel, who were partners in Y&S Crop Service. She attended Tuslaw High School and earned her bachelor's degree from the College of the Ozarks. She holds a master's degree and Ph.D. in sport philosophy from Kent State University. Stoll, who is recognized as a passionate advocate for and expert on character development, directs the Center of ETHICS* (www.webpages.uidaho.edu/center_for_ethics/) at the University of Idaho and lectures nationally on moral education, moral reasoning, and moral development. She has served as a consultant to the USMA, U.S. Navy, U.S. Air Force, President's Commission of the NCAA, National Youth Sport Coaches Association, and NFHS. She has evaluated moral development in sport and developed and taught intervention techniques to enhance the moral reasoning of high school, college, and professional athletes. She has been featured in the national electronic and print media as an influential sport educator, and in 2007 she was named as one of the 100 most influential sports educators in America.

Charlene Vivian (Stoner) Stringer (March 16, 1948–)

Born in Edenborn, Pennsylvania, Stringer credited her parents Buddy, a coal miner, and Thelma, a housewife, as her great inspirations. She earned bachelor's and master's degrees in health and physical education from Slippery Rock University. Stringer was the first women's coach to take teams from three different institutions—Cheney University of Pennsylvania, the University of Iowa, and Rutgers University—to the NCAA Final Four. She has coached these teams to over 950 wins, the third most victories in college women's basketball, and received numerous Coach of the Year recognitions. In 1993, Stringer was honored with the Carol Eckman Award given by the Women's Basketball Coaches Association to the coach who demonstrates spirit, courage, integrity, commitment, leadership, and service to women's basketball. She was inducted into the Women's Basketball Hall of Fame in 2001 and Naismith Memorial Basketball Hall of Fame in 2009. The U.S. Sports Academy honored her in 2002 by naming its annual women's coaching award as the C. Vivian Stringer Medallion Award of Sport for Women's Coaching. In her inspirational autobiography, *Standing Tall: A Memoir of Tragedy and Triumph*, published in 2008, Stringer describes the challenges of her life, including her daughter's special needs due to contracting childhood meningitis, her husband's sudden death from a heart attack, and surviving breast cancer.

Jim Thompson (February 20, 1949–)

The son of William and Marjorie, a farmer and an elementary school teacher, respectively, Thompson earned a bachelor's degree in elementary education from the University of North Dakota, a master's degree in public affairs from the University of Oregon, and a master's degree in business administration from Stanford University. Thompson founded (1998) and serves as chief executive officer of the Positive Coaching Alliance (PCA), which works to transform the culture of youth sports and help develop character in young athletes. The message of the PCA has been delivered nationally to thousands of sport administrators, parents, and athletes. Thompson is tireless in his efforts to help coaches enrich the positive experiences of young athletes so they will learn life lessons while enjoying their sport experiences. Thompson has authored eight books, including *Positive Coaching: Building Character and Self-Esteem through Sports, Positive Sports Parenting, The Power of Double-Goal Coaching*, and *Elevating Your Game: Becoming a Triple-Impact Competitor*.

LeRoy T. Walker (June 4, 1918–April 23, 2012)

The youngest of 11 children, Walker was born in Atlanta, Georgia, and grew up in Harlem, New York City. Walker displayed outstanding academic and athletic skills in football and basketball at Benedict College, graduating in 1940. He immediately earned his master's degree from Columbia University and later his doctorate from New York University. Walker coached and taught at Benedict College, Bishop College, and Prairie View A&M University, before going to North Carolina Central University where he spent the majority of his career. As a track-and-field coach, he coached numerous All-Americans, national champions, and Olympians. Prior to becoming the U.S.'s first African American Olympic track-and-field coach in 1976, he coached Olympic teams from Ethiopia, Israel, Jamaica, Kenya, and Trinidad-Tobago. He shared some of his expertise in track and field in two books, *Championship Techniques in Track and Field* and *Track and Field: A Guide for the Serious Coach and Athlete*. Walker was a member of the USOC Board of Directors and then served as USOC treasurer (1986–1992) and president (1992–1996). His many honors and recognitions include induction into the National Track and Field Hall of Fame (1983) and United States Olympic Hall of Fame (1987). Walker, who dedicated much of his life to the advancement of track and field nationally and internationally, always did so with grace and humility while honoring others. Throughout his long and distinguished career, he served as a role model of respect, responsibility, and justice.

Hazel Virginia (Hotchkiss) Wightman (December 20, 1886–December 5, 1974)

Wightman was born in Healdsburg, California, where she played tennis to strengthen herself physically. In 1911, she graduated from the University of California at Berkeley. Between 1909 and 1911, Wightman swept the U.S. tennis championships in singles, women's doubles, and mixed doubles. During her long career, she won 43 adult U.S. titles, the last at age 68 and a total of 16 U.S. championship titles. Wightman won gold medals in women's doubles (with Helen Wills Moody) and mixed doubles (with Dick Williams) at the 1924 Paris Olympic Games.

She helped organize the Ladies International Tennis Challenge between British and American teams in 1923, played on five teams, and served as captain for 13 years. The winner of these annual competitions (the last one was in 1989) received the Wightman Cup, a sterling silver vase Wightman donated as the trophy. She was called the "Queen Mother of American Tennis" because of her lifelong participation in, achievements in, and promotion of women's tennis. Wightman, the mother of five, taught tennis to many young people, without charge; wrote a short instructional book, *Better Tennis*; and welcomed aspiring champions into her home when they traveled to Boston to play in tournaments. In 1940, a group of New England women initiated the Service Bowl Award, a trophy given in her honor to the player who annually made notable contributions to sportsmanship, fellowship, and service to tennis. Wightman was the first recipient, as well as a 1946 recipient after this award became a national honor given by the United States Tennis Association. Wightman was inducted into the International Tennis Hall of Fame in 1957. "Lady Tennis" aptly symbolized her unparalleled reputation for sportsmanship as well as her grace and manners on and off the court.

John Wooden (October 14, 1910–June 4, 2010)

Wooden was born in Hall, Indiana, to Roxie and Joshua Wooden. He led his Martinsville High School team to three consecutive state championship finals, winning the title in 1927. He earned three-time All-American honors at Purdue University, graduating in 1932 with a degree in English. While teaching and coaching in high school, Wooden played professional basketball in the former National Basketball League. Following service in the U.S. Navy during World War II, Wooden earned his master's degree from Indiana State University. From 1946 to 1948, Wooden served as basketball coach and athletic director at Indiana State. Then during 27 seasons as UCLA's coach, beginning in 1948, his teams amassed a 620–147 record, including 10 NCAA championships, an 88-game winning streak, and four 30–0 seasons. Wooden's honors include induction into the Naismith Memorial Basketball Hall of Fame as a player (1960) and coach (1973), induction into the National Collegiate Basketball Hall of Fame in its founding class (2006), and the Presidential Medal of Freedom (2003). Long after he retired, Wooden remained a highly respected teacher of the game of basketball and life lessons. In his first book, *Practical Modern Basketball*, Wooden shared some of his tactical coaching strategies. His autobiographical book, *They Call Me Coach*, provided insights into the values that made Wooden a remarkable person and highly successful coach. He wrote about the importance of effort and achieving individual potential and shared numerous maxims and philosophical building blocks in several other books, including *Wooden: A Lifetime of Observations and Reflections On and Off the Court.* Wooden taught and modeled the virtues and characteristics of character in his highly acclaimed Pyramid of Success. This one-page model described the characteristics of individuals who would be successful in life and basketball if they acted in accordance with the values that Wooden identified. He believed that his legacy in coaching was revealed through the successes of his players, not on the court, but in their lives.

Organizations

This section describes 139 sport and sport-related organizations in the United States and internationally that govern sports for athletes in this country. In the first major group, following the USOC, are the 39 national governing bodies for sports in the summer (31) and winter (8) Olympic Games and the International Sport Federation (ISF) for each. In addition, eight other sport governing bodies recognized by the USOC are included. The second major group is comprised of 22 single-sport organizations, which focus on youth or specific age groups. The third major group contains 19 organizations offering competitions in several sports, which may or may not be age specific. The fourth major group contains 21 sport-related organizations that contribute to the experiences of athletes.

As appropriate, these organizations have been placed in historical context. The brief descriptions connect the scope of work of these organizations with sport ethics and ethical behavior in sport. Each sport governing organization is responsible for ensuring that athletes, coaches, and sport managers demonstrated the highest level of ethical conduct through rule compliance and displaying sportsmanship and fair play. For example, the national governing bodies educate about sport-specific rules and permissible training equipment and impermissible drugs. Another example of the work of sport organizations is to offer sport development opportunities for individuals of all ages and ability levels. Many of these organizations have codes of ethics or conduct for athletes, coaches, sport managers, and even fans to emphasize the importance of playing by the rules and being a good sport.

United States Olympic Committee and the National Governing Body for Each Olympic Sport

United States Olympic Committee (USOC)

Founded in 1894 and authorized by the Amateur Sports Act in 1978, the USOC serves as the national Olympic committee for the United States. In partnership with sport governing bodies, the USOC selects and enters athletes for the summer and winter Olympic Games, Pan American Games, and Paralympic Games. As a nonprofit, nongovernmental organization, it depends on sponsorships and donations to provide training centers, financial support, and coaching to elite athletes. It is responsible for overall rule compliance of teams representing the United States in international competitions. The USOC's Coaching Ethics Code ensures that those who train and guide the development of elite international athletes adhere to the highest ethical conduct.

Summer Sports

UNITED STATES TENNIS ASSOCIATION (USTA)

The USTA, since its establishment initially for only males in 1881, has been dedicated to the growth of tennis, which today ranges from Quick Start Tennis for youth to championships for players of all ages to the U.S. Open for professionals. The USTA oversees professional tour events and selects teams for the Davis Cup (for men), Fed Cup (for women), Olympic Games, and Paralympic Games.

International Sport Federation: International Tennis Federation (ITF)

U.S. EQUESTRIAN FEDERATION (USEF)

The Association of American Horse Shows, which was organized in 1917, unified males and females from all regions of the country with the purpose of clean competition and fair play in the show ring. Its successor, USEF, advances the level of horsemanship beginning at the junior level, ensures the well-being of horses, and pursues excellence in the Olympic Games and other international competitions.

International Sport Federation: International Equestrian Federation (FEI)

U.S. ROWING

Organized rowing traces its history to the National Association for Amateur Oarsmen founded in 1872 for men. U.S. Rowing promotes lifelong participation in rowing by offering youth, junior, scholastic, collegiate, adaptive, and masters educational programs and competitions and selects the men's and women's national teams that compete in the Olympic Games and other international competitions. Rowers use either two oars (sculls) or one oar (sweeps). The events include single sculls, double sculls, and quadruple sculls, coxless pair, coxless four, and eight with coxswain, who faces the direction the boat is traveling, steers it, and coordinates the power and rhythm of the rowers.

International Sport Federation: International Federation of Rowing Associations (FISA)

U.S. SAILING

Sailing traces its origin to 1897 when the North American Yacht Racing Union was organized to promote yacht racing and unify the rules. U.S. Sailing promotes getting started in sailing through learning symposiums and sailing festivals. It offers 18 national championships in fleet, match, and team racing in skiff, dinghy, windsurfer, keelboat, and multihull boats, and selects sailors for the Olympic and Paralympic Games.

International Sport Federation: International Sailing Federation (ISAF)

USA ARCHERY

USA Archery seeks to develop the interest and abilities of individuals of all ages in archery with the goal of producing Olympic, Pan American, and world champions. USA Archery's junior program for individuals from ages 8 to 18 includes club activities and tournaments for beginners through world competitions. Its junior programs emphasize character development as well as skill development.

International Sport Federation: World Archery Federation (World Archery)

USA BADMINTON

Since it began as the American Badminton Association in 1936, USA Badminton has promoted the game and prepared players for national competitions. Badminton became an Olympic sport in 1992. USA Badminton encourages recreational players to compete through clubs and a grassroots national championship for nonelite players. In addition to players developing their talents and performing to their highest levels, the stated goal is for players at all levels to enhance the quality of their lives.

International Sport Federation: Badminton World Federation (BWF)

USA BASKETBALL

USA Basketball selects and prepares teams for international competitions. It began in 1974 as the Amateur Basketball Association of the United States of America, but changed to USA Basketball after international competitions welcomed professional players. It also sponsors developmental programs like Hoop Summit and national teams to compete in U17 and U19 international championships.

International Sport Federation: International Basketball Federation (FIBA)

USA Boxing

USA Boxing promotes Olympic-style boxing, which is limited to four two-minute rounds, and national competitions. Beginning in 2016, professional boxers may qualify and participate. While there are nine weight classes for males and three for females in the Olympic Games, the Junior Olympic program is based on age and weight categories. Since 1993, USA Boxing has allowed females to box against females in sanctioned competition.

International Sport Federation: International Boxing Association (AIBA)

USA Canoe/Kayak (USACK)

USACK promotes flatwater sprint and whitewater slalom and selects elite athletes for Olympic and international competitions. In addition to promoting canoe and kayak racing, it sanctions recreational paddling sports, including dragon boat, freestyle, marathon, surfski, wildwater, outrigger, canoe polo, canoe sailing, and stand-up paddleboard.

International Sport Federation: International Canoe Federation (ICF)

USA Cycling

Track cycling traces its history in the United States back to the late 1800s. USA Cycling promotes several types of cycling and selects teams for the Olympic Games and other international competitions. USA Cycling sanctions over 3,000 local, regional, and national events including road, track (on a velo-drome, which is a steeply banked oval track), mountain (such as cross country, slalom, and downhill), cyclo-cross, and BMX (bicycle motocross for racing and freestyle with 20-inch wheel cycles).

International Sport Federation: International Cycling Union (UCI)

USA DIVING

Diving developed as a sport when German and Swedish gymnasts practiced their movements over water, which helps explain the relationship between these two sports. USA Diving selects and prepares teams to represent the United States in the Olympic Games and other international competitions. It promotes and offers a variety of programs for all ages and skills levels, including junior (under 18 years of age), senior (elite), and master (over 21 years who no longer compete) divers.

International Sport Federation: International Swimming Federation (FINA)

USA FENCING (USFA)

In 1891, the Amateur Fencers League of America was established to promote this sport. Its successor, USFA, works with local clubs and colleges to offer amateur competitions for juniors, collegians, and veterans and selects and prepares elite fencers for international competitions, including the Olympic Games. Fencing includes three weapons: foil, a light-weight sword often used to train for duels; epee, a freestyle dueling sword; and saber, a slashing cavalry sword.

International Sport Federation: International Fencing Federation (FIE)

USA FIELD HOCKEY

Possibly because field hockey was introduced into the United States by a woman, played in many women's colleges, and the

United States Field Hockey Association in 1922 was organized by women, this sport has been played almost exclusively by females in the United States. USA Field Hockey supports programs like grassroots development programs, camps, championships, and high-performance training centers and selects the national teams for international competitions.

International Sport Federation: International Field Hockey Federation (FIH)

USA Golf

USA Golf selects and prepares future elite American golfers for competitive success in Olympic, Paralympic, and Pan American competition.

International Sport Federation: International Golf Federation (IGF)

USA Gymnastics

USA Gymnastics selects and prepares teams to represent the United States in the Olympic Games and World Championships. It develops men's and women's artistic gymnastics, rhythmic gymnastics, acrobatic gymnastics, and trampoline and tumbling at the grassroots through national levels.

International Sport Federation: International Gymnastics Federation (FIG)

USA Judo

The martial art of judo involves throwing and grappling on the ground including pins, arm locks, and control holds. Strict rules govern competition and ensure safety, making it open to individuals of all ages and skill levels, with separate weight divisions for men, women, boys, and girls. It oversees instructional programs and competitive opportunities for juniors, seniors, Team USA, and Paralympic athletes.

International Sport Federation: International Judo Federation (IJF)

USA Pentathlon

The founder of the modern Olympic Games initiated this event in 1912 because he believed it would test a man's (and since 2000 a woman's) moral qualities as well as physical resources and skills. The pentathlon consists of fencing through one-touch bouts against every other competitor using epee swords; swimming in a freestyle race over 200 meters; riding or equestrian show jumping, while riding a randomly assigned horse, jump over 12 hurdles (15 jumps) over a course length of 335 to 450 meters; and a combined event of shooting and hitting down five targets, running 1,000 meters, and repeating this twice for a total of 15 targets and 3,000 meters, with all events completed on one grueling day. USA Pentathlon selects the men's and women's teams that represent the United States in the Olympic Games.

International Sport Federation: International Modern Pentathlon Union (UIPM)

USA Rugby

USA Rugby was founded as the United States of America Rugby Football Union and fielded its first national team in 1975. It develops the game at all levels with over 115,000 members, including four national teams.

International Sport Federation: World Rugby

USA Shooting

USA Shooting manages shooting development programs, sanctions events at local, state, regional, and national levels, and prepares shooters to win medals at the Olympic Games. The shooting disciplines include pistol, rifle, and shotgun (skeet, trap, and double trap).

International Sport Federation: International Shooting Sport Federation (ISSF)

USA Soccer (Football in the Olympic Games)

USA Soccer, originally founded in 1913 as the United States Football Association, seeks to popularize this sport recreationally through the Olympic and World Cup levels. It works with and through USA Youth Soccer, the American Youth Soccer Association, SAY Soccer, U.S. Club Soccer, United States Adult Soccer Association, its development academy, and the professional soccer leagues in integrating player participation and development.

International Sport Federation: Federation of Association Football (FIFA)

USA SWIMMING

USA Swimming is committed to three core objectives: build a base by encouraging young people to discover swimming as an activity they can enjoy throughout their lives; promote the sport so more people support and participate in swimming; and achieve sustained competitive success. USA Swimming offers camps and clinics and selects the open water, short course, and junior and national teams for the Olympic Games and other international competitions.

International Sport Federation: International Swimming Federation (FINA)

USA SYNCHRO

Perhaps because of Esther Williams, who was a freestyle swimming champion and popularized water ballet through performances in the San Francisco World's Fair Aquacade in 1940, the following year the AAU offered the first competitive duet and team events in synchronized swimming. Since 1979, USA Synchro has promoted this sport for females beginning in clubs through national teams. Individuals, duets, or teams combine incredible water skills and breath control with strength, endurance, flexibility, grace, and artistry from gymnastics, with elaborate moves precisely timed to music and the other swimmers. It became an Olympic sport for women in 1984. While the United States changed its rules to allow men to compete with women in 1978, men are not allowed to compete in this sport in the Olympic Games.

International Sport Federation: International Swimming Federation (FINA)

USA Table Tennis (USATT)

USATT is comprised of members who play table tennis in over 250 clubs, and it offers over 350 annual tournaments. USATT oversees the Olympic and cadet, junior, and national teams that compete internationally.

International Sport Federation: International Table Tennis Federation (ITTF)

USA Taekwondo

Taekwondo, a Korean martial art that emphasizes fighting with the fists and feet, seeks to enhance life through the development of mind and body. USA Taekwondo seeks to develop world-class athletes for the achievement of sustained competitive excellence and works through an athlete development process beginning with junior programs leading to national teams in four categories: base programming, developmental, high-performance, and world-class.

International Sport Federation: World Taekwondo Federation (WTF)

USA Team Handball

Team handball, which is most popular in European nations, has seven players (one of whom is a goalkeeper) who pass or bounce a ball into the opponent's goal, which is similar to, but smaller than, a soccer goal. USA Team Handball recruits intercollegiate athletes in baseball, football, soccer, softball, triathlon, volleyball, and water polo to play this team sport and selects the teams to represent the United States in international competitions.

International Sport Federation: International Handball Federation (IHF)

USA Track and Field (USATF) (called Athletics in the Olympic Games)

USATF traces its organizational history to the late nineteenth-century athletic clubs that offered track-and-field competitions. Today, USATF fosters sustained competitive excellence, interest, and participation in track and field, long-distance running, and race walking. USATF begins with running programs at the grassroots level, sanctions over 4,000 events annually, and selects national teams that compete in the Olympic Games and other international competitions. The USATF has around 100,000 members and 2,500 affiliated local clubs.

International Sport Federation: International Association of Athletics Federations (IAAF)

USA Triathlon (USAT)

Triathlon sanctions over 4,300 races for its nearly 500,000 members and seeks to create interest and participation through camps, clinics, races, and educational opportunities. USA Triathlon selects and prepares teams to represent the United States in the Olympic Games and other international competitions in this endurance event over varying distances in swimming, cycling, and running.

International Sport Federation: International Triathlon Union (ITU)

USA Volleyball

After being developed at a YMCA in 1895 and spread internationally through the YMCA, in 1928 the United States Volleyball Association was formed and sponsored its first tournament. USA Volleyball sponsors championships for youth and juniors, indoor and beach programs for adults, and indoor and beach national teams, and three disabled national teams and selects and trains teams for international competition in volleyball on indoor courts and beach volleyball.

International Sport Federation: International Volleyball Federation (FIVB)

USA WATER POLO

USA Water Polo seeks to grow this fast-paced team game that emphasizes swimming, passing, and scoring throughout the United States and win gold medals in Olympic, World Championship, and Pan American Games. U.S. leagues provide a low-cost, entry-level membership for water polo clubs for competition in indoor and outdoor events, while Masters Water Polo encourages and promotes participation in lifelong fitness and competitive water polo.

International Sport Federation: International Swimming Federation (FINA)

USA WEIGHTLIFTING

USA Weightlifting conducts Olympic development programs and selects male and female competitors for the Olympic Games and other international events. In addition to local weightlifting competitions sponsored by affiliates at the school age, junior, senior, and master levels, it sanctions national championships.

International Sport Federation: International Weightlifting Federation (IWF)

USA WRESTLING

In 1968, the United States Wrestling Federation was established, with leadership provided by college coaches. The successor, USA Wrestling, promotes wrestling through developmental programs and camps, educational programs for coaches, and competitive opportunities up through the Olympic Games. USA Wrestling conducts competitions in 13 categories for males and nine for females.

International Sport Federation: United World Wrestling

Winter Sports

UNITED STATES SKI AND SNOWBOARD ASSOCIATION (USSA)

USSA supports athletic excellence in Olympic skiing (alpine; freestyle; Nordic; and freeskiing) and snowboarding. It provides education, development, and competitive events for young athletes and selects athletes for the Olympic Games.

International Sport Federation: International Ski Federation (FIS)

U.S. SPEEDSKATING

U.S. Speedskating sponsors grassroots programs, such as development camps, and selects and trains Olympic speed skaters in short-track and long-track events.

International Sport Federation: International Skating Union (ISU)

USA BIATHLON (USBA)

Biathlon, which combines the physical demands of cross-country skiing with the precision of rifle marksmanship, while relatively unknown in the United States, is the top-rated winter sport on European television. Since 1980, USBA's promotional efforts since 1980 have grown biathlon to over 1,000 members who compete in the winter and summer (with running rather than skiing) versions of the sport.

International Sport Federation: International Biathlon Union (IBU)

USA BOBSLED AND SKELETON FEDERATION (USBSF)

USBSF promotes and develops athletes for the Olympic Games in bobsledding and skeleton. Bobsled competitions consist of four-man (a pilot, a brakeman, and two pushers), two-man (without the two pushers), and two-woman teams making timed runs down a narrow, twisting, banked, and iced track on gravity-powered sleds. Skeleton (sometimes called tobogganing) is an individual sport in which the athlete lies in a prone, head-first position and drives the sled as fast as possible down an iced track. Given the virtual obscurity of these winter sports in the United States, many athletes on the national teams are recruited from other sports. Athletes from sports requiring strength and speed have become pushers in bobsled.

International Sport Federation: International Bobsleigh and Tobogganing Federation (FIBT)

USA Curling (USAC)

Teams of four players take turns sliding a heavy, polished granite stone down the ice, while two of the players using brooms seek to help position the stone closest to the target. Women in 1948 and men in 1958 organized national associations for curling. USAC chooses teams for the Olympic Games and Paralympic Games.

International Sport Federation: World Curling Federation (WCF)

USA Figure Skating

Local ice skating clubs sponsored competitions beginning in the mid-nineteenth century, long before the United States Figure Skating Association was established in 1921. USA Figure Skating begins with instructional programs in basic skills and offers competitive levels for figure skaters as they increase their proficiency. Elite skaters compete in regional, sectional, and national championships and international events like the Olympic Games and World Championships.

International Sport Federation: International Skating Union (ISU)

USA Hockey

USA Hockey has over 610,000 ice and inline hockey players, coaches, officials, and volunteers and supports programs at the grassroots through elite levels. It offers programs for youth, junior, disabled, college, and adult players. USA Hockey selects and manages national team development, national sled (disabled), and men's and women's national teams.

International Sport Federation: International Ice Hockey Federation (IIHF)

USA LUGE

In luge, one or two athletes lay supine and feet first on a sled while speeding along an iced track with banked curves and walled-in straights. USA Luge recruits, prepares, and equips the national luge team for international and Olympic competition and promotes the growth of this sport.

International Sport Federation: International Luge Federation (FIL)

Non-Olympic Sports with National Governing Bodies

ASA/USA Softball

Begun in 1933, ASA evolved into the strongest softball organization in the United States through grassroots programs through national teams competing internationally. ASA conducts over 100 championships in fast pitch, slow pitch, and modified pitch for players of all ages.

International Sport Federation: World Baseball Softball Confederation (WBSC)

United States Bowling Congress (USBC)

The USBC was formed in 2005 from a merger of the American Bowling Congress, Women's International Bowling Congress, Young American Bowling Alliance, and USA Bowling to serve over 2,600,000 amateur adult and youth bowlers.

International Sport Federation: World Bowling Federation

U.S. Squash

U.S. Squash traces its roots to 1904 when the United States Squash Racquets Association was founded and became a pioneer in promoting competition for females as well as males. It conducts tournaments and governs the nearly 17,000 members who play this racket and ball game in over 1,000 facilities nationwide.

International Sport Federation: World Squash Federation (WSF)

USA Baseball

USA Baseball governs more than 12,000,000 amateur players and between 1992 and 2008 chose and prepared the Olympic team, and will again for 2020. Among the baseball teams it selects for international competitions are Premier12, 12 and under, 14 and under, 15 and under, 17 and under, 18 and under, collegiate national team, and the women's national team.

International Sport Federation: World Baseball Softball Confederation (WBSC)

USA Karate

Karate is an attacking martial art that uses kicks, punches, strikes, and blocking movements. Classes begin for students as early as four years old and continue throughout life. Through its educational programs and competitions, USA Karate emphasizes helping participants develop healthier minds and bodies as they work to improve personal defense skills.

International Sport Federation: World Karate Federation (WKF)

USA Racquetball

This organization traces its founding to 1969, the year after this sport was developed. Racquetball is played by all ages and skill levels from local tournaments through international competitions for the top players.

International Sport Federation: International Racquetball Federation (IRF)

USA Roller Sports (USARS)

USARS creates, enhances, and conducts programs and competitions in roller sports, including figure skating, inline hockey, rink hockey, roller derby, slalom, and speed skating along with fitness and recreational activities for beginners through elite athletes.

International Sport Federation: International Roller Sports Federation (FIRS)

USA Water Ski

USA Water Ski promotes the growth and development of recreational water skiing, and organizes and governs competitive water skiing, working with local water ski clubs serving over 15,000 members. Nearly 80 percent of its members compete in annual tournaments.

International Sport Federation: International Waterski and Wakeboard Federation (IWWF)

Single-Sport Organizations

American Canoeing Association (ACA)

Founded in 1880, the ACA promotes the paddle sports of canoeing, kayaking, rafting, and stand up paddleboarding as wholesome lifetime recreational activities through event sponsorship, safety education, instructor certification, waterway stewardship, water trails, and paddler's rights and protection. Approximately 800,000 individuals participate in nearly 4,300 ACA-sanctioned paddle sport events annually.

American Youth Football and Cheer (AYF)

AYF, established in 1996, promotes the development of youth through football and cheerleading with over 830,000 youth participants nationally and internationally. A hallmark of AYF is its commitment to giving back to the community, such as providing financial grants to leagues, working with corporate sponsors to provide shoes for players and fields for teams, and sending inner-city kids to football camps.

American Youth Soccer Organization (AYSO)

Begun in 1964 for boys, with girls included since 1971, the AYSO has grown to involve over 500,000 players. AYSO is committed to ensuring every child plays and has fun running and kicking.

Babe Ruth League, Inc.

The Babe Ruth League was founded in 1951 to provide wholesome baseball for boys ages 13 to 15 and expanded to include baseball players ages between 4 and 18. In 1984, Babe Ruth Softball for girls ages 4 to 18 was added. Its Bambino Division for players between 4 and 12 was renamed Cal Ripken Baseball, a Division of Babe Ruth League, Inc.

Biddy Basketball International

Founded in 1951, Biddy Basketball's developmental program adapts the size of the ball, height of the goal, and distance for shooting free throws, so boys and girls from ages 7 to 14 can learn basketball skills as they grow and mature. Athletes compete in local, district, regional, and international championships.

Boston Athletic Association (BAA)

The BAA was established in 1887 to manage athletic events, especially running events, and promote a healthy lifestyle through sports. BAA conducted its first road race, which became known as the Boston Marathon, in 1897. This marathon, the world's oldest annual marathon, is regarded by most as the most prestigious in the world. The BAA remains an active running club for recreational through elite runners and sponsors races for all ages.

The First Tee

The mission of this junior golf program is to provide young people with golf programs that build character, instill life-enhancing values, and promote healthy choices through its character education and life skills programs. This international youth development organization uses golf to teach and reinforce these nine core values: honesty, integrity, sportsmanship, respect, confidence, responsibility, perseverance, courtesy, and judgment. Its Code of Conduct stresses respect for self, others, and surroundings. Since 1997, the First Tee has involved over 10 million children and adolescents, including over 7,000 elementary school that have introduced The First Tee National School Program.

Little League Baseball and Softball

Little League Baseball began in 1939 to provide organized baseball competitions for 9- to 12-year-old boys and has expanded nationally and internationally (over 80 countries). In 1974, Little League Baseball began to allow girls to play on baseball teams. Today, there are baseball leagues for boys and girls ages 4 to 18 and for girls in softball.

National Softball Association (NSA)

The NSA focuses on meeting the needs of parks and recreation departments and softball complex owners to serve youth through adult players. It provides state, regional, and world tournaments to NSA-sanctioned leagues through qualifying tournaments.

PONY

PONY, an acronym for Protect Our Nation's Youth, began in 1951 to sponsor baseball for boys ages 13 and 14 to help them grow into healthier and happier adults. PONY Baseball is organized into teams in two-year age increments starting at age 5 through 18. Even though girls may play in the baseball leagues, PONY began offering fast-pitch and slow-pitch softball in 1976 and now serves girls between ages 12 and 18. PONY Baseball and Softball serves over 500,000 players.

Pop Warner Little Scholars (PWLS)

This program, named for the legendary Hall of Fame coach Glenn "Pop" Warner, began in 1929 to provide youth football programs, now expanded to 42 states and internationally. The program was renamed Pop Warner Little Scholars in 1959 in recognition of its emphasis on academic achievement in an atmosphere conducive to developing sound character while having fun. In the 1970s, cheerleading was officially recognized as a competitive program and majorettes, pom squads, dancing boots, and pep squads also have been added. Pop Warner programs serve about 325,000 boys and girls ages 5 to 16.

Soccer Association for Youth (SAY)

SAY, established in 1967, provides recreational grassroots soccer programs for children, emphasizing low fees, balanced teams, and equal participation. SAY serves over 150,000 players.

T-Ball USA Association

The T-Ball USA Association seeks to develop the game of T-ball by offering a variety of programs and services for over 2 million boys and girls ages four to eight. It works with local, regional, and national youth baseball leagues and community groups such as parks and recreation departments.

United States Adult Soccer Association (USASA)

USASA, along with 54 national state organizations, is dedicated to participation in and growth of adult soccer as a game for life. It supports developmental leagues and premier leagues for male and females.

United States Golf Association (USGA)

USGA sponsors programs for players of all ages and annually conducts 13 national championships, including the U.S. Open, U.S. Women's Open, U.S. Senior Open, and national amateur championships and state team championships. Since its founding in 1894, USGA has worked with the Royal and Ancient Golf Club in St. Andrews, Scotland, to write and interpret the rules of golf, which include playing by the letter, spirit, and etiquette of the game.

United States Masters Swimming (USMS)

USMS is dedicated to serving over 60,000 adult swimmers. It provides organized workouts, competitions, clinics, and workshops for noncompetitive and competitive swimmers who seek to improve their fitness through swimming.

U.S. Club Soccer

U.S. Club Soccer since 2000 supports competitive soccer clubs and the development of elite players through planning, marketing, managing, and financing programs. U.S. Club Soccer sponsors events from the id2 National Identification and Development Program to the National Cup for teams U-11 through U-18–19 through the National Premier Leagues.

U.S. Lacrosse

In 1998, U.S. Lacrosse unified youth, men's, and women's lacrosse and now serves youth, interscholastic, and college lacrosse through 67 chapters.

U.S. Youth Soccer

Over 600,000 volunteers and administrators and 300,000 coaches enable U.S. Youth Soccer to serve over 3,000,000 youth players ages 5 to 19. Its programs include underserved areas, athletes with physical disabilities, recreational players, competitive athletes, and elite athletes.

USA Football

This organization, which does not sponsor leagues or teams, hosts educational programs for coaches, officials, and administrators and skill development programs for young players. Through its program Heads Up Football it seeks to advance player safety. Its Fundamentals program teaches basic football skills, and its Protection Tour educates about equipment fitting, tackling fundamentals, and concussions. Organizations can receive fitness and field grants based on need and merit.

USA Pickleball Association (USAPA)

USAPA was established in 1984 to promote the development and growth of pickleball in the United States and internationally. The game evolved in the 1960s as a racket sport hitting a perforated plastic ball over a lowered badminton net. Pickleball is played in thousands of community centers, physical education classes, YMCA facilities, and retirement communities.

USA Ultimate

Formed in 1968 by high school students, ultimate combines the athletic skills of running, catching, and throwing (a flying disc). One of the fastest-growing team sports in the United States, players self-officiate as they move quickly between offense and defense and attempt to score by catching a pass in the opposing team's end zone. Governed by the Spirit of the Games with its tradition of sportsmanship, it is played by millions worldwide at all skill levels.

Youth Basketball of America (YBOA)

YBOA promotes youth basketball worldwide through an international camp and national championships for boys in grades 2 to 12 and girls in grades 3 to 12.

Multiple Sport Organizations

Amateur Athletic Union (AAU)

After its establishment in 1888, the AAU led this nation's participation in the Olympic Games by serving as the national sport federation for several sports. Beginning with swimming and track and field in 1967, the AAU's Junior Olympics now serves over 16,000 boys and girls representing all 50 states and several U.S. territories participate at the grassroots level and advance to national competitions in over 20 sports. Today, the AAU through over 60,000 volunteers serves over 670,000 participants through its "Sports for All, Forever" philosophy and sport programs.

BlazeSports

A legacy organization of the 1996 Paralympic Games in Atlanta, BlazeSports serves over 13,000 youth and adults with physical disabilities through adaptive sport and recreation. It offers youth programs, veterans' programs, international programs, training and education, and camps.

Disabled Sports USA (DS/USA)

Disabled Sports USA offers nationwide sport rehabilitation programs in summer sports, winter sports, warfighter sports (for wounded warriors and their families), race development (skiing and snowboarding), and for youth. These are open to individuals with a permanent disability, including visual impairments, amputations, spinal cord injury, dwarfism, multiple sclerosis, head injury, cerebral palsy, and other neuromuscular and orthopedic conditions.

International Olympic Committee (IOC)

The IOC has 206 affiliated national Olympic committees and 35 international sport federations. In addition to hosting the largest multisport international sport festivals in the summer and winter Olympic Games, the IOC emphasizes fair competition by seeking to eliminate performance-enhancing drugs. The IOC Ethics Commission (see https://www.olympic.org/ethics-commission) advocates for ethical principles, through its Code of Ethics, and emphasizes the values and principles enshrined in the Olympic Charter.

International Paralympic Committee (IPC)

Olympic-style games for individuals with disabilities began in 1960 and have grown to include over 4,500 athletes from over 140 nations. This global governing body organizes the summer Paralympic Games in 20 sports and winter Paralympic Games in 5 sports, and coordinates world championships and other competitions. By IOC policy, all host cities for the summer and winter Olympic Games also host the Paralympic Games.

National Association of Intercollegiate Athletics (NAIA)

Formed in 1952 by smaller institutions that had previously conducted a postseason basketball tournament, the NAIA (now with nearly 300 members and over 60,000 athletes) has grown to include championships in 11 sports for males. In 1980, the NAIA began national championships for females and now offers them in 11 sports. Launched in 2000, the Champions of Character program emphasizes how student-athletes and coaches should model core values of respect, responsibility, integrity, servant leadership, and sportsmanship.

National Association of Police Athletic/Activities League (National PAL)

National PAL provides local chapters with resources and opportunities to organize young athletes ages 5 to 18 for competing in a championship environment in sports. One goal is for young athletes in the over 700 cities with PAL programs will learn to respect the police officers and the laws they enforce.

National Christian College Athletic Association (NCCAA)

Established in 1968, the NCCAA seeks to produce winners in the game of life through the promotion of intercollegiate athletic competition with a Christian perspective. It conducts national championships in nine sports each for men and women.

National Collegiate Athletic Association (NCAA)

The NCAA, which began in 1906, is comprised of three divisions based on enrollment, number of sports, and the awarding of grants-in-aid. (Division I has 351 members; Division II has 325 members; Division III has 450 members.) The NCAA offers national championships in each of these divisions in 24 sports each for males and females.

National Congress of State Games (NCSG)

NCSG is comprised of summer (31) and winter (10) state games organizations. It supports member organizations in promoting health, fitness and character building through multisport competitions and physical activities.

National Federation of State High School Associations (NFHS)

Since 1920, the NFHS has provided leadership to and supported educationally based interscholastic sports. Over 7,800,000 students participate in interscholastic sports. The most popular sports for girls are outdoor track and field, basketball, and volleyball, while more boys participate in football, outdoor track and field, and basketball. In addition to providing sport-specific rules for high school sports, the NFHS offers professional development opportunities for coaches and officials so these important individuals are better prepared to facilitate the all-around growth and development of adolescents.

National Intramural-Recreational Sports Association (NIRSA)

NIRSA was established in 1950 and now provides professional development to nearly 4,500 members, who serve an estimated million students. Through its members, NIRSA fosters quality recreational programs, facilities, and services for diverse populations within colleges and universities.

National Junior College Athletic Association (NJCAA)

The NJCAA, which began in 1938, offers national champion-ships in 14 sports for males and 12 sports for females in its over 430 member institutions. NJCAA promotes intersectional and national competitions for athletes in two-year institutions in ways consistent with the educational missions of member institutions.

National Senior Games Association (NSGA)

NSGA is dedicated to motivating men and women over 50 to lead healthy lives through participating in state through national senior athletic events. The biennial Summer National Senior Games, which began in 1987, include competitions in archery, badminton, basketball, bowling, cycling, golf, horse-shoes, pickleball, race walk, racquetball, road race, shuffle-board, softball, swimming, table tennis, tennis, track and field, triathlon, and volleyball.

Special Olympics

Begun as a day camp in 1962 and expanded into the first Inter-national Special Olympics Games in 1968, the Special Olym-pics annually provide educational and competitive experiences for over 4,500,000 individuals with intellectual disabilities in over 170 countries. In local through international competi-tions in 35 summer and winter sports, the Special Olympics empower individuals to become physically fit, productive, and respected members of society.

Sports and Fitness Industry Association (SFIA)

SFIA is a trade association of sports and fitness brands, suppliers, and retailers. Working with industry leaders, it promotes brands and products connected to sports, fitness, and active lifestyles.

United States Association of Blind Athletes (USABA)

Since its establishment in 1976, USABA has been committed to enhancing the lives of blind and visually impaired individuals.

It conducts sport competitions and recreation programs to help people learn the skills needed to participate in sports and life alongside their sighted peers. USABA athletes compete in cycling, judo, powerlifting, alpine and Nordic skiing, swimming, tenpin bowling, track and field, wrestling, five-a-side football, showdown (a table game with the goal of hitting a ball into the goal pocket at the end of a table), and goalball (a team sport with the objective to throw a ball with embedded bells into the opponent's goal).

United States Collegiate Athletic Association (USCAA)

The USCAA sponsors national championships in seven sports for men and six sports for women who attend small colleges. It is comprised of three conferences, Hudson Valley Intercollegiate Athletic Conference, Penn State University Athletic Conference, and Yankee Small College Conference.

USA Deaf Sports Federation (USADSF)

Since 1945, when the American Athletic Union of the Deaf was established, sport competitions have been offered to individuals without hearing. USADSF selects athletes for teams in international competitions in basketball, bowling, curling, cycling, golf, handball, ice hockey, martial arts, orienteering, shooting, ski and snowboard, soccer, swimming, tennis, track and field, triathlon, volleyball, and wrestling.

Wheelchair and Abulatory Sports, USA (WSUSA)

Since its establishment in 1956 as the National Wheelchair Athletic Association, Wheelchair Sports, USA has focused on providing participation and competitive sport opportunities for athletes with disabilities. It provides programs for juniors, adults, and quadriplegics (those with paralysis in upper and lower extremities) in archery, handcycling, powerlifting, shooting, swimming, table tennis, and track and field.

Sport-Related Organizations

American College of Sports Medicine (ACSM)

Founded in 1954, ACSM is dedicated to the integration of research, education, and practical application of sports medicine and exercise science to maintain and enhance physical performance, fitness, health, and quality of life. The over 50,000 regional, national, and international members of ACSM apply knowledge about medicine and exercise science to promote healthier lifestyles for people and excellence in sports, including the diagnosis, treatment, and prevention of sports-related injuries.

Boys and Girls Clubs

Sports often attract youth to local Boys and Girls Clubs, where they can develop their skills, make friends, and have fun. Boys and Girls Clubs are positive places for kids and help instill in them a sense of competence, usefulness, belongingness and influence.

Josephson Institute

Since 1987, the Josephson Institute has developed and delivered services and materials to increase ethical commitment, competence, and practice in all segments of society. The Josephson Institute's character education program for youth, Character Counts, emphasizes trustworthiness, respect, responsibility, fairness, caring, and citizenship. The Pursuing Victory with Honor program applies these six pillars of character to sport.

momsTeam (National Youth Sports Safety Foundation, NYSSF)

NYSSF, established in 1989, promotes the healthy development, safety, and well-being of youth by keeping them physically active and participating in sports for life. Given that over 5,000,000 youth athletes require treatment in hospital emergency rooms because of sports injuries, NYSSF is dedicated to reducing the number and severity of injuries youth sustain in sports and fitness activities by educating health professionals, program administrators, coaches, parents, and athletes through educational information for parents and young athletes.

National Alliance for Youth Sports (NAYS)

This organization partners with national, state, and community-based organizations, including parks and recreation departments, Boys and Girls Clubs, National PAL, and STOP Sports Injuries. The NAYS educates volunteer coaches, parents, officials, and administrators of youth sport programs to help them meet national standards for quality programs for children.

National Association for Athletics Compliance (NAAC)

NAAC seeks to foster the highest possible professional and ethical standards in athletics compliance and uphold the ideals of higher education.

National Association of Collegiate Directors of Athletics (NACDA)

NACDA provides professional development opportunities and serves as an advocate in addressing the nature, scope, issues, and challenges facing intercollegiate athletics. It seeks to develop a collegial and mutually beneficial relationship among athletic administrators, faculty, and students.

National Athletic Trainers' Association (NATA)

The NATA, established in 1950, is comprised of over 35,000 certified athletic trainers who seek to enhance the quality of health care they provide. NATA sets standards for professionalism, education, certification, research, and practice. Its code of ethics is an example of the high standard of professionalism expected of certified athletic trainers who assist athletes of all

ages through the prevention, assessment, treatment, and rehabilitation of sports injuries.

National Consortium for Academics and Sports (NCAS)

NCAS focuses on the educational attainment of students who
also are athletes and uses the power and appeal of sport to positively affect social change. Established in 1985, over 280 member institutions agree to provide free tuition to former athletes
who did not complete their degree requirements if these individuals participate in school outreach and community service
programs addressing social issues of America's youth.

National Council of Youth Sports (NCYS)

NCYS works to enhance the experiences of youth in sports
through member organizations that serve 60,000,000 children. Local communities emphasize children in youth sports
having fun through healthy physical activities and developing
self-esteem, fair play, and good citizenship.

National High School Athletic Coaches Association (NHSACA)

NHSACA is committed to meeting the needs of administrators, coaches, athletes, and parents who make up the athletic
community in schools. In addition to offering a coach certification program, it provides information to help coaches attain
and maintain the professional expertise to fulfill their responsibility to develop the sports skills and character of young people.

National Recreation and Park Association (NRPA)

NRPA advocates for making parks, open spaces, and recreational opportunities available to everyone to increase their
quality of life. Through coalitions and partnerships with allied
organizations, NRPA facilitates community initiatives to use
parks and recreational activities to enhance people's emotional,
social, and physical needs.

National Sports Center for the Disabled (NSCD)

Courage, strength, and determination are the qualities that describe the individuals served since 1970 by NSCD, one of the largest therapeutic recreation and adaptive sports agencies in the world. Through its programs, the lives of over 3,000 children and adults with physical or mental challenges are positively impacted on ski slopes, in canoes, on mountain trails, and on golf courses as they learn more about sports and themselves.

National Strength and Conditioning Association (NSCA)

Since its establishment in 1978, the NSCA has grown to nearly 30,000 members in 72 countries. NSCA members disseminate and apply research-based knowledge on strength training and conditioning practices to improve athletic performance and fitness.

National Youth Sports Health and Safety Institute

The National Youth Sports Health and Safety Institute through its leaders advocates for advancing and disseminating educational information and recommendations to enhance the health and safety of youth in sports. In making youth sports a public-health solution, it focuses on sports trauma and concussions, environmental challenges like heat illness, training and competition overload and overuse, and playing with chronic disease and disability, such as Type 1 diabetes.

Positive Coaching Alliance (PCA)

PCA seeks to transform youth sports so sports can transform youth with the goal of "Better Athletes, Better People." It works with youth sport partner organizations, leagues, schools, and cities; conducts workshops for youth sport coaches, parents, organizational leaders, and athletes; and provides helpful resources on its website. The PCA stresses that youth athletes honor the game by striving to win through a positive, character-building environment while learning life lessons.

STOP Sports Injuries

STOP (Sports Trauma and Overuse Prevention) Sports Injuries was founded by American Orthopaedic Society for Sports Medicine in 2007. This public outreach program seeks to raise awareness about the importance of sports safety and provides educational materials and public service announcements about the problems of overuse and trauma to help ensure that youth develop a love of healthy physical activity.

United States Anti-Doping Agency (USADA)

USADA is committed to ensuring clean sport by eliminating doping in sport and preserving the well-being of Olympic, Paralympic, Pan American, and Parapan American sport. As the national anti-doping organization, its mission is to preserve the integrity of competition, inspire true sport, and protect the right of athletes.

World Anti-Doping Agency (WADA)

In its fight against the use of performance-enhancing drugs, WADA takes a seven-prong approach: worldwide compliance with the World Anti-Doping Code; scientific research, publication of the prohibited substances and methods, and laboratory accreditation; anti-doping coordination; global anti-doping development fostering a clean sport culture worldwide; preventative methods such as values-based educational programs; athlete outreach to raise awareness; and cooperation with law enforcement.

Young Men's Christian Association (YMCA)

The YMCA serves as a change agent to meet the critical social needs of children and adults of all ages, races, faiths, backgrounds, abilities, and income levels. The YMCA's foci are youth development, healthy living, and social responsibility as it seeks to help kids and families in need reach their full potential.

Young Women's Christian Association (YWCA)

The YWCA's mission is to eliminate racism, empower women, support social justice, and strengthen communities through job training, career counseling, providing child care, and developing the health and fitness of members. Its mission includes advocacy for racial justice and civil rights, employment and economic advancement of women and girls, and the health and safety of women and girls.

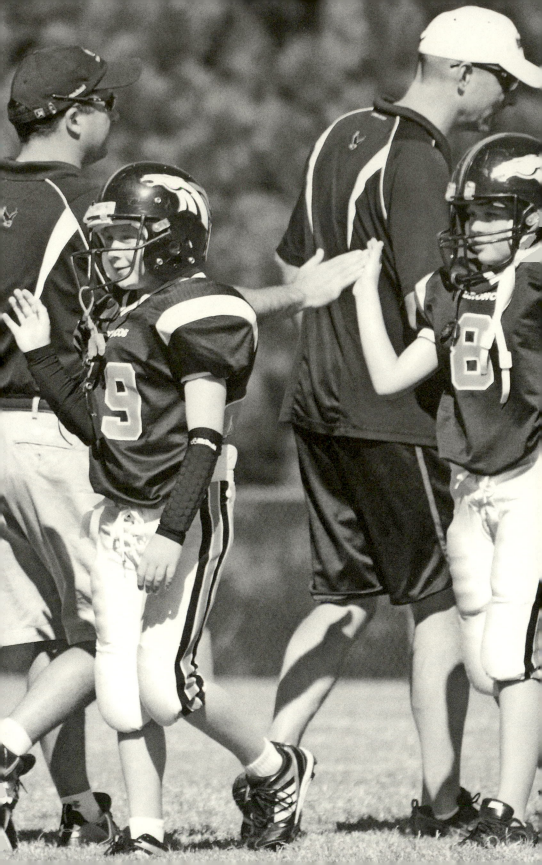

This chapter provides facts, statistics, and documents to help readers contextualize significant events, issues, and challenges as they impact the operation of sports on an ethical or unethical basis. While the information and data will illustrate historical and current practices, the documents provide guidance about how unfair or non-sportsmanship behaviors could be replaced by values-based actions and displays of character. One goal of providing this information is to broaden the perspective about how each level of sport has not, but potentially could have, succeeded in developing the values that it claims result from sport participation. Another goal is to provide context for continuing ethical problems that have not yet been resolved, but need to be addressed if sport is to overcome cheating, an overemphasis on winning, the use of performance-enhancing drugs, discriminatory treatment of females and ethnic minorities, and gamesmanship. The information and data are provided in a chronological manner, beginning with youth sports through the Olympic Games, along with sections addressing some ethical issues associated with females and African Americans in sports.

Youth Sport

Children play because they have fun. They enjoy exploring the world around them and discovering and expanding their abilities

---

Football players congratulate the opposing team's players and coaches at the close of a youth football game. This postgame tradition inspires good sportsmanship. (Susan Leggett/Dreamstime.com)

to move. They mimic the activities of adults as they learn to throw, catch, and kick balls. Since parents want to provide safe play spaces, they increasingly have organized sport opportunities for their children. As early as age three, children are enrolled in organized classes, programs, and teams in figure skating, gymnastics, ice hockey, soccer, and other sports. Despite questions from educators and physicians about whether young children are developmentally ready for competitive sports at such early ages, many very young children engage in structured practices each week almost year-round. So, it should not be surprising when ethical problems begin to impact sport participants from a young age, especially with an adult-imposed emphasis on winning. Table 5.1 lists several of the ethical challenges facing youth sport, as well as proposes what could be the rights of youth sport athletes. It could be argued these rights represent morally reasoned ways to address each of the challenges.

Table 5.1   Ethical Challenges Facing Youth Sports Contrasted with the Ethical Rights of Youth Sport Athletes

Ethical Challenges Facing Youth Sports	Ethical Rights of Youth Sport Athletes
1. Coaches and parents taking the fun out of youth sports by putting too much pressure on young athletes.	1. The right to have fun playing.
2. Coaches and parents sending the message that winning is the important thing as shown by rewarding winning more than anything else.	2. The right to receive positive reinforcement for showing effort, playing hard, and doing one's best.
3. Adults allowing anyone to coach youth in sports.	3. The right to have qualified coaches whose abilities have been certified and who have cleared criminal background checks.
4. Coaches and parents insisting young athletes dedicate themselves to playing only one sport year-round.	4. The right to play or not play any sport and to have time off from sports.

Ethical Challenges Facing Youth Sports	Ethical Rights of Youth Sport Athletes
5. Coaches and parents expecting young athletes to be tough and play through injuries.	5. The right to have injuries evaluated properly, to be given needed medical care, and to allow injuries to heal before being expected to play.
6. Coaches arguing with officials when they do not agree with a call and allowing young athletes to argue with officials about calls.	6. The right to have coaches and parents model showing respect to officials and the right to be expected to show respect to officials.
7. A parent demanding a coach should give a child more playing time or play a child in a certain position.	7. The right to play various positions, against balanced competition, and for approximately the same amount of time as all other players.
8. Coaches focusing on developing the skills and advancement of the best athletes.	8. The right to play at a level commensurate with their abilities with the dual goals of seeking to win and learning life lessons.
9. Coaches modeling their actions after professional and collegiate models along with having unrealistic performance expectations of young athletes.	9. The right to learn basic skills and fundamental strategies in developmentally appropriate ways and receive positive coaching.
10. Coaches teaching and encouraging young athletes to intentionally violate game rules and taunt opponents to gain competitive advantages.	10. The right to play sports according to the rules without fear of violence or harm and receive respect from opponents coupled with the responsibility to play by the rules and show respect to opponents.

While youth sport has been praised by parents and youth sport coaches for teaching character and life lessons to children, sometimes positive values are not learned. Instead, myths persist because adults want to believe things that have not been proved to be true.

Ethical problems associated with youth sports have led to the formation of numerous organizations dedicated to helping youth sports teach positive values. For example, the Positive Coaching Alliance (PCA) has established national partnerships with organizations like Little League (baseball), Pop Warner (football), and the American Youth Soccer Association with the goal of transforming youth sports.

Many people talk about sportsmanship, or what it means to be a "good sport." What does it mean to you to be a good sport? Answers to this question vary widely. Sadly, PCA has even heard stories of coaches telling their teams that if they win the Sportsmanship Award at a tournament, they will spend the entire following week conditioning! Why might a coach say this? Unfortunately, some coaches equate being a good sport with being soft or weak.

PCA believes the time has come to unite behind "The Power of Positive," which is described in Document 5.1. Coaches, parents, and athletes need to realize that this perspective needs to replace the common win at all cost perspective. If a coach and his or her team have to dishonor the game to win it, what is this victory really worth, and what sort of message is this sending young athletes?

Document 5.1

The Power of Positive

Why Positive Is Powerful

A positive approach gets the most from youth and high school athletes, which is what coaches, parents and the athletes themselves want. Staying positive also helps youth get the most out of sports.

Encouraging athletes with positive reinforcement helps them hear and heed the necessary corrections. With that winning combination of truthful, specific praise and constructive criticism, athletic performance improves and so do the chances that kids stick with sports longer and learn all the valuable life lessons inherently available through organized competition.

Academic research and real-world scoreboard results from millions of coaches, parents and athletes that PCA has trained and educated prove what the pro and college coaches on PCA's National Advisory Board already know: Positive is powerful.

The Core Concepts

Elm Tree of Mastery

Focusing on what you can control is the key to performance and success. Great coaches teach this! And a tremendous body of research backs this up! The scoreboard is an important part of youth and high school sports. . .but still just a part. Winning is neither everything nor the only thing. While youth learn how to compete, a necessary lesson now and throughout their lives, they also should take a mastery approach to sports. That means focusing on what they can control: their Effort, Learning and Ability to persist through mistakes and adversity.

Honoring the Game

Sports provide a great framework for cultivating ethical behavior. Winning and losing gracefully are hallmarks of people equipped to live in and lead a civil society. And learning to treat people with dignity, especially under the pressure of competition, is one of the most valuable life lessons sports can offer. In sports, this is "Honoring the Game," respect for Rules, Opponents, Officials Teammates and Self. These are the ROOTS of positive competition and a healthy team culture!

Filling Emotional Tanks

Each person has an "Emotional Tank" that works like the gas tank of a car. When the tank is empty, we go nowhere. When the tank is full, we can go nearly anywhere. Athletes with full E-Tanks feel connected to their team and coach, which enables them to learn, perform and compete better! The best mix for a full Emotional Tank is five parts specific, truthful praise for each piece of constructive correction. 5:1 is the Magic Ratio!

Development Zone

Youth and high school sports can provide a "Development Zone" environment for developing Better Athletes, Better People, but only if coaches, parents, administrators and student-athletes intentionally make it so. Insuring that young athletes get to learn and compete in a Development Zone Culture (as opposed to a win-at-all-cost culture) is a great gift youth and high school sports leaders can make possible for their communities. That's why PCA Founder Jim Thompson's latest book, his ninth, is titled *Developing Better Athletes, Better People: A Leader's Guide to Transforming High School and Youth Sports into a Development Zone*. And that's why our website of 1,000+ free printable and audio-video tips and tools is called the Development Zone Resource Center.

Source: Positive Coaching Alliance. "The Power of Positive." 2016. Available at http://www.positivecoach.org/the-power-of-positive/ (used by permission).

Children will not learn how to honor the game if they are not actively involved with sports. Today, most schools fail to meet the physical activity, fitness, and sport skill instructional needs of children because too many physical education programs have been eliminated due to budgetary constraints or pressures to increase the amount of the school day dedicated to instruction in reading, mathematics, or other subjects. According to the Centers for Disease Control and Prevention, about 17 percent (12.7 million) of children and teens ages 2 to 19, based on 2011–2012 data, are obese. While viewing television, playing video games, and surfing the Internet may be contributing factors, so, too, are super-sized fast foods and concern about safe play spaces.

Since most children do not participate in daily physical education in schools, parents and interested citizens have continued to expand the number of youth sport programs. While many of these programs advocate for children having fun while learning sport skills in developmentally appropriate ways and times, other children participate in highly competitive sport teams when their bodies, psychological development, and emotional maturity are not ready for the pressures of winning and performing as miniature college or professional athletes. Yet, national championships, beginning at very young ages and continuing for older children, abound in numerous sports as listed in Table 5.2.

Table 5.2 Examples of National Championships for Young Athletes

Age Groups	Sexes	Sponsoring Organizations	National Championships
Eight and under	Boys and girls	Amateur Athletic Union	AAU Basketball National Championships
Nine-year old boys and girls	Boys and girls	Amateur Athletic Union	AAU Junior Olympic Swimming Meet
Ten years and under	Girls	Amateur Athletic Union	AAU Girls Junior National Volleyball Championships
Ten years and under	Boys and girls	Babe Ruth League	Cal Ripken Baseball 10-Year-Old World Series
Weight divisions beginning with 106 lb.	Boys	Golden Gloves	National Golden Gloves Tournament of Champions
Nine to twelve	Boys and girls	Little League	Little League Baseball World Series
Nine to twelve	Girls	Little League	Little League Softball World Series
Eight through eleven with weight limits	Boys	Pop Warner	Junior Pee Wee Pop Warner Super Bowl
Eight through eleven	Girls	Pop Warner	Junior Pee Wee Cheer and Dance Championships
Nine and under	Boys and girls	US Club Soccer	Youth World Series

An ethical concern is that seeking victories to qualify for and succeed in national championships, in programs modeled after professional sports with fully uniformed children playing with all the trappings of commercialized sport, may be teaching life lessons other than character development. Except for winners pictured with their trophies, every other team or athlete in qualifying events and these championships ends the season having lost on the scoreboard. The pressures from coaches, who have dedicated huge amounts of time and emotional energy, and parents, who have spent large sums of money and made major psychological investments, may be teaching these young athletes the only thing that really matters is winning. Also, when children play in national championships at an early age, it is not surprising some parents begin to envision their children as potential superstars. It is important to note that many of these competitors, as well as those who compete in national championships in their older years, often do not persist in sports, choosing instead to drop out of them.

Interscholastic Sports

When young athletes drop out of sports, they are deprived of potential physical, psychological, emotional, and social benefits. Instead of what many individuals claim is an overemphasis on only the most successful players, should opportunities for individuals of all skill levels be provided? One way to decrease the increased prevalence of overweight and obese adolescents could be to provide more sport opportunities characterized more by fun and learning life lessons than on competitions among the most highly skilled. Often the world of sports is viewed as a pyramid, with fewer and fewer people playing sports as they age as the demand for higher skilled performances increases. Maybe a way to address the ethical dilemma of sport excluding people could be to broaden and widen the base by providing lifelong participation opportunities in sport along with allowing those with advanced skills to continue to compete at their level in high school, college, and professionally. This alternative approach to sport opportunities is illustrated in Figure 5.1. If this approach were to be implemented, more children, adolescents, and adults would have opportunities to play sports at levels commensurate with their skill levels.

Since 1920, the National Federation of State High School Associations (NFHS) has advocated for and led in the development of interscholastic sports based on an educational model. Through school-sponsored sport competitions, students could learn values that would help them succeed in their lives. NFHS's leadership of interscholastic sports and other extracurricular activities has consistently advocated for academic achievement, good citizenship, healthy lifestyles, and fair play.

Historically, interscholastic sports promoted by NFHS were exclusively for boys. Occasionally girls attending rural schools were allowed to play on basketball teams, although most educators and parents believed girls were not interested in sports

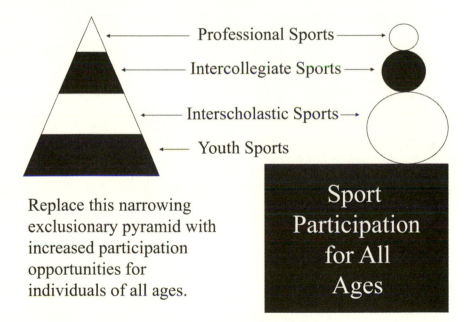

Figure 5.1   Model for Increased Participation in Sports

or did not possess sport skills. Societal attitudes through the 1960s reinforced the traditional perspective that boys played sports and girls cheered for them. Girls seldom had opportunities to learn sport skills, maybe through the lack of parental encouragement, sports equipment, instructional programs, or teams on which to play. Some have argued this limitation of females in sports was unfair.

When the federal government passed the Education Amendments in 1972 (P. L. 92–318), educational opportunities for females in schools began to expand. Title IX in Section 1681 of this legislation, as amended by section 3 of P. L. 93–568 in 1975, prohibits discrimination on the basis of sex in any federally funded education program or activity. It states, " 'No person in the United States shall, on the basis of sex, be excluded from participation in, be denied the benefits of, or be subjected to discrimination under any education program or activity receiving Federal financial assistance." Although these 37 words do not specifically mention athletics or sports, this law forever changed the world of sports in the United States for females.

P. L. 93–568 describes the reach of nondiscrimination on the basis of sex in educational programs or activities receiving federal financial assistance. Section 106.41 on athletics states,

> no person shall, on the basis of sex, be excluded from participation in, be denied the benefits of, be treated differently from another person or otherwise be discriminated against in any interscholastic, intercollegiate, club or intramural athletics offered by a recipient, and no recipient shall provide any such athletics separately on such basis.

While broadly disallowing disparate treatment in all educational programs and services, this federal law specifically requires equal opportunity in interscholastic sports. Figure 5.2

illustrates how this law and changing societal attitudes toward females participating in sport have resulted in an over 1,000 percent increase in girls playing interscholastic sports in the years since the passage of the 1972 Education Amendments. It also should be noted that over this same time period, participation opportunities for boys increased 23.2 percent.

With 7.8 million adolescents playing interscholastic sports, it is not surprising many of these athletes and their parents believe they will receive grants-in-aid to pay for a college education based on their athletic abilities. Oftentimes, this expectation is accompanied by pressures to win, playing only one sport year-round, overuse injuries, and burnout leading to their dropping out of sports. As Table 5.3 describes, the likelihood of receiving a college athletic scholarship is quite small. Some athletes will get the opportunity to play intercollegiate sports. Few

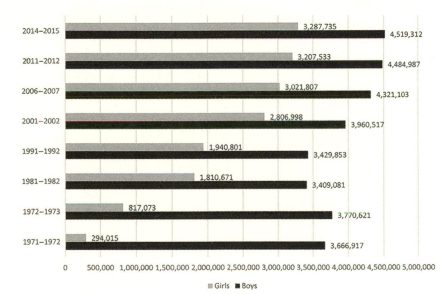

Figure 5.2 Participation Numbers by Sex in Interscholastic Sports

Source: National Federation of State High School Associations. 2016. "2014–15 High School Athletics Participation Survey Results." p. 53 (Copyright NFHS 2016; used by permission).

will play professionally. (The data in Table 5.3 include only athletes in NCAA institutions and do not include athletes who play in institutions governed by the NAIA, NJCAA, or other intercollegiate athletic governing organization.)

Table 5.3   Estimated Probability of Competing in Athletics beyond the High School Level

Student-Athletes	Men's Basketball	Women's Basketball	Football	Baseball	Men's Ice Hockey	Men's Soccer
High School Student Athletes	538,676	433,120	1,086,627	474,719	35,198	410,982
High School Senior Student Athletes	153,907	123,749	310,465	135,655	10,057	117,423
NCAA Student Athletes	17,984	16,186	70,147	32,450	3,964	23,365
NCAA Freshman Roster Positions	5,138	4,625	20,042	9,271	1,133	6,676
NCAA Senior Student Athletes	3,996	3,597	15,588	7,211	881	5,192
NCAA Student Athletes Drafted	46	32	254	678	7	101
Percentage High School to NCAA	3.3%	3.7%	6.5%	6.8%	11.3%	5.7%
Percentage NCAA to Professional	1.2%	0.9%	1.6%	9.4%	0.8%	1.9%
Percentage High School to Professional	0.03%	0.03%	0.08%	0.50%	0.07%	0.09%

Source: National Collegiate Athletic Association. "Estimated Probability of Competing in Athletics beyond the High School Interscholastic Level." 2013. © 2013 National Collegiate Athletic Association. (Used by permission.)

Arizona Sports Summit Accord

Since the last time many individuals will play organized sports is in high school, coaches, parents, and educators should take advantage of the opportunity to teach character and other positive values through sport. Depending on the leadership of interscholastic sports, these values may be taught, or different lessons may be learned. Given the numerous examples of ethical misbehaviors in interscholastic sports, many in sport have stated there was the need to raise the consciousness of sport managers, coaches, athletes, parents, and the general public about these problems. So, in 1999, the Josephson Institute Center for Sports Ethics brought together 50 influential leaders in sports. This group issued the Arizona Sports Summit Accord, provided in Document 5.2, which calls for a greater emphasis on building character and behaving ethically in sports.

Document 5.2

Arizona Sports Summit Accord

Preamble

At its best, athletic competition can hold intrinsic value for our society. It is a symbol of a great ideal: pursuing victory with honor. The love of sports is deeply embedded in our national consciousness. The values of millions of participants and spectators are directly and dramatically influenced by the values conveyed by organized sports. Thus, sports are a major social force that shapes the quality and character of the American culture. In the belief that the impact of sports can and should enhance the character and uplift the ethics of the nation, we seek to establish a framework of principles and a common language of values that can be adopted and practiced widely.

It is therefore agreed:

1. The essential elements of character-building and ethics in sports are embodied in the concept of sportsmanship and six core principles: trustworthiness, respect, responsibility, fairness, caring, and citizenship. The highest potential of

sports is achieved when competition reflects these "'Six Pillars of Character.'"

2. It is the duty of sports leadership—including coaches, athletic administrators, program directors, and officials—to promote sportsmanship and foster good character by teaching, enforcing, advocating, and modeling these ethical principles.

3. To promote sportsmanship and foster the development of good character, sports programs must be conducted in a manner that enhances the mental, social, and moral development of athletes and teaches them positive life skills that will help them become personally successful and socially responsible.

4. Participation in athletic programs is a privilege, not a right. To earn that privilege, athletes must conduct themselves, on and off the field, as positive role models who exemplify good character.

5. Sports programs should establish standards for participation by adopting codes of conduct for coaches, athletes, parents, spectators, and other groups who impact the quality of athletic programs.

6. All sports participants must consistently demonstrate and demand scrupulous integrity and observe and enforce the spirit as well as the letter of the rules.

7. The importance of character, ethics, and sportsmanship should be emphasized in all communications relating to the recruitment of athletes, including promotional and descriptive materials.

8. In recruiting, educational institutions must specifically determine that the athlete is seriously committed to getting an education and has or will develop the academic skills and character to succeed.

9. The highest administrative officer of organizations that offer sports programs must maintain ultimate responsibility for the quality and integrity of those programs. Such officers

must assure that education and character-development responsibilities are not compromised to achieve sports performance goals and that the academic, emotional, physical, and moral well-being of athletes is always placed above desires and pressures to win.

10. The faculties of educational institutions must be directly involved in and committed to the academic success of student-athletes and the character-building goals of the institution.

11. Everyone involved in athletic competition has a duty to treat the traditions of the sport and other participants with respect. Coaches have a special responsibility to model respectful behavior and the duty to demand that their athletes refrain from disrespectful conduct including verbal abuse of opponents and officials, profane or belligerent trash-talking, taunting, and unseemly celebrations.

12. The leadership of sports programs at all levels must ensure that coaches, whether paid or voluntary, are competent to coach. Minimal competence may be attained by training or experience. It includes basic knowledge of 1) the character-building aspects of sports, including techniques and methods of teaching and reinforcing the core values comprising sportsmanship and good character, 2) first-aid principles and the physical capacities and limitations of the age group coached, and 3) coaching principles and the rules and strategies of the sport.

13. Because of the powerful potential of sports as a vehicle for positive personal growth, a broad spectrum of sports experiences should be made available to all of our diverse communities.

14. To safeguard the health of athletes and the integrity of the sport, athletic programs must discourage the use of alcohol and tobacco and demand compliance with all laws and regulations, including those relating to gambling and the use of drugs.

15. Although economic relationships between sports programs and corporate entities are often mutually beneficial, institutions and organizations that offer athletic programs must safeguard the integrity of their programs. Commercial relationships should be continually monitored to ensure against inappropriate exploitation of the organization's name or reputation and undue interference or influence of commercial interests. In addition, sports programs must be prudent, avoiding undue financial dependency on particular companies or sponsors.

16. The profession of coaching is a profession of teaching. In addition to teaching the mental and physical dimensions of their sport, coaches, through words and example, must also strive to build the character of their athletes by teaching them to be trustworthy, respectful, responsible, fair, caring, and good citizens.

Source: Josephson Institute. "Arizona Sports Summit Accord." 1999. Available at http://sports.josephsoninstitute.org/resources-sport/accord/ (used by permission).

Before discussing intercollegiate sports, the next section examines females in sport. This interlude in the sequential presentation of data and documents seems appropriate since federal legislation and participation opportunities have most dramatically impacted females at the interscholastic and intercollegiate levels.

Females in Sports

Females of all ages have historically been excluded from sports. Traditional and societal roles and domestic responsibilities as wives and mothers limited their participation in sports. Until recent decades, physicians, women physical educators, and many women warned that females' physical and emotional makeup predisposed them to less vigorous and competitive physical exertion. Also, most sports were developed, governed, and participated in by males, who usually dismissed females as incapable of matching their stronger and faster athletic achievements. It also was perceived that most females were simply not interested in competing in sports. But, as the events and individuals described in Table 5.4 illustrate, significant changes occurred as females no longer accepted discriminatory exclusion and sought opportunities to achieve their athletic potential.

Table 5.4   Significant Events Affecting the Exclusion and Inclusion of Females in Sports

Date	Noteworthy Event	Effect or Implication
1850	Amelia Bloomer popularizes wearing loose-fitting pants worn under a skirt (these became known as bloomers).	Bloomers become the costume worn by females in gymnasiums, which frees them to play basketball and other sports in the late 1800s and early 1900s.
1874	Tennis, first introduced in the United States by a female, gains societal acceptance as a sport for females because it can be played in Victorian-style clothing and at a leisurely pace.	In 1884, the first women's singles tennis championship is contested at the All England Lawn Tennis Club at Wimbledon. In 1887, the first women's national tennis championship is held in the United States.
1892	Senda Berenson teaches the new game of basketball to Smith College students and modifies the rules to restrict players to one-third of the court to protect them from overexertion.	Basketball becomes the most popular sport for college women and schoolgirls. Basketball as played by most females remains a half-court game until 1938. Most colleges begin to play the game full court in 1970.
1896	Stanford plays the University of California in the first women's intercollegiate basketball game.	Only a few institutions offer athletic teams for females in basketball or any other sport for several decades because competitive sports are perceived as too physically and emotionally demanding.
1896	The International Olympic Committee (IOC) excludes females from participation in the modern Olympic Games.	IOC members state females are incapable physically and emotionally of competing in elite-level sports. However, the first females compete in the 1900 Paris Olympic Games in tennis and golf.

(continued)

Table 5.4 (*continued*)

Date	Noteworthy Event	Effect or Implication
1901	A British woman, Constance Applebee, introduces field hockey to females in the United States.	Some women play field hockey in colleges and on club teams, including against teams internationally, while males in the United States choose not to play what they perceive is a feminine sport. Females are not permitted to play field hockey in the Olympic Games until 1980 (males begin to play field hockey in the 1908 London Olympic Games).
1926	The first female, Gertrude Ederle at age 19, swims the English Channel in a time two hours faster than the men's record.	Ederle, who was a 1924 Olympic champion in swimming, receives a ticket tape parade in New York City. Her remarkable achievement in swimming the English Channel is viewed as the exception to females' interests and abilities in athletics.
1932	Babe Didrikson wins the Amateur Athletic Union (AAU) national team championship by winning the javelin, shot put, baseball throw, 80-meter hurdles, and broad jump and tying for first in the high jump.	Didrikson captures a silver medal in the high jump and gold medals in the javelin and 80-meter hurdles in the 1932 Los Angeles Olympic Games. A three-time AAU All-American basketball player who also excels in several other sports, Didrikson wins numerous amateur and professional golf championships.
1943	Chicago Cubs owner Philip Wrigley establishes the All-American Girls Professional Baseball League.	Over 600 female athletes play professional baseball in small Midwestern towns for 11 years. The league folds due to a decentralization of the league and loss of attendance.
1944	Swimmer Ann Curtis becomes the first female to win the Sullivan Award, presented by the AAU to the outstanding amateur athlete in the United States.	Since its initiation in 1930, 21 female athletes (including twins Coco and Kelly Miller in 1999) have received this award, which honors their athletic achievements as well as sportsmanship.
1954	The Iowa Girls' High School Athletic Union establishes a statewide program for girls' sports equal to that for boys.	This organization focuses on promoting greater sport opportunities for junior and senior high school girls in Iowa and is notably linked with the six-on-six basketball game played in Iowa through 1993.
1966	The Commission on Intercollegiate Athletics for	This organization, which becomes the Association for Intercollegiate Athletics

Date	Noteworthy Event	Effect or Implication
	Women begins to conduct national intercollegiate championships in gymnastics and track and field.	for Women (AIAW) in 1971, expands to provide 42 championships in 19 sports.
1967	Katherine Switzer registers as K. V. Switzer and becomes the first female to officially enter and run in the Boston Marathon.	When a male race official realizes a female has entered, he tries to tear her number from her back during the race. Females are allowed to officially run in the Boston Marathon in 1972.
1972	Congress passes the Education Amendments. Title IX of this legislation requires equal opportunity in all educational programs including athletics.	After Congress refuses to exclude athletics from this law and states its application to sport in educational institutions, the participation of females on school teams grows from under 300,000 to over three million and on college teams from around 16,000 to over 250,000.
1974	Billie Jean King establishes the Women's Sports Foundation.	Dedicated to advocacy and research on sport issues for women, this organization advocates for sports for females of all ages and skill levels.
1976	NJCAA offers its first national championships for females.	The NJCAA offers 22 national championships in 12 sports for women.
1978	U.S. Congress passes the Amateur Sports Act.	This act prohibits sex discrimination in amateur sports, thus making training facilities and money more available to women.
1980	NAIA offers its first national championships for females.	The NAIA offers 12 national championships in 11 sports for women.
1981	NCAA offers its first national championships for females.	The NCAA offers 48 national championships across its three divisions for females.
1984	Joan Benoit wins marathon in Olympic Games.	Females are allowed to run Olympic races longer than 1,500 meters including their first marathon.
1991	U.S.'s soccer team wins the first Women's World Cup.	Myths about the endurance and physical skills of females continue to be debunked
1997	Women's National Basketball Association plays its first season.	Failed attempts of women's professional basketball leagues are replaced by this successful league.
2012	Females comprise 44.2 percent of the participants in the London Olympic Games.	Females have advanced from exclusion to nearly full inclusion in the Olympic Games.

When the AIAW was established, it offered females an educational model for intercollegiate athletics different from the males' college sport governing organizations. The policies of the AIAW sought to prevent or control abuses afflicting men's athletics, such as ethical problems dealing with academics, recruiting, and commercialism. This different approach, however, met its demise when the NCAA, NAIA, and NJCAA began to offer national championships for females. The financial incentives offered by the NCAA to its member institutions were so substantial that athletic directors and presidents chose to abandon the AIAW, leading to its demise in 1982. Today, intercollegiate athletic programs operate following the men's model, with the same ethical problems the women's model attempted to prevent.

It is important to analyze the significance of Title IX of the 1972 Education Amendments to intercollegiate athletics. Given considerable uncertainty about the breadth of its application and resistance from many males (especially football coaches) to extend equal opportunity to females in intercollegiate athletics, the federal government in 1979 issued a clarifying policy interpretation. The original legislation and this policy interpretation make it clear intercollegiate athletic programs must provide equal opportunity to all students in three broad categories, as described in Table 5.5.

To fully understand the resistance and challenges to Title IX, Table 5.6 places this legislation in historical context. This table also demonstrates the consistency in application of Title IX to intercollegiate athletics.

Since federal law requires equal opportunity in all educational programs including athletics, it is informative to know the extent to which these institutions have added competitive opportunities for females. While the number of teams tells only part of the story, it does indicate whether or not a good faith effort has been made to provide sport teams for females. Table 5.7 provides historical through current data showing growth in the number of sport teams offered to females attending NCAA (but does not report on NAIA and NJCAA)

Table 5.5 Basic Requirements of Title IX for Intercollegiate Athletics

Area	Language from Title IX of the 1972 Education Amendments and A Policy Interpretation: Title IX and Intercollegiate Athletics
Financial assistance or athletic grants-in-aid must be available on a substantially proportional basis	"To the extent that a recipient awards athletic scholarships or grants-in-aid, it must provide reasonable opportunities for such awards for members of each sex in proportion to the number of students of each sex participating in interscholastic or intercollegiate athletics." [Section 106.37(c)(1) of P.L. 93–568 and Section IV of A Policy Interpretation]
Program areas so males and females receive equivalent treatment, benefits, and opportunities	Equal athletic opportunity to: (section 106.41c P.L. 93–568 and Section IV of A Policy Interpretation) <ul><li>The provision of equipment and supplies</li><li>Scheduling of games and practice time</li><li>Travel and per diem allowance</li><li>Opportunity to receive coaching and academic tutoring</li><li>Assignment and compensation of coaches and tutors</li><li>Provision of locker rooms, practice, and competitive facilities</li><li>Provision of medical and training facilities and services</li><li>Provision of housing and dining facilities and services</li><li>Publicity</li><li>Recruitment of athletes (added in A Policy Interpretation)</li><li>Support services for athletes (added in A Policy Interpretation)</li></ul>
Interests and abilities of male and female students are effectively accommodated	"The regulation requires institutions to accommodate effectively the interests and abilities of students to the extent necessary to provide equal opportunity in the selection of sports and levels of competition available to members of both sexes." (Section VII C.1 of A Policy Interpretation) That is, the regulation requires the Director to consider whether the selection of sports and levels of competition effectively accommodate the interests and abilities of members of both sexes.

(*continued*)

Table 5.5   (*continued*)

Area	Language from Title IX of the 1972 Education Amendments and A Policy Interpretation: Title IX and Intercollegiate Athletics
	Institutions may choose any one of three options for meeting this requirement: (Section VII C.5(a) of A Policy Interpretation) (1) "Whether intercollegiate level participation opportunities for male and female students are provided in numbers substantially proportionate to their respective enrollments; or (2) Where the members of one sex have been and are underrepresented among intercollegiate athletes, whether the institution can show a history and continuing practice of program expansion which is demonstrably responsive to the developing interest and abilities of the members of that sex; or (3) Where the members of one sex are underrepresented among intercollegiate athletes, and the institution cannot show a continuing practice of program expansion such as that cited above, whether it can be demonstrated that the interests and abilities of the members of that sex have been fully and effectively accommodated by the present program."

Source: Available at http://www2.ed.gov/about/offices/list/ocr/docs/t9interp.html.

institutions. This table also documents that over half of the female athletes in NCAA institutions are coached by males. Most of the athletic programs in which female athletes participate are administered by males. This disparity is gradually changing.

Table 5.6   Application of Title IX to Intercollegiate Athletics

Date	Legislation, Court Decisions, Letters of Clarification, and Other Significant Actions
June 23, 1972	Congress prohibits discrimination on the basis of sex in any federally funded education program or activity.
1974; 1975; 1977	Proposed amendments to Title IX, bills restricting its application to intercollegiate athletics, and resolutions and bills to curtail enforcement of Title IX are repeatedly defeated in Congress.
July 21, 1975	The Department of Health, Education, and Welfare (HEW) issues the final Title IX regulations. It allows an adjustment period of three years for secondary schools and colleges, as long as work toward compliance is expeditious.
December 11, 1979	HEW issues "A Policy Interpretation: Title IX and Intercollegiate Athletics." This policy interpretation includes a three-prong test that details how to provide equal opportunity and specifies how to assess compliance.
May 4, 1980	The Department of Education (DOE) begins operation and includes responsibility for the oversight of Title IX through the Office of Civil Rights (OCR).
February 28, 1984	In the *Grove City vs. Bell* decision, the U.S. Supreme Court removes the application of Title IX to athletics unless this program receives direct federal financial assistance.
March 22, 1988	The Civil Rights Restoration Act states that educational institutions, if they receive any type of federal financial assistance, must comply with Title IX in their athletic programs.
April 2, 1990	DOE publishes the Title IX Investigative Manual, which replaces the Interim Title IX Intercollegiate Athletics Manual, which had been distributed on July 28, 1980.
February 26, 1992	In *Franklin vs. Gwinnett County Public Schools*, the U.S. Supreme Court rules that if a defendant intentionally avoids complying with Title IX, a plaintiff filing a lawsuit based on Title IX may receive punitive damages.
July 26, 1993	The NCAA publishes its first Gender Equity Study. It documents that women • Comprise 35 percent of varsity athletes • Receive 30 percent of athletic grant-in-aid dollars • Are allocated 17 percent of recruiting dollars • Receive 23 percent of operating budget dollars • Have access to 37 percent of participation opportunities on teams

(continued)

Table 5.6 *(continued)*

January 16, 1996	OCR issues a Letter of Clarification that restates, but does not change, the requirements that institutions may choose any of three approaches to demonstrate effective accommodation of the participation needs of the underrepresented sex.
October 1, 1996	The Equity in Athletics Disclosure Act (EADA), which was passed by Congress in 1994, goes into effect. EADA requires each institution receiving federal financial assistance to annually report specific information about all intercollegiate athletic programs.
July 23, 1998	OCR issues a Letter of Clarification that describes the meaning of "substantially equal" relative to providing financial aid to male and female athletes.
February 26, 2003	The Commission on Opportunities in Athletics, appointed by the Secretary of Education in 2002, recommends weakening the application of Title IX to athletics. Due to a minority report and public criticism of the recommendations, DOE makes no revisions in the regulations of Title IX relative to athletics.
July 11, 2003	OCR issues a Letter of Clarification reaffirming the regulations and policies of Title IX.
March 18, 2005	OCR issues a Letter of Clarification that permits colleges to determine through an e-mail survey whether the interests and needs in participation opportunities for the underrepresented sex are being met (withdrawn in April 2010).
September 17, 2008	OCR issues a Letter of Clarification to provide guidance to ensure male and female students are provided equal opportunities to participate in intercollegiate athletic programs.
April 20, 2010	OCR issues Guidance on Accommodating Students' Athletic Interests and Abilities: Standards for Part Three of the "Three-Part Test" that reaffirms Title IX's nondiscrimination requirements.

Sources: Compiled by the author from government documents available at http://www2.ed.gov/about/offices/list/ocr/docs/tix_dis.html; http://www2.ed.gov/about/offices/list/ocr/qa-sex.html; http://www2.ed.gov/about/offices/list/ocr/athleticresources.html; http://www2.ed.gov/about/offices/list/ocr/frontpage/pro-students/issues/sex-issue04.html; http://www2.ed.gov/finaid/prof/resources/athletics/eada.html; https://www.law.cornell.edu/supremecourt/text/503/60; http://www.fhwa.dot.gov/environment/environmental_justice/legislation/restoration_act.cfm; http://www.oyez.org/cases/1980–1989/1983/1983_82_792/; http://www2.ed.gov/about/offices/list/ocr/docs/t9interp.html.

Table 5.7   Females in Intercollegiate Athletics in NCAA Institutions

Year	Average Number of Teams	Head Coaches of Women's Teams	Head Administrators over Women's Programs	Number of Athletic Directors Division I	Number of Athletic Directors Division II	Number of Athletic Directors Division III
1972	Not available	Over 90%	Over 90%			
1978	5.61	58.2%	Not available			
1982	6.59	52.4%	Not available			
1986	7.15	50.6%	15.2%			
1990	7.24	47.3%	15.9%			
1992	7.09	48.3%	16.8%			
1996	7.53	47.7%	18.5%			
2000	8.14	45.6%	17.8%	27	45	99
2004	8.32	44.1%	18.5%	28	47	113
2006	8.45	42.4%	18.6%	31	50	110
2008	8.65	42.8%	21.3%	29	53	142
2010	8.64	42.6%	19.3%	30	43	128
2012	8.73	42.9%	20.3%	36	46	133
2014	8.83	43.4%	22.3%	37	69	133

Source: Acosta, V.R., and L.J. Carpenter. "Women in Intercollegiate Sport. A Longitudinal, National Study Thirty-Seven Year Update." 2014. (Used by permission; full report is available at: www.acostacarpenter.org)

Intercollegiate Athletics

In addition to an increase in the number of teams offered to females in NCAA member institutions, it is important to compare the number of teams for male and female athletes, which is provided using data from the 2014 institutional reports submitted in compliance with the Equity in Athletics Disclosure Act. These are shown in the trend data in Figure 5.3. Specifically, in the 10 conferences in the NCAA FBS (i.e., the highest competitive level), the average number of teams for female athletes (17) exceeds the average number of teams for male athletes (12.4). The actual numbers of male and female participants on these teams in the 10 conferences in the FBS are provided in Figure 5.4.

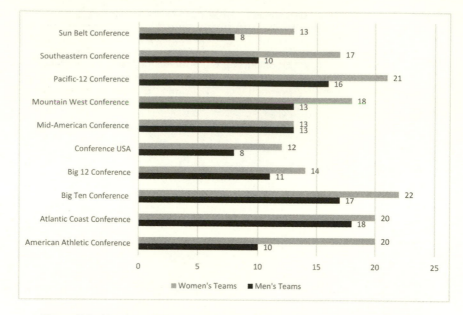

Figure 5.3   Number of Men's and Women's Sport Teams (Including Coed Teams) in the 10 Conferences in the NCAA FBS in the 2014 Reporting Year

Source: Data compiled by the author from U.S. Office of Postsecondary Education, Equity in Athletics Data Analysis Cutting Tool, 2016. Available at http://ope.ed.gov/athletics/.

The higher average numbers of teams and female athletes in FBS institutions fail to fully reveal the number of sport opportunities for male and female athletes. So, it is important to document whether Title IX or other factors have contributed to equitable participation opportunities across all competitive levels. Figures 5.5 and 5.6 provide data from the 2014 institutional reports submitted in compliance with the Equity in Athletics Disclosure Act. Figure 5.5 shows a comparison by sex for 509 institutions in the NJCAA, 261 institutions in the NAIA, and 1,093 institutions in the NCAA. Disparities by sex are further broken out in Figure 5.6 by division within each governing organization.

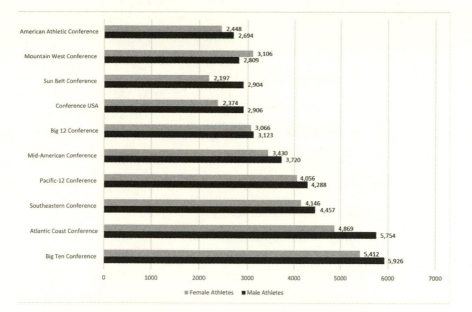

Figure 5.4   Number of Male and Female Participants in the 10 Conferences in the NCAA FBS in 2014

Source: Data (i.e., grand total participants) compiled by the author from U.S. Office of Postsecondary Education, Equity in Athletics Data Analysis Cutting Tool, 2016. Available at http://ope.ed.gov/athletics/.

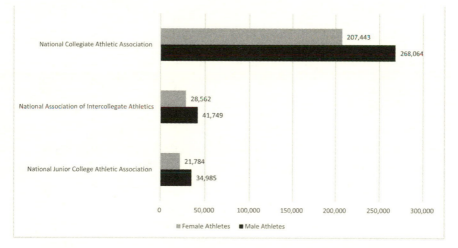

Figure 5.5   Number of Athletes by Sex and Governing Organizations in 2014

Source: Data compiled by the author from U.S. Office of Postsecondary Education, Equity in Athletics Data Analysis Cutting Tool, 2016. Available at http://ope.ed.gov/athletics/.

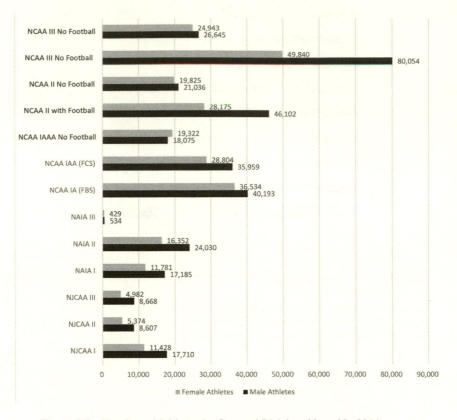

Figure 5.6   Number of Athletes by Sex and Divisional Level in 2014

Source: Data compiled by the author from U.S. Office of Postsecondary Education, Equity in Athletics Data Analysis Cutting Tool, 2016. Available at http://ope.ed.gov/athletics/.

As Figures 5.5 and 5.6 illustrate, across competitive levels, except NCAA IAAA without football, there are thousands more males than females participating in intercollegiate athletics. However, in the decades since the enactment of the 1972 Education Amendments that included Title IX, the gap between the sport participation opportunities for males and females in colleges gradually lessened.

When institutions offer males more competitive opportunities than females, it may be due to the large number of athletes playing on football teams. Others argue there are more male athletes because females are not as interested as males in playing intercollegiate sports; not as many females are skillful enough to play intercollegiate sports; more male athletes are willing to participate on teams even though their playing time may be limited, while females are not; and male athletes should be the primary beneficiaries of the revenues earned by males in football and basketball. Another perspective is that athletic directors and other decision makers continue to resist providing sport opportunities for females despite the federal requirement for equitable educational opportunities in athletics.

Another controversial issue facing intercollegiate athletics is the amount of financial support provided to men's and women's athletics. Title IX requires equal opportunity not only in participation opportunities, but also for grants-in-aid and program areas such as recruiting, travel, and coaching. To examine this issue, data were compiled and analyzed from the 2014 institutional reports required by the Equity in Athletics Disclosure Act. While 57 percent of college undergraduate students nationally are females, Figure 5.7 shows that in 2014 females received 45.5 percent of the funding for grants-in-aid, 36.1 percent of the support for team expenses, and 33.4 percent of the funds for recruiting. One approach to determining if institutions are complying with Title IX is that if one sex would accept the financial support and sport opportunities provided to the other sex, then equity likely exists. These percentages suggest equity has not yet been realized.

Most institutions playing in the NCAA FBS operate their programs as commercial businesses. Some critics allege this makes these programs ancillary to higher education, even though the NCAA states maintaining intercollegiate athletics as an integral part of an institution's educational mission is its fundamental purpose. As illustrated comparatively in Figures 5.8 and 5.9, the most media-hyped teams in football and men's basketball in the 10 conferences in the FBS play in

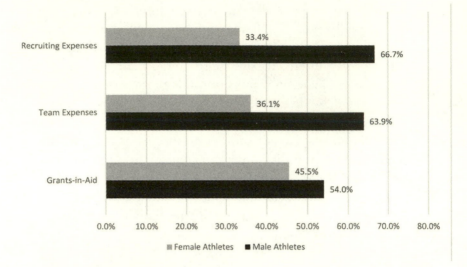

Figure 5.7   Comparison of Financial Support for Male and Female Athletes in Intercollegiate Athletics in 2014

Source: Data compiled by the author from U.S. Office of Postsecondary Education, Equity in Athletics Data Analysis Cutting Tool, 2014. Available at http://ope. ed.gov/athletics/.

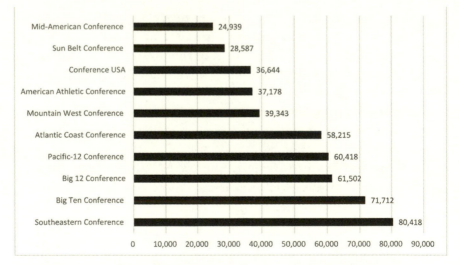

Figure 5.8   Average Football Stadium Capacities in the 10 Conferences in the NCAA FBS

Source: Compiled by the author data from the http://ope.ed.gov/athletics/ and https://en.wikipedia.org/wiki/List_of_NCAA_Division_I_FBS_football_stadiums.

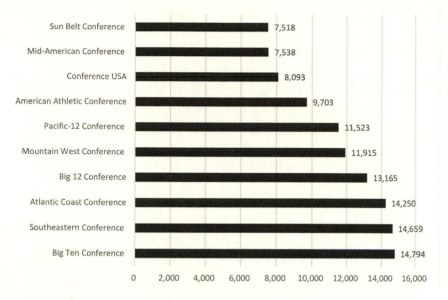

Figure 5.9 **Average Basketball Arena Capacities in the 10 Conferences in the NCAA FBS**

Source: Compiled data by the author from the http://ope.ed.gov/athletics/ and https://en.wikipedia.org/wiki/List_of_NCAA_Division_I_basketball_arenas.

stadiums and arenas that were built and expanded to maximize their revenue-producing potential.

These teams are engaged in an athletics "arms race" of trying to keep up with nationally ranked teams, and especially those in their conferences. Since winning games leads to sold-out stadiums and arenas, coaches must successfully recruit the best athletes. Coaches claim their football and basketball practice facilities, locker rooms, and training and conditioning facilities must be as good, if not better than, those against whom they compete when recruiting prospective athletes. These same coaches, who are fixated on winning to keep their jobs, demand multimillion-dollar salaries, or else they will leave for institutions that will pay them what they believe they deserve for winning games.

In addition to this ever-escalating arms race, many people question whether this money-making push of operating intercollegiate athletic programs in the FBS as commercialized businesses reinforces a belief that colleges have difficulty justifying operating as quasi-farm systems for the NFL and NBA. Further evidence of this commercialized, rather than educational, model is the number of athletes who play these sports who do not earn college degrees. A lack of seriousness concerning academics characterizes those who view playing football and basketball as a required step in becoming professional athletes.

The overwhelming majority of tickets to intercollegiate football and men's basketball games are sold to nonstudents, further distancing these two sports from the concept athletes are students first. In reality, almost every athlete on these teams has been recruited and is receiving financial support dependent on his continued participation on these teams. Since the grants-in-aid received by these athletes are most often awarded for only one year, there is no guarantee of continued receipt of this financial support unless the athlete performs on the field or court, conducts himself in a way consistent with coach expectations, and maintains academic eligibility in conformity with NCAA, conference, and institutional requirements. Some individuals argue one-year grants overemphasize athletics over academics and give coaches too much control over athletes' lives.

These data could indicate equity for both sexes has not been fully achieved. It also could verify that athletic departments invest more money in football and men's basketball because it takes money to make money. However, most athletic departments, including their football and men's basketball teams, do not make more money than they spend.

Football and men's basketball teams are caught up in an arms race according to the Knight Commission on Intercollegiate Athletics. The football stadiums, basketball arenas, and the often palatial training and locker room facilities associated with them, which are funded through institutional support and private donations, are believed to be essential in attracting potential recruits. These recruits are then expected to help win games, which will attract more fans, broadcast rights fees, licensed merchandise sales, and private donations. Because of the problems associated with this arms race and the commercialization of intercollegiate athletics, the Knight Commission on Intercollegiate Athletics, as stated in Document 5.3, has concluded institutions should initiate reforms in their athletic programs to reconnect them with the educational mission of higher education.

Document 5.3

Quoted Excerpts from "A Call to Action" from the Knight Commission on Intercollegiate Athletics

. . . The Commission has pursued this work over the years because it believes the nation's best purposes are served when colleges and universities are strong centers of creative, constant renewal, true to their basic academic purposes. In the opening years of the new century, however, those basic purposes are threatened by the imbalance between athletic imperatives and the academy's values. To say it again, the cultural sea change is now complete. Big-time college football and basketball have been thoroughly professionalized and commercialized.

Nevertheless, the Commission believes that the academic enterprise can still redeem itself and its athletic adjunct. It is still possible that all college sports can be reintegrated into the moral and institutional culture of the university. Indeed, in sports other than football and basketball, for the most part that culture still prevails. Athletes can be (and are) honestly recruited. They can be (and are) true "student-athletes," provided with the educational opportunities for which the university exists. The joys of sport can still be honorably celebrated.

But the pressures that have corrupted too many major athletic programs are moving with inexorable force. If current trends continue, more and more campus programs will increasingly mirror the world of professional, market-driven athletics. What that could look like across the board is now present in high-profile form: weakened academic and amateurism standards, millionaire coaches and rampant commercialism, all combined increasingly with deplorable sportsmanship and misconduct.

. . . It is time to make a larger truth evident to those who want bigger programs, more games, more exposure, and more dollars. It is this: Most Americans believe the nation's colleges and universities are about teaching, learning and research, not about winning and losing. Most pay only passing attention to athletic success or failure. And many big donors pay no attention at all to sports, recognizing in Bart Giamatti's words that it is a "sideshow."

Part of this larger truth requires understanding something that sports-crazed fans are inclined to ignore or denigrate: Loss of academic integrity in the arenas and stadiums of the nation's colleges and universities is far more destructive to their reputations than a dozen losing seasons could ever be.

. . . In its earlier reports, the Commission defined a "one-plus-three" model, with the "one"—presidential control—directed toward the "three"—academic integrity, financial integrity, and certification. The Commission here proposes a new "one-plus-three" model for these new times—with the "one," a Coalition of Presidents, directed toward an agenda of academic reform, de-escalation of the athletics arms race, and de-emphasis of the commercialization of intercollegiate athletics. The Coalition of Presidents' goal must be nothing less than the restoration of athletics as a healthy and integral part of the academic enterprise.

. . . the Commission makes the following recommendations for the Coalition's agenda:

Academics. Our key point is that students who participate in athletics deserve the same rights and responsibilities as all other students. Within that broad framework, the Coalition should focus on the following recommendations:

> Athletes should be mainstreamed through the same academic processes as other students. These specifically

include criteria for admission, academic support services, choice of major, and requirements governing satisfactory progress toward a degree. Graduation rates must improve. By 2007, teams that do not graduate at least 50 percent of their players should not be eligible for conference championships or for postseason play. Scholarships should be tied to specific athletes until they (or their entering class) graduate. The length of playing, practice and postseasons must be reduced both to afford athletes a realistic opportunity to complete their degrees and to enhance the quality of their collegiate experiences. The NBA and the NFL should be encouraged to develop minor leagues so that athletes not interested in undergraduate study are provided an alternative route to professional careers. These recommendations are not new. What is novel is the Commission's insistence that a new and independent structure is needed to pursue these proposals aggressively.

The Arms Race. The central point with regard to expenditures is the need to insist that athletic departments' budgets be subject to the same institutional oversight and direct control as other university departments. The Coalition should work to:

Reduce expenditures in big-time sports such as football and basketball. This includes a reduction in the total number of scholarships that may be awarded in Division I-A football. Ensure that the legitimate and long-overdue need to support women's athletic programs and comply with Title IX is not used as an excuse for soaring costs while expenses in big-time sports are unchecked. Consider coaches' compensation in the context of the academic institutions that employ them. Coaches' jobs should be primarily to educate young people. Their compensation should be brought into line with prevailing norms across the institution. Require that agreements for coaches' outside income be negotiated with institutions, not individual coaches. Outside income should be apportioned in the context of an overriding reality: Advertisers are buying the institution's reputation no less than the coaches'. Revise the plan for distribution of revenue from the NCAA contract with CBS for broadcasting rights to the Division I men's basketball championship. No such revenue should be distributed based on commercial values such as winning and losing. Instead, the revenue distribution plan should reflect values centered on improving academic performance, enhancing athletes' collegiate experiences, and achieving equity for both sexes.

Again, the recommendations put forth here have been heard before. The Coalition offers a chance to make progress on them at long last.

Commercialization. The fundamental issue is easy to state: Colleges and universities must take control of athletics programs back from television and other corporate interests. In this regard, the Coalition should: Insist that institutions alone should determine when games are played, how they are broadcast, and which companies are permitted to use their athletics contests as advertising vehicles. Encourage institutions to reconsider all sports-related commercial contracts against the backdrop of traditional academic values. Work to minimize commercial intrusions in arenas and stadiums so as to maintain institutional control of campus identity. Prohibit athletes from being exploited as advertising vehicles. Uniforms and other apparel should not bear corporate trademarks or the logos of manufacturers or game sponsors. Other athletic equipment should bear only the manufacturer's normal label or trademark. Support federal legislation to ban legal gambling on college sports in the state of Nevada and encourage college presidents to address illegal gambling on their campuses. The Commission is not naïve. It understands that its recommendations governing expenditures and commercialization may well be difficult to accept, even among academics and members of the public deeply disturbed by reports of academic misconduct in athletics programs. The reality is that many severe critics of intercollegiate athletics accept at face value the arguments about the financial exigencies of college sports. In the face of these arguments, they conclude that little can be done to rein in the arms race or to curb the rampant excesses of the market. Nothing could be further from the truth. The athletics arms race continues only on the strength of the widespread belief that nothing can be done about it. Expenditures roar out of control only because administrators have become more concerned with financing what is in place than rethinking what they are doing. And the market is able to invade the academy both because it is eager to do so and because overloaded administrators rarely take the time to think about the consequences. The Coalition of Presidents can rethink the operational dynamics of intercollegiate athletics, prescribe what needs to be done, and help define the consequences of continuing business as usual. . . .

Source: Knight Commission on Intercollegiate Athletics. 2001. "A Call to Action: Reconnecting College Sports and Higher Education," pp. 22–23, 26–29, 2001. (Used by permission).

The Knight Commission on Intercollegiate Athletics has continued to monitor intercollegiate athletics and issue reports and statements calling for reforms. For example, "Restoring the Balance: Dollars, Values, and the Future of College Sports," issued in 2010, is a blueprint for restoring educational values and priorities and strengthening accountability. Specifically, the Commission urged reporting of athletic expenditures with greater transparency, making academic values a priority, and treating athletes, not as professionals, but as students. At its May 16, 2016, meeting, the Commission called upon the NCAA to restrict the use of 100 percent of the revenues from its March Madness tournament to institutions for support of athletes, including their health and safety. The Commission also urged the NCAA to reward academic outcomes and not just athletic outcomes in its revenue distribution plan.

Race and Ethnicity

Another ethical issue facing intercollegiate athletics and professional sports is whether equity and fairness have been achieved or if discriminatory practices based on race and ethnicity persist. Table 5.8 provides information about past practices in several sports to document the historical exclusion experienced by African Americans in the United States.

While most overt racism has been eliminated from sports by law or societal changes, it is important to determine if progress has been made by African Americans and other minorities in gaining access to competitive opportunities in colleges and

Table 5.8   Examples in Several Sports of Discrimination against and Effects on African Americans

Date	Discriminatory Treatment	Effect or Implication
Baseball		
1884	Moses Fleetwood Walker, who had played baseball at Oberlin College and the University of Michigan, becomes the first African American to play professional baseball with the Toledo Blue Stockings in the American Association. He experiences racist taunts and abuse throughout his one season in the major leagues.	The American Association joins with the National League in a "gentleman's agreement" banning African Americans from professional baseball. Due to this ban, African Americans form a series of professional Negro Baseball Leagues. At times, African American athletes in the Negro Baseball Leagues compete against and often defeat Caucasian professional players in barnstorming games.
1945	Jackie Robinson signs a professional contract with the Brooklyn Dodgers and plays the season with its minor league affiliate in Montreal.	The "gentleman's agreement" ends when Robinson plays for the Brooklyn Dodgers beginning on April 15, 1947. Robinson is subjected to racist taunting and abuse including death threats, but he does not retaliate to help open the door to MLB to other African Americans. Not until 1959 does the final MLB team, the Boston Red Sox, include African American players.

Date	Discriminatory Treatment	Effect or Implication
Basketball		
1923–1949	The New York Renaissance (Rens) dominates basketball among African American teams, but due to segregation, this team is seldom allowed to compete against Caucasian teams.	In 1939, the Rens are permitted to play in the National Basketball League's World Professional Basketball Tournament, which the Rens win. Robert Douglas, who owns and coaches the Rens to over 2,500 victories, is the first African American inducted into the Naismith Memorial Basketball Hall of Fame in 1972.
1925	The American Basketball Association, the first true professional basketball league, begins, with African Americans banned from playing.	The Harlem Globetrotters, comprised of African Americans since the team's formation in the 1920s, display outstanding basketball skills as an entertaining barnstorming team.
Early 1940s	Several African Americans join teams in the National Basketball League.	African Americans are banned from the new Basketball Association of America when it forms in 1946.
1950	Chuck Cooper with the Boston Celtics, Nat Clifton with the New York Knicks, and Earl Lloyd with the Washington Capitols become the first African Americans to play in the NBA.	During the 2014–2015 season, 74.4 percent of players in the NBA are African Americans.
1966	Bill Russell becomes coach of the Boston Celtics, the first African American in the NBA. He is preceded by John McLendon who is hired in 1961 to coach the Cleveland Pipers in the American Basketball League.	During the 2014–2015 season, 30 percent of the head coaches in the NBA are African Americans.
Cycling		
1894	Founded in 1880, the League of American Wheelmen votes to exclude African Americans with a "white-only" clause for membership. This prohibition bans African Americans from most races in the United States.	Despite this ban, African American Marshal Taylor wins several cycling races as an amateur and a professional. Excluded from many cycling races in the United States, however, he competes mostly internationally in the early 1900s.

(*continued*)

Table 5.8 *(continued)*

Date	Discriminatory Treatment	Effect or Implication
Football		
1920	Fritz Pollard, after starring at Brown University in 1915–1917 and earning All-American acclaim in 1916, becomes one of the two African American players in the new American Professional Football Association (now NFL).	The NFL discriminates against African American players by adhering to a "gentleman's agreement" to exclude them between 1934 and 1946.
1923	Jack Trice, playing his first game for Iowa State University, suffers a broken collarbone, but he continues to play until he is trampled by three University of Minnesota players sending him off the field on a stretcher. Trice dies three days later from internal bleeding.	Although a few colleges permit outstanding African Americans to play on their teams, they often are victims of brutality from racist opponents. The football stadium at Iowa State University is named Jack Trice Stadium.
1946	Kenny Washington and Woody Strode with the Los Angeles Rams and Marion Motley and Bill Willis with the Cleveland Browns re-integrate the NFL.	The Washington Redskins are the last team to sign African American players in 1962. In 2015, 68.7 percent of NFL players are African Americans.
1951	During a game, Wilbanks Smith playing for Oklahoma A&M repeatedly attacks Drake University's Johnny Bright and then deliberately hits him in the face with his fist breaking Bright's jaw.	This vicious, racist attack is captured on film, with the sequence of photos winning a Pulitzer Prize. The football field at Drake University is named Johnny Bright Field.
Late 1800s through 1960s	In inter-regional football games, most coaches acquiesced to the demands of Southern segregationists and denied African American players the right to compete by	Bigotry persists in the former Southwest Conference and especially the SEC. The University of Georgia and University of Mississippi are the last SEC institutions to integrate their football teams in 1972.

Date	Discriminatory Treatment	Effect or Implication
	leaving them at home or on the bench. Many Southern teams choose to maintain their exclusionary practices by playing against only teams from the South.	
1989	Art Shell becomes the second African American head coach in the NFL. He is preceded by Fritz Pollard, who in 1921 becomes the first African American head coach in the NFL.	In 2015, 15.6 percent of NFL head coaches are African Americans.
Golf		
1960	Charlie Sifford integrates the PGA and in 1967 wins the Hartford Open, a PGA event.	Charlie Sifford is never permitted to enter The Masters because at the time it excludes African Americans.
1964	Althea Gibson integrates the LPGA.	Only six African American women have ever played in LPGA events, and none has ever won a LPGA title.
1975	Lee Elder becomes the first African American allowed to play in The Masters.	Tiger Woods wins The Masters in 1997.
Tennis		
1948	Reginald Weir becomes the first African American to play in a United States Lawn Tennis Association (USLTA) tournament when he is allowed to enter the National Indoor Tennis Championship.	Most tennis tournaments continue to be held at segregated clubs. African Americans compete in tennis events sponsored by the American Tennis Association (ATA), beginning with the first national championships in 1917.
1950	Althea Gibson, who previously had won 10 consecutive ATA singles titles beginning in 1947, is invited to play in the USLTA National Championship.	Althea Gibson wins 11 major titles, including the Wimbledon singles crowns and USLTA singles titles in 1957 and 1958.

(continued)

Table 5.8   (*continued*)

Date	Discriminatory Treatment	Effect or Implication
Track and Field		
1866	Track and field is organized in the United States by segregated athletics clubs, such as the New York City Athletic Club.	Some African Americans compete in this sport in clubs, segregated YMCAs, and on teams at northeastern colleges or in historically black colleges and universities.
1936	Jesse Owens becomes the first American to win four gold medals in a single Olympic Games in Berlin, thereby shattering Adolf Hitler's claim of the superiority of the Aryan race.	Owens is subjected to segregation, racism, and bigotry while a collegiate athlete and later in his life, even after winning the 100 meters, 200 meters, long jump, and as a member of the 4 × 100 meter relay team.
1948	Alice Coachman sets a new world record in the high jump in the London Olympic Games, as she becomes the first African American woman to win a gold medal.	Despite growing up in the segregated South, Coachman takes advantage of attending Tuskegee Institute, where she wins national championships in the 50-meter dash, 100-meter dash, 400-meter relay, and high jump.

on professional teams. The number of athletes is one way to illustrate this, as shown in Table 5.9, which provides data for colleges by sex and ethnicity. According to the 2010 U.S. Census, 13 percent of the population is African American, so the number of African American athletes for both sexes is higher than would be expected based on the population. The low participation numbers for Hispanics and Latinos does not reflect their 16 percent of the population in the 2010 U.S. Census.

With so much emphasis placed on recruiting the best athletes in football and men's basketball to help increase revenues through winning at the highest competitive level, many coaches, athletic directors, and institutions are accused of placing more emphasis on winning games than on students earning degrees. In the decades since institutions could not discriminate against African Americans in their admission policies, many

Table 5.9   College Athletes in NCAA Division I Institutions by Sex and Ethnicity

	Caucasian	African American	Latino	American Indian/ Alaskan Native	Asian	Non-Resident Alien	Other
2014-15							
Male	58.9%	22.1%	4.5%	0.3%	1.9%	4.8%	3.9%
Female	66.8%	12.5%	4.5%	0.4%	2.3%	5.9%	3.5%
2012-13							
Male	60.0%	22.4%	4.4%	2.0%	2.0%	4.7%	3.7%
Female	68.5%	12.7%	4.3%	2.4%	2.4%	5.2%	3.6%
2010-11							
Male	62.9%	21.2%	4.1%	0.4%	1.9%	4.6%	3.0%
Female	70.1%	12.6%	4.1%	0.4%	2.3%	5.4%	3.0%
2008-09							
Male	66.7%	21.5%	4.0%	0.1%	2.0%	N/A	5.0%
Female	74.0%	13.0	4.0%	0.2%	2.3%	N/A	5.0%
2006-07							
Male	64.2%	24.7%	3.8%	0.4%	1.6%	N/A	5.3%
Female	72.1%	15.7%	3.7%	0.4%	2.3%	N/A	5.8%
2004-05							
Male	62.2%	24.8%	3.7%	0.4%	1.7%	4.1%	3.1%
Female	70.5%	15.4%	3.3%	0.4%	2.2%	4.9%	3.3%
2002-03							
Male	62.6%	24.6%	3.3%	0.4%	1.6%	4.1%	3.4%
Female	71.9%	14.8%	2.9%	0.3%	2.0%	4.5%	3.7%
2000-01							
Male	61.6%	24.3%	3.3%	0.4%	1.4%	4.7%	4.4%
Female	70.4%	14.8%	2.6%	0.4%	1.7%	5.4%	4.8%

Source: Lapchick, R., and D. Baker. "The 2015 Racial and Gender Report Card: College Sport." 2016. Available at http://nebula.wsimg.com/5050ddee56f2fcc88 4660e4a03297317?AccessKeyId=DAC3A56D8FB782449D2A&disposition=0&all oworigin=1 (used by permission).

institutions have recruited an increasing number of African Americans to play on these two sport teams. The percentages of African Americans on football and men's basketball teams in NCAA Division I institutions continue to grow.

Like the NFL and NBA, the percentage of African American intercollegiate players in NCAA Division I competition continue to exceed the percentage of the population in the United States. Similarly, there are a small number of African American and other minority head coaches in these two sports. The differences between the number of Caucasian players and coaches in comparison with the number of African American players and coaches in Division I are shown in Figure 5.10 for football and Figure 5.11 for basketball.

Similar concerns exist relative to the wide disparities between the number of African American players and head coaches in

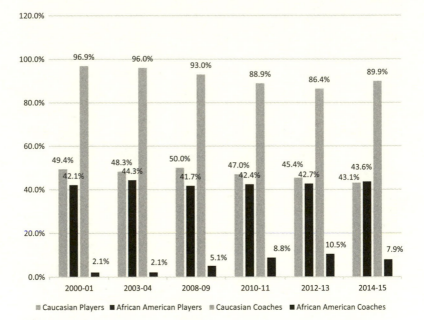

Figure 5.10 Percentage of Caucasian and African American Football Coaches and Players in NCAA Division I

Source: Lapchick, R., and D. Baker. "The 2015 Racial and Gender Report Card: College Sport." 2015. Available at http://nebula.wsimg.com/5050ddee56f2fcc88 4660e4a03297317?AccessKeyId=DAC3A56D8FB782449D2A&disposition=0&all oworigin=1 (used by permission).

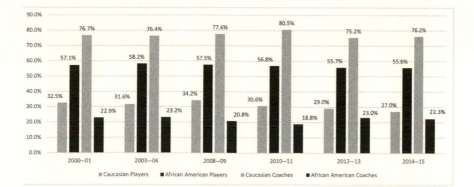

Figure 5.11 Percentage of Caucasian and African American Basketball Coaches and Players in NCAA Division I

Source: Lapchick, R., and D. Baker. The 2015 Racial and Gender Report Card: College Sport, 2015. Available at http://nebula.wsimg.com/5050ddee56f2fcc884 660e4a03297317?AccessKeyId=DAC3A56D8FB782449D2A&disposition=0&allo worigin=1 (used by permission).

National Football League

Figure 5.12 Percentage of Players, Coaches, Owners, and Top Management in Three Professional Leagues

Source: Lapchick, R. E. "Racial and Gender Report Card for the 2015 National Football League," "Racial and Gender Report Card for the 2015 National Basketball Association," and "Racial and Gender Report Card for the 2016 Major League Baseball." Available at http://nebula.wsimg.com/91f862c7e055dd1842f 9ceb52428ae2c?AccessKeyId=DAC3A56D8FB782449D2A&disposition=0&allo worigin=1, http://nebula.wsimg.com/6e1489cc3560e1e1a2fa88e3030f5149?Acc essKeyId=DAC3A56D8FB782449D2A&disposition=0&alloworigin=1, and http:// nebula.wsimg.com/811d6cc2d0b42f3ff087ac2cb600ebeb?AccessKeyId=DAC3 A56D8FB782449D2A&disposition=0&alloworigin=1 (used by permission).

National Basketball Association

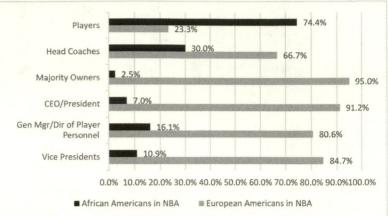

Major League Baseball

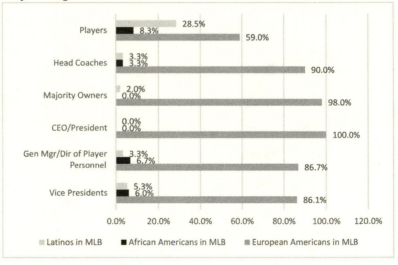

Figure 5.12   (*continued*)

professional football, basketball, and baseball. The continued domination by Caucasian head coaches, owners, presidents, general managers or directors of player personnel, and vice presidents in comparison to African Americans and Latinos (in Major League Baseball) in these positions is shown in Figure 5.12.

Olympic Sports

The use of performance-enhancing drugs threatens the integrity of all sports, and especially at the highest competitive levels. While professional sports have dealt with doping in sports in differing ways over the past few years, there has been a more consolidated effort in international sport. As an outgrowth of worldwide conferences that included representatives of governments, the Olympic Movement at all levels, the International Paralympic Committee, athletes, and numerous other stakeholders, the World Anti-Doping Code was developed, adopted, and then implemented on January 1, 2004. One purpose of this code is to protect each athlete's right to participate in doping-free sport while promoting health, fairness, and equality. A second purpose is to coordinate anti-doping programs internationally through detection, deterrence, and prevention of doping. This code harmonizes anti-doping policies, rules, and regulations, and helps implement international standards regarding testing, laboratories, therapeutic use exemptions, and prohibited substances and methods. The code provides universal criteria for determining whether a substance should be banned from use based on whether it enhances performance, poses a threat to athlete health, and violates the spirit of sport. The code also provides standards for sanctions, while permitting flexibility depending on the circumstances.

Not everyone agrees, however, that the use of performance-enhancing drugs should be banned. Table 5.10 lists several positives and negatives about this ethical issue.

The Olympic Games have grown into the most acclaimed international sport festival in the world. The growth in the number of nations sending athletes (from only 14 in the first Olympic Games to over 200 provides evidence of their popularity and prestige. Throughout the years, though, there have been several ethical controversies. Strong opposition to athletes receiving money based on their athletic ability was a passion of IOC presidents Pierre de Coubertin and Avery Brundage.

Table 5.10   Pros and Cons of Using Performance-Enhancing Drugs in Sports

Pros for the Use of Performance-Enhancing Drugs	Cons against the Use of Performance-Enhancing Drugs
1. Enhances physical health and well-being	1. Breaks the law when they are obtained illegally
2. Builds strength, muscle mass, and endurance	2. Gives unfair advantages (i.e., which is cheating)
3. Improves athletic performance and recovery	3. Results in harmful physical side effects
4. Has been developed through medical advances and should be treated no differently than technological, training, or other pharmacological enhancements	4. Violates medical opinion that these drugs should be used only by prescription for legitimate medical reasons
5. Excites fans who demand superior performances	5. Causes dependency on muscular development, increased endurance, or other benefits of using these drugs
6. Levels the playing field when these drugs are made available to all athletes	6. Makes sports impure or artificial, with competitions based on chemicals not on the limits of natural human potential
7. Replaces declining levels of testosterone	7. Costs large sums of money, which could be wasteful or associated with crime
8. Redirects money from wasteful drug testing to more productive sport enhancements to benefit athletes	8. Results in financial and personal losses if an athlete fails a drug test

Between 1980 and 2001, IOC president Juan Antonio Samaranch led the Olympic Games into an era welcoming professional athletes and commercialized the Olympic Games. Wars and aftermaths of wars, boycotts, judging scandals, state-subsidized athletes, and recognition or nonrecognition of nations also have plagued the Olympic Games.

Another issue has been should females be allowed to participate in the Olympic Games, and, if so, in what events? Table 5.11 documents the evolution in competitive opportunities for males and females.

Table 5.11   Sports for Males and Females in the Olympic Games

Summer Sports	Years for Males	Years for Females
Archery	1900–1908; 1920; 1972–present	1904–1908; 1972–present
Athletics (track and field)	1896–present	1928–present
Badminton	1992–present	1992–present
Baseball	1992–2008	
Basketball	1936–present	1976–present
Beach volleyball	1996–present	1996–present
Boxing	1904–present; except 1912	2012–present
Canoe/kayak slalom	1972; 1992–present	1972; 1992–present
Canoe/kayak sprint	1936–present	1948–present
Cycling BMX	2008–present	2008–present
Cycling mountain bike	1996–present	
Cycling road	1896–present, except 1912	1984–present
Cycling track	1896–present, except 1900, 1904, and 1908	1988–present
Diving	1904–present	1912–present
Equestrian/Dressage	1900; 1912–present	1952–present in mixed events
Equestrian/Eventing	1900; 1912–present	1952–present in mixed events
Equestrian/Jumping	1912–present	1956–present
Fencing	1896–present	1924–present
Football (soccer)	1900–present, except 1932	1996–present
Golf	1900–1904; 2016	1900; 2016
Gymnastics Artistic	1896–present	1928; 1956–present
Gymnastics Rhythmic		1984–present
Handball	1936; 1972–present	1976–present
Hockey (field)	1908; 1920–present	1980–present
Judo	1964; 1972–present	1992–present
Modern pentathlon	1912–present	2000–present

(continued)

Table 5.11 *(continued)*

Summer Sports	Years for Males	Years for Females
Rowing	1900–present	1976–present
Rugby	1900; 1908; 1920–1924; 2016	2016
Sailing	1900; 1908–present (mixed team); 1988–present	1900; 1908–present (mixed team); 1988–present
Shooting	1896–present (males) except 1904 and 1928 1968–1992 (mixed team)	1984–present (females) 1968–1992 (mixed team)
Softball		1996–2008
Swimming	1896–present	1912–present
Synchronized swimming		1984–present
Table tennis	1988–present	1988–present
Taekwondo	2000–present	2000–present
Tennis	1896–1924; 1988–present	1900; 1908–1924; 1988–present
Trampoline	2000–present	2000–present
Triathlon	2000–present	2000–present
Volleyball	1964–present	1964–present
Water polo	1900; 1908–present	2000–present
Weightlifting	1896; 1904; 1920–present	2000–present
Wrestling freestyle	1904–1908; 1920–present	2004–present
Wrestling Greco-Roman	1896; 1908–present	

Winter Sports	Years for Males	Years for Females
Alpine skiing	1936–present	1936–present
Biathlon	1924; 1960–present	1992–present
Bobsleigh	1924–1956; 1964–present	2002–present
Cross country skiing	1924–present	1952–present
Curling	1924; 1998–present	1998–present
Figure skating	1908; 1920; 1924–present	1908; 1920; 1924–present

Winter Sports	Years for Males	Years for Females
Freestyle skiing	1992–present	1992–present
Ice hockey	1920; 1924–present	1998–present
Luge	1964–present	1964–present
Nordic combined	1924–present	
Short-track speed skating	1992–present	1992–present
Skeleton	1928; 1948; 2002–present	2002–present
Ski jumping	1924–present	2014–present
Snowboard	1998–present	1998–present
Speed skating	1924–present	1960present

Source: Compiled by the author from information available on the International Olympic Committee website, 2016. Available at http://www.olympic.org/sports.

While sports for female athletes were slowly added to the Olympic Games, sports like figure skating, golf, swimming, and tennis open to females were viewed as more appropriate than other sports for females. Track and field, which was the premier sport for males, was not considered acceptable for females. Due to pressures placed on the all-male IOC and the hosting of another international competition for females in track and field, in the 1928 Amsterdam Olympic Games, five track-and-field events (100 meters; 4 × 100m relay; 800 meters; discus; and high jump) were opened to female athletes. The 800-meter race, because some believed this distance was too demanding for females to run, was eliminated and not resumed until the 1960 Rome Olympic Games. A longer-distance race for females, the 1,500 meters, began in the 1972 Munich Olympic Games. The marathon for females was added in the 1984 Los Angeles Olympic Games. The winner, Joan Benoit, won in 2 hours, 24 minutes, and 52 seconds, a time that would have won 13 of the 20 previous men's Olympic marathons.

Specific data about the number of nations, events, and athletes by sex illustrate the spreading internationalism of the Olympic Games, as well as the dramatic expansion in opportunities for female athletes. From zero females in 1896, participation of female athletes grew to 44.2 percent in the 2012 London Olympic Games. However, much of this expansion in opportunities has occurred in recent years due to increases in the number of sports for females as listed in Table 5.11 and events within the summer and winter Olympic Games as shown in Tables 5.12 and 5.13.

Table 5.12   Participation Numbers in the Summer Olympic Games

Olympiad	Year	City	Nations	Events	Males	Females	Athletes
I	1896	Athens, Greece	14	43	241	0	241
II	1900	Paris, France	24	95	975	22	997
III	1904	St. Louis, MO	12	91	645	6	651
IV	1908	London, England	22	110	1,971	37	2,008
V	1912	Stockholm, Sweden	28	102	2,359	48	2,407
VI	1916	Berlin, Germany	canceled	due	to	war	
VII	1920	Antwerp, Belgium	29	154	2,561	65	2,626
VIII	1924	Paris, France	44	126	2,954	135	3,089
IX	1928	Amsterdam, Holland	46	109	2,606	277	2,883
X	1932	Los Angeles, CA	37	117	1,206	126	1,332
XI	1936	Berlin, Germany	49	129	3,632	331	3,963
XII	1940	Tokyo, Japan	canceled	due	to	war	
XIII	1944	London, England	canceled	due	to	war	
XIV	1948	London, England	59	136	3,714	390	4,104
XV	1952	Helsinki, Finland	69	149	4,436	519	4,955
XVI	1956	Melbourne, Australia	72	145	2,938	376	3,314

Olympiad	Year	City	Nations	Events	Males	Females	Athletes
XVII	1960	Rome, Italy	83	150	4,727	611	5,338
XVIII	1964	Tokyo, Japan	93	163	4,473	678	5,151
XIX	1968	Mexico City, Mexico	112	172	4,735	781	5,516
XX	1972	Munich, Germany	121	195	6,075	1,059	7,134
XXI	1976	Montreal, Canada	92	198	4,824	1,260	6,084
XXII	1980	Moscow, USSR	80	203	4,064	1,115	5,179
XXIII	1984	Los Angeles, CA	140	221	5,263	1,566	6,829
XXIV	1988	Seoul, Korea	159	237	6,197	2,194	8,391
XXV	1992	Barcelona, Spain	169	257	6,652	2,704	9,356
XXVI	1996	Atlanta, Georgia	197	271	6,806	3,512	10,318
XXVII	2000	Sydney, Australia	199	300	6,582	4,069	10,651
XXVIII	2004	Athens, Greece	201	301	6,296	4,329	10,625
XXIX	2008	Beijing, China	204	302	6,450	4,746	11,196
XXX	2012	London, England	204	302	5,892	4,676	10,568

Source: Information compiled by the author from information available on the International Olympic Committee website, 2016. Available at http://www.olympic.org/uk/index_uk.asp.

Table 5.13 Participation Numbers in the Winter Olympic Games

Olympiad	Year	City	Nations	Events	Males	Females	Athletes
I	1924	Chamonix, France	16	16	247	11	258
II	1928	St. Moritz, Switzerland	25	14	438	26	464
III	1932	Lake Placid, New York	17	14	231	21	252

(continued)

Table 5.13 *(continued)*

Olympiad	Year	City	Nations	Events	Males	Females	Athletes
IV	1936	Garmisch-Parkenkirchen, Germany	28	17	566	80	646
V	1948	St. Moritz, Switzerland	28	22	592	77	669
VI	1952	Oslo, Norway	30	22	585	109	694
VII	1956	Cortina d'Ampezzo, Italy	32	24	687	134	821
VIII	1960	Squaw Valley, CA	30	27	521	144	665
IX	1964	Innsbruck, Austria	36	34	892	199	1,091
X	1968	Grenoble, France	37	35	947	211	1,158
XI	1972	Sapporo, Japan	35	35	801	205	1,006
XII	1976	Innsbruck, Austria	37	37	892	231	1,123
XIII	1980	Lake Placid, NY	37	38	840	232	1,072
XIV	1984	Sarajevo, Yugoslavia	49	39	998	274	1,272
XV	1988	Calgary, Canada	57	46	1,122	301	1,423
XVI	1992	Albertville, France	64	57	1,313	488	1,801
XVII	1994	Lillehammer, Norway	67	61	1,215	522	1,737
XVIII	1998	Nagano, Japan	72	68	1,389	787	2,176
XIX	2002	Salt Lake City, UT	77	78	1,513	886	2,399
XX	2006	Turin, Italy	80	84	1,548	960	2,508
XXII	2010	Vancouver, British Columbia	82	86	1,522	1,044	2,566
XXIII	2014	Sochi, Russia	88	98	1,753	1,120	2,873

Source: Information compiled by the author from information available on the International Olympic Committee website, 2016. Available at http://www.olympic.org/uk/index_uk.asp.

Conclusion

The ethical challenges facing youth sports can be addressed by ensuring the rights of young athletes are placed foremost. Adults might consider giving the games back to youth so they can have fun, develop sport skills, and learn positive values like respect and honesty along with sportsmanship and teamwork. Instead of national championships for preteen youth, playing multiple sports and positions as they explore their favorites, developing their social and leadership skills, and learning life lessons are more likely to characterize morally sound youth sport programs.

Interscholastic sports are beneficial extracurricular experiences. When the emphasis is on further developing sport skills, being a part of a team and striving collectively to reach goals, and learning character lessons about self-discipline, responsibility, and hard work, interscholastic sports are educational. Playing sports in high school can be a highlight of a young person's life.

Females, by law, can no longer be excluded from sports as they must be provided opportunities to play in sport programs conducted by schools and colleges. Females have demonstrated at the youth through Olympic levels they are interested in, dedicated to, and capable of achieving at high levels of performance. Many of the discriminatory practices against females have been eliminated, as females increased their participation levels to 40 percent or higher on most college campuses. Females have made progress toward, but not yet fully achieved, receiving comparable financial support for grants-in-aid and other operational support.

Athletic departments in institutions in the NCAA FBS have become commercialized businesses as they seek to maximize wins and revenues. Attracting and entertaining alumni and other fans require winning, so some coaches and athletes have chosen to behave unethically to increase their chances of winning. While many coaches and athletes follow the rules, violations of recruiting and academic regulations occur when there is a singular emphasis on winning. To make intercollegiate athletics more educationally and ethically sound, having athletes earn degrees to prepare for life, rather than a career in professional sports, and keeping winning in perspective to rein in the arms race and commercialization seem more laudatory goals.

A regretful time in sports in the United States was characterized by segregation and racism. Thankfully, as integration and civil rights were enforced, most discriminatory practices were eliminated. Some African Americans, however, continue to suffer from fewer educational opportunities and limited jobs as coaches and sport managers. The moral imperative remains to eliminate prejudice and bias as these negatively affect sports and all those involved.

Performance-enhancing drugs have been used by athletes to gain competitive advantages in professional sport leagues, Olympic Games, intercollegiate athletics, interscholastic sports, and sometimes even youth sports. Banning performance-enhancing drugs and testing for use of these drugs are attempts to prevent cheating. This fight to level the playing field, however, is challenged by the huge rewards associated with being the most successful athletically.

Athletes and all others associated with sport should keep their focus on behaving in morally responsible and ethically appropriate ways. The information and data included in this chapter provide evidence that unethical actions have not yet been fully eliminated, so everyone needs to be vigilant with the moral courage in helping to make sport ethical.

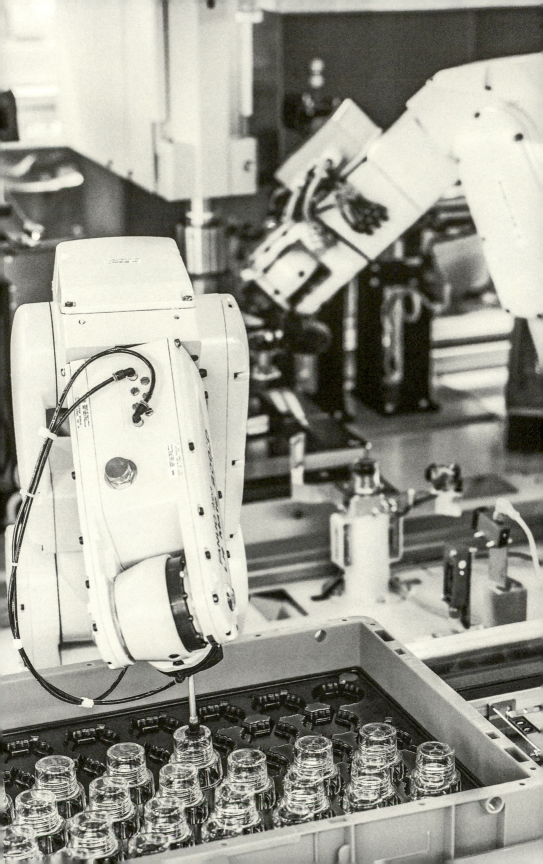

6   Resources

This chapter includes selected and annotated bibliographies of print resources, including reference works, books, scholarly journal articles, and nonprint resources of databases, DVDs, and Internet sites. For ease in locating information of specific interest, these resources are organized by five topics: sport for all, youth sport, interscholastic sport, intercollegiate sport, and international sport.

Print Resources

Ethical Issues in Sport for All

Reference Works

Ashe, A. R., Jr. 1988. *A Hard Road to Glory: A History of the African-American Athlete* (194 pp.); *A Hard Road to Glory: A History of the African-American Athlete, 1919–1945* (497 pp.); *A Hard Road to Glory: A History of the African-American Athlete since 1946* (571 pp.). New York: Warner Books.

> These books tell the historical story of discriminatory treatment of African American athletes as they sought equal opportunities to demonstrate their talents in sports.

The latest generation of BEREG-KIT antidoping bottles from Berlinger Special AG of Switzerland makes an appearance at the 2016 Summer Olympic Games in Rio de Janeiro, Brazil. This latest version of these special bottles, which are used to prevent tampering with antidoping samples, has been manufactured in Switzerland since the end of April 2016 under the tightest security conditions and is globally acknowledged to be the most secure of its kind. (Berlinger Special AG via AP Images)

Written by a former African American tennis champion, these volumes graphically recount the barriers experienced by athletes seeking a level-playing field regardless of their race.

Bartlett, R., C. Gratton, and C. Rolf, eds. 2006. *Encyclopedia of International Sports Studies.* London: Routledge, 3 vols., 1520 pp.
> This reference work includes entries in sports medicine, sport science, social science of sport, sport engineering, and technology in sport. It includes discussions of psychological and sociological aspects of sports.

Cashmore, E. 2000. *Sports Culture: An A–Z Guide.* New York: Routledge, 482 pp.
> The author presents information about issues, events, organizations, and people and places, each in a social and cultural context.

Christensen, K.A., A. Guttmann, and G. Pfister, eds. 2001. *International Encyclopedia of Women and Sports.* New York: Macmillan, 3 vols.
> These volumes include detailed information about the history of and current situation in women's sports. They include more than 230 biographies, 170 sports entries, and 75 country profiles; plus, this work examines cultural, social, and ethical issues of women's sports.

Deardorff, D. L. II. 2000. *Sports: A Reference Guide and Critical Commentary, 1980–1999.* Westport, CT: Greenwood Press, 361 pp.
> The author examines sport as it relates to history, business, law, education, race and ethnicity, sex, literature, philosophy and religion, popular culture, psychology, science and technology, and sociology.

Frank, A. M. 2003. *Sports and Education: A Reference Handbook.* Santa Barbara, CA: ABC-CLIO, 226 pp.

> This chronology helps the reader learn about sport and significant issues, individuals, and organizations in sport.

Jones, D. G., with E. L. Daley. 1992. *Sports Ethics in America: A Bibliography, 1970–1990*. Westport, CT: Greenwood Press, 320 pp.

> This comprehensive bibliography provides nearly 2,900 entries listing books, journal articles, magazines, and newspapers published in the United States since 1970. Although the citations are not annotated, they are topically arranged into five categories: general works; teams, players, and coaches; the game, competition, and contestants; sports and society; and reference works.

Levinson, D., and K. Christensen, eds. 1999. *Encyclopedia of World Sport: From Ancient Times to the Present*. New York: Oxford University Press, 488 pp.

> This comprehensive volume is filled with detailed information about hundreds of sports and how they are played. It also explores issues in sport as a part of the human experience.

Wiggins, D. K., ed. 2004. *African Americans in Sports*. Armonk, NY: Sharpe Reference, 2 vols.

> Numerous authors provide information about African American players, sports, teams, institutions, organizations, and other key personnel. Within the listings are descriptions of cultural themes and social issues that place each entry in historical context.

Books

Coakley, J. J. 2015. *Sports in Society. Issues and Controversies*, 11th ed. New York: McGraw-Hill, 697 pp.

> This book examines the major issues in the interface between sports and society, including racial and equity for both sexes, violence, deviance, economic issues, social class, the media, politics, and socialization. In this

comprehensive book, the author examines many of these issues from an ethical perspective.

Cooper, C. E. 2012. *Run, Swim, Throw, Cheat: The Science behind Drugs in Sport.* Oxford, England: Oxford University Press, 305 pp.

> The limits of human performance can be expanded through every day to exotic performance-enhancing drugs, but not without breeching ethical boundaries, violating the rules, and breaking laws.

Eitzen, D. S. 2012. *Fair and Foul: Beyond the Myths and Paradoxes of Sport*, 5th ed. Lanham, MD: Rowman and Littlefield Publishers, 311 pp.

> The author uses a point-counterpoint approach in discussing the role of sport in society, including how race, class, and sex relate to an uneven playing field in sports. He examines ethical issues such as whether sport unites or divides, is fair or foul, is healthy or destructive, is expressive or controlled, and whether it is myth or reality that sport serves as a pathway to success.

Feezell, R. M. 2004. *Sport, Play, and Ethical Reflection.* Urbana: University of Illinois Press, 173 pp.

> After discussing sport's playful nature, the author contrasts sportsmanship and cheating in sports. The case is made that character can be enhanced through sport, but only through respecting the game.

Finley, P. S., and L. L. Finley. 2006. *The Sports Industry's War on Athletes.* Westport, CT: Praeger, 198 pp.

> The authors expose the big, bad world of sports and the lack of ethical behavior therein. They discuss doping, eating disorders, playing while hurt, cheating, dirty play, violence, recruiting scandals, academic fraud, hazing, racism, and sexism.

Lumpkin, A., S.K. Stoll, and J.M. Beller. 2012. *Practical Ethics in Sport Management.* Jefferson City, NC: McFarland and Company, Inc., 260 pp.

This book focuses on applying basic ethical principles to many of the problems facing sport. The authors discuss intimidation, gamesmanship, violence, eligibility, elimination, commercialism, equity for both sexes, racial equity, performance-enhancing drugs, and technology and provide numerous ethical dilemmas to encourage the use of moral reasoning to address real sport issues.

McCloskey J., and J.E. Bailes. 2005. *When Winning Costs Too Much: Steroids, Supplements, and Scandal in Today's Sports.* Lanham, MD: Taylor Trade Publishing, 344 pp.

Doping in sports is examined, from kids using steroids through the BALCO scandal with elite athletes using designer drugs. The physical, social, and ethical issues associated with seeking to gain advantages by using drugs in sports are discussed.

McNamee, M.J., ed. 2010. *The Ethics of Sport: A Reader.* New York: Routledge, 505 pp.

Numerous authors contribute examinations of pivotal ethical issues and dilemmas. The book is divided into seven sections: the roots of sport ethics; fair contests, rules, spoiling, and cheating; doping, genetic modification, and the ethics of enhancement; cultures of equality and difference; ethical development in and through sports; commercialism, corruption, and exploitation in sports; and ethics and adventurous activity.

Murray, T.H., K.J. Maschke, and A.A. Wasunna, eds. 2009. *Performance-Enhancing Technologies in Sports: Ethical, Conceptual, and Scientific Issues.* Baltimore, MD: Johns Hopkins University Press, 280 pp.

Ethical issues surrounding doping in sport, genetic enhancement, endurance-enhancing technologies, human subject research, and athlete attitudes are among the topics examined in this edited work.

Rhoden, W.C. 2006. *$40 Million Slaves: The Rise, Fall, and Redemption of the Black Athlete.* New York: Crown Publishers, 286 pp.

This historical examination of African Americans in sport describes how they have been discriminated against, excluded, and exploited in sport. The author argues African American athletes remain largely on the periphery of power in the multibillion-dollar sport industry their talents helped build.

Simon, R. L., C. R. Torres, and P. F. Hager. 2015. *Fair Play: The Ethics of Sport*, 4th ed. Boulder, CO: Westview Press, 272 pp.

The authors examine issues in competitive athletics as they relate to ethical theory and moral dilemma. The moral issues involving youth and fans and the moral foundations of winning are explored.

Journal Articles

Flett, M. R., D. R. Gould, A. L. Paule, and R. P. Schneider. 2010. "How and Why University Coaches Define, Identify, and Recruit 'Intangibles.'" *International Journal of Coaching Science* 4 (2), 15–35.

This study explored psychosocial development in collegiate sports from coaches' perspectives. Specifically, how do coaches identify and assess intangibles such as toughness or resiliency, social character, work ethic, trustworthiness, and motivation?

Howe, L. A. 2004. "Gamesmanship." *Journal of the Philosophy of Sport* 31 (2): 212–225.

The author discusses competition, excellence, fairness, sportsmanship, winning and losing, and competition and suggests how these concepts interact in the world of sports.

Kretchmar, R. S. 2005. "Why Do We Care So Much about Mere Games? (And Is This Ethically Defensible?)" *Quest* 57 (2): 181–191.

>People of all ages and for many eras of time seem to care a great deal about the outcome of games, even though more pressing issues like world poverty, war, and political injustice exist. The author suggests it is easy to understand why humans gravitate to less serious games with their artificial problems for recreational respite and to escape from the demands of life.

Lindsay, P. 2008. "Representing Redskins: The Ethics of Native American Team Names." *Journal of the Philosophy of Sport* 35 (2): 208–224.

>Nicknames of professional sport teams, such as the Washington Redskins and Atlanta Braves, are derogatory and unethical. The author encourages opponents of such nicknames to persuade sport fans they are hurtful.

Lomax, S. 2008. "Whatever Happened to America's Ethical Values?" *Business and Economic Review* 55 (1): 15–18.

>Cheating and other unethical activities are prevalent among corporate executives, government officials, and athletes as widespread cheating characterizes the educational system and workplace. The author stresses the importance of parents serving as role models for positive values and children's ethical development.

Mathias, M. B. 2004. "The Competing Demands of Sport and Health: An Essay on the History of Ethics in Sports Medicine." *Clinics in Sports Medicine* 23 (2): 195–214.

>Historically, tension has existed between the emphasis on winning in sport and health of athletes. At times, athletes, athletic trainers, and physicians have pursued victory at the cost of athletes' health of athletes.

Nucci, C., and K. Young-Shim. 2005. "Improving Socialization through Sport: An Analytic Review of Literature on Aggression and Sportsmanship." *Physical Educator* 62 (3): 123–129.

The authors discuss aggression and sportsmanship in sports. They also describe how socialization and the development of social skills can potentially occur in and through sports.

Rudd, A. 2005. "Which 'Character' Should Sport Develop?" *Physical Educator* 62 (4): 205–211.

The author examines two types of character that can potentially be developed through sports: social values and moral values. The recommendation is sport should emphasize the development of moral character.

Stovitz, S.D., and D.J. Satin. 2004. "Ethics and the Athlete: Why Sports Are More Than a Game but Less Than a War." *Clinics in Sports Medicine* 23 (2): 215–225.

The authors review key ethical concepts and provide a practical framework for interpreting and assessing the moral status of an athlete's behavior. They suggest a close relationship exists between ethics and athletes' behaviors.

Tatum, L. 2002. "Girls in Sports: Love of the Game Must Begin at an Early Age to Achieve Equality." *Seton Hall Journal of Sport Law* 12 (2): 281–310.

The author provides a strong rationale, based on a review of equal protection clauses and litigation at the college, school, and community levels, that only through a broad and an early expansion of opportunities in sports can females finally achieve equality.

Other Types of Print Works

Women's Sports Foundation. 2013. "Progress and Promise. Title IX at 40 Conference, a White Paper." Available at https://www.womenssportsfoundation.org/en/home/research/articles-and-reports/equity-issues/progress-and-promise-title-ix-at-40

Equity in sports for females reflects the ethic of fair play and equal opportunity as legislated in educational programs based on Title IX. Research evidence affirms the progress made and promise of greater advancements for female athletes.

Ethical Issues in Youth Sport

Books

Bigelow, B., T. Moroney, and L. Hall. 2001. *Just Let the Kids Play: How to Stop Other Adults from Ruining Your Children's Joy and Success in Youth Sports*. Deerfield Beach, FL: Health Communications Incorporated, 336 pp.

> The authors describe several problems in youth sports, such as elite teams excluding players, out-of-control adults, and physical and psychological injuries to young athletes. To address unethical conduct associated with youth sport, the authors suggest playing by the rules and adapting the games to children; plus, they provide success stories that yield ideas for change.

Cantu, R. C., and M. Hyman. 2012. *Concussions and Our Kids: America's Leading Expert on How to Protect Young Athletes and Keep Sports Safe*. Boston: Houghton Mifflin Harcourt, 181 pp.

> This guide provides provocative yet essential advice to parents and coaches about what concussions are, how to treat them, and how to protect youth from the adverse consequences of head trauma.

Farrey, T. 2008. *Game On: The All-American Race to Make Champions of Our Children*. New York: ESPN Books, 383 pp.

> This investigative work examines in detail the major societal and ethical concerns associated with children's involvement in sports. Using the framework of ages 3 through 14, the author explores the various choices parents face in deciding how much emphasis to place on sports for their children.

Gatz, M., M. A. Messner, and S. J. Ball-Rokeach. 2002. *Paradoxes of Youth and Sport.* Albany: State University of New York Press, 277 pp.

This book examines ethical issues, including violence, racial and sexual inequity, the media, the obsession to win, and commercialization, and given these problems, whether youth sport can build character. Special emphasis is placed on the role of sport in the lives of youth in urban settings.

Hyman, M. 2009. *Until It Hurts: America's Obsession with Youth Sports and How It Harms Our Kids.* Boston: Beacon Press, 146 pp.

The author begins with the story of ignoring his son's tired arm and as his coach sends him out to pitch. The author described how, in the quest for tomorrow's superstar athletes, overzealous parents push and exploit their children until they breakdown physically and emotionally. He also gives hope for breaking this destructive cycle.

Hyman, M. 2012. *The Most Expensive Game in Town: The Rising Cost of Youth Sports and the Toll on Today's Families.* Boston: Beacon Press, 160 pp.

The over-exposure of adolescent athletes in the media, towns' investments in facilities for youth sport competitions, corporate sponsorships of sport academies, and national competitions for preschoolers through precollege adolescents illustrate the burgeoning of the business of youth sports. Often nudged aside is the development of character and values used to justify youth sports.

Murphy, S. 1999. *The Cheers and the Tears: A Healthy Alternative to the Dark Side of Youth Sports Today.* San Francisco: Jossey-Bass, 230 pp.

Alleging a crisis in youth sport, the author provides guidance to parents for avoiding the pitfalls of an overemphasis on sports for their children. This sport psychologist advocates ensuring young athletes enjoy positive sport experiences.

Selleck, G.A. 2003. *Raising a Good Sport in an In-Your-Face World: Seven Steps to Building Character on the Field—and Off.* Chicago: Contemporary Books, 194 pp.
    The author discusses moral and ethical aspects of sport with an emphasis on sportsmanship and how a person lives.

Sheehy, H., and D. Peary. 2002. *Raising a Team Player: Teaching Kids Lasting Values on the Field, on the Court, and on the Bench.* North Adams, MA: Storey Books, 152 pp.
    A small-town coach shares his life-tested wisdom on work ethic, goal setting, winning and losing, competition, enthusiasm, sportsmanship, and character.

Thompson, J. 1995. *Positive Coaching: Building Character and Self-Esteem through Sports.* Portola, CA: Warde Publishers, 400 pp.
    This book focuses on helping coaches, parents, and teachers build the character and self-esteem of youth playing sports. The author suggests specific strategies that address the psychological health of young athletes.

Thompson, J. 2003. *The Double-Goal Coach—Positive Coaching Tools for Honoring the Game and Developing Winners in Sports and Life.* New York: HarperCollins, 346 pp.
    Written by the founder of the Positive Coaching Alliance, this book provides best-practices coaching tools. The author offers a framework for how coaches and parents can help youth enjoy sports while they learn valuable life lessons.

Thompson, J. 2009. *Positive Sports Parenting: How "Second-Goal" Parents Raise Winners in Life through Sports.* Portola Valley, CA: Balance Sports Publishing, 60 pp.
    The author suggests advice to parents about how they can help their children learn life lessons through sports.

Practical tools and ideas will help parents keep winning in perspective while supporting their children and working effectively with coaches.

Journal Articles

Bach, G. 2002. "Youth Sports Organizers Call Time Out: An Estimated 70% of All Youth Sports Programs Are Operated by Parent-Interest Groups; and Each Parent's Motives and Morals Influence How the Program Is Run." *Parks and Recreation* 37 (6): 60–63.

This article discusses the Recommendations for Communities, a joint initiative of the National Recreation and Park Association and National Alliance for Youth Sports.

Dougherty, N. 2007. "Rules for Rowdiness." *Athletic Management* 19 (4): 59–63.

Examples of negative behaviors in high school and college sports are described. The author discusses efforts made by school administrators to curtail these ethical problems.

Goldstein, J. D., and S. E. Iso-Ahola. 2006. "Promoting Sportsmanship in Youth Sports: Perspectives from Sport Psychology." *Journal of Physical Education, Recreation, and Dance* 77 (7): 18–24.

After examining theoretical and practice information about sportsmanship in youth sport, the authors offer suggestions for providing a better sporting environment for youth.

Lee, M., J. Whitehead, and N. Ntoumanis. 2007. "Development of the Attitudes to Moral Decision-Making in Youth Sport Questionnaire (AMDYSQ)." *Psychology of Sport and Exercise* 8 (3): 369–392.

The authors developed a questionnaire to assess the attitudes of young competitors toward moral decision making in sport. They report males, older athletes, team sport athletes, and athletes competing at higher levels score higher than females, younger athletes, and individual sport athletes on acceptance of cheating and gamesmanship. Female athletes were more likely to keep winning in perspective.

Lumpkin, A. 2008. "Teaching Values through Youth and Interscholastic Sports." *Strategies: A Journal for Physical and Sport Educators* 21 (4): 19–23.

After discussing the goals for youth and adolescents in sports and some issues of concern, the author suggests numerous strategies for teaching character and moral values through sports. By explaining, demonstrating, modeling, and reinforcing respect and responsibility and related values, keeping winning in perspective, and making sports fun, youth and adolescent athletes are more likely to develop character through their participation in sports.

McCallister, S. G., E. M. Blinde, and W. M. Weiss. 2000. "Teaching Values and Implementing Philosophies: Dilemmas of the Youth Sport Coach." *Physical Educator* 57 (1): 35–45.

Through interviews of coaches, this study examines the values and life skills that they view as important and extent to which they seek to teach these to young athletes. Even though coaches recognize the importance of teaching a wide range of positive values and life skills, those interviewed struggle to instill these values and life skills in young athletes.

Ryska, T. A. 2003. "Sportsmanship in Young Athletes: The Role of Competitiveness, Motivational Orientation, and Perceived Purposes of Sport." *Journal of Psychology* 137 (3): 273–293.

This study found intrinsic reasons for sport participation by young athletes predicted higher levels of sportsmanship, while extrinsic purposes for participation in sports, such as to obtain social status and a high-status career, contributed to lower levels of sportsmanship. The author recommends developing a competitive sport setting to promote ethical standards of behavior by young sport participants.

Sage, G. H. 1998. "Does Sport Affect Character Development in Athletes?" *Journal of Physical Education, Recreation, and Dance* 69 (1): 15–18.

The author states that despite claims to the contrary, there is no evidence sport builds character. Rather, organized sport for youth may adversely affect moral development as an "anything goes" pursuit of winning shapes athletes' values in negative ways.

Wells, M. S., G. D. Ellis, K. P. Paisley, B. Arthur, and D. Skye. 2005. "Development and Evaluation of a Program to Promote Sportsmanship in Youth Sports." *Journal of Park and Recreation Administration* 23 (1): 1–17.

The authors discuss the serious and growing problem of poor sportsmanship in youth sports. They describe the "Play Hard, Play Fair, Play Fun" youth basketball program as an example of how to shift the focus from winning to an atmosphere characterized by sportsmanship, cooperation, and positive relationships among participants on competing teams. Effective strategies used to enhance sportsmanship include introducing the players and referees, posting signs supporting sportsmanship, rewarding players for good sportsmanship, resetting the score to zero when the score discrepancy between the two teams became too large, hosting a postgame social event for players and coaches, and providing a league Web site with photographs of each team's weekly sportsmanship award winner.

Wiersma, L. D., and C. P. Sherman. 2005. "Volunteer Youth Sport Coaches' Perspectives of Coaching Education/Certification and Parental Codes of Conduct." *Research Quarterly for Exercise and Sport* 76 (3): 324–338.

Based on focus group interviews with 25 volunteer youth sport coaches, the authors identify areas of need for educating coaches, barriers and problems faced in and recommendations for offering coaching education, and the importance of codes of conduct for parents.

Other Types of Print Works

Aspen Institute. "Sport for All: Play for Life," 50 pp.

This reports describes an ambitious plan to reimagine organized youth sports. Project Play prioritizes health and inclusion and emphasizes unstructured play for all children.

National Alliance for Youth Sports. 2007. National Standards for Youth Sports. Available at: https://www.nays.org/resources/nays-documents/national-standards-for-youth-sports/, 9 pp.

Nine standards should guide operations and outcomes of youth sport programs according to individuals involved with organizing and managing these programs. The sixth standard calls on everyone involved to display sportsmanship.

Women's Sports Foundation. 2008. "Go Out and Play: Youth Sports in America." Available at: www.womenssportsfoundation.org/home/research/articles-and-reports/mental-and-physical-health/go-out-and-play, 192 pp.

Reporting on a nationwide survey of youth in grades 3 through 12 and parents, sports are found to have a positive impact on family satisfaction and linked with improved physical and emotional health, academic achievement, and quality of life. This report concludes a gap exists between the sexes, with males benefiting from greater sport opportunities in rural and urban areas. Ethnic minority females are discriminated against by race and sex, while youth with disabilities are disadvantaged because of fewer participation opportunities in sports.

Ethical Issues in Interscholastic Sport

Books

Alberts, C. L. 2003. *Coaching Issues and Dilemmas: Character Building through Sport Participation.* Reston, VA: National Association for Sport and Physical Education, 187 pp.

> This book describes the importance of coaches modeling positive values and developing character. Practical scenarios are provided to help guide coaches in dealing with ethical issues.

Bissinger, H. G. 1990. *Friday Night Lights: A Town, a Team, and a Dream.* Reading, MA: Addison-Wesley Publishing Company, 357 pp.

> This eyewitness account of a football season at Permian High School in Odessa, Texas, reveals one community's obsession with its team's success. The author describes many of the social, racial, and sexual problems associated with football shaping a town's identity.

Brown, B. E. 2003. *Teaching Character through Sport: Developing a Positive Coaching Legacy.* Monterey, CA: Coaches Choice, 140 pp.

> The author provides coaches with specific strategies for teaching values and developing character through sport.

Carocci, V. P. 2008. *Building Character—Harry's Way: The Story of Harry DeFrank and the Value of Sport in the Lives of Our Youngsters When Done the Right Way by the Right People.* Carlisle, PA: Tuxedo Press, 196 pp.

> This book tells the story of Harry DeFrank, a high school girls' basketball team coach. He teaches players values and how to play the game of basketball and conduct their lives the right way.

Dohrmann, G. 2010. *Play Their Hearts Out: A Coach, His Star Recruit, and the Youth Basketball Machine.* New York: Ballantine Book, 422 pp.

This story depicts corruption in grassroots basketball and the high-stakes competition for adolescent talent. Through exploiting the romanticized hoop dreams of basketball prodigies, an AAU coach can exploit parents and adolescents.

Fay, G. 2013. *Sports: The Ultimate Teen Guide (It Happened to Me)*. Lanham, MD: Scarecrow Press. 338 pp.

Optimally playing sports requires proper nutrition, physical training, avoidance of performance-enhancing drugs, preventing and caring for injuries, and psychological preparation. Achieving these goals can lead to the sheer joy of competing and developing a lifelong love of sports.

Lewis, M. 2007. *The Blind Side*. New York: W.W. Norton & Company.

Overcoming an absent father, crack-addicted mother, and poverty on the streets, Michael Oher's need for an education is fulfilled through the adoption by an evangelical family and the opportunity to display his amazing football prowess in a private school they support. Oher maximizes his talent, graduates high school (barely), and qualifies academically in creative ways to receive a football scholarship at his new parents' alma mater.

May, R. A. B. 2008. *Living through the Hoop: High School Basketball, Race, and the American Dream*. New York: New York University Press, 243 pp.

The author explores high school basketball through the lens of race with specific reference to the impact of drugs, drinking, and delinquency of athletes. It is challenging for sportsmanship and an overemphasis on winning to coexist.

Ripken, C., and R. Wolff. 2006. *Parenting Young Athletes the Ripken Way: Ensuring the Best Experience for Your Kids in Any Sport.* New York: Gotham Books, 240 pp.

> After his Hall of Fame career when he played baseball with sportsmanship and class, Cal Ripken Jr. has focused on youth. He offers advice as a father and coach about how to reduce the overemphasis on winning and emphasize the fun of playing sports.

Journal Articles

Camire, M., and P. Trudel. 2010. "High School Athletes' Perceptions on Character Development through Sport Participation." *Physical Education & Sport Pedagogy* 15 (2): 193–207.

> High school athletes as do school administrators and coaches believe sports can teach and develop character. Despite this belief, gamesmanship persists and has become recognized by athletes as part of the game.

Fierberg, D. E. 2000. "High School, Where Hazing Is Amazing." *Education Digest* 66 (4): 48–51.

> Hazing is behavior that threatens or causes physical or psychological harm to an athlete as a condition of participating on a team. School administrators and coaches have not been diligent enough to prevent hazing, which is illegal.

Gaines, S. A. 2012. "Theory into Practice: Developing Individual and Team Character in Sport." *Strategies* 25 (8): 30–33.

> Developing character through sports does not happen automatically. Rather, coaches and sport managers must establish goals and guidelines of appropriate behavior, such as sportsmanship, and provide opportunities to observe and enact values, such as respect, responsibility, honesty, and fairness.

Marsh, H. W., and S. Kleitman. 2003. "School Athletic Participation: Mostly Gain with Little Pain." *Journal of Sport and Exercise Psychology* 25 (2): 205–228.

The authors claim playing interscholastic sports leads to positive effects on academic performance, self-esteem, subsequent college enrollment, and eventual educational attainment. These positive outcomes hold true across the range of participation levels and demographic subgroups of socioeconomic status, sex, and ethnicity.

Said, E., and S. N. Blair: 2005. "Sports Gone beyond Wild . . . But Not Completely without Hope." *Physician and Sportsmedicine* 33 (7): 6–7.

An orthopedic surgeon and exercise physiologist address problems in school sports. Specifically, they discuss the use of anabolic steroids, aggressive parents and fans, unethical behaviors of coaches, and a "winning-at-all-costs" approach.

Sloan, T. 2003. "It's Not Cheating Unless You Get Caught." *Referee* 28 (2): 24–28.

The author discusses the fine line between gamesmanship and cheating in sports. Using examples from baseball, football, and soccer, the author explains how officials sometimes contribute to the confusion leading to more unethical behavior in sports.

Vandenabeele, R. 2004. "S.O.S.: Save Our Sportsmanship." *Coach and Athletic Director* 74 (1): 72.

The author discusses strategies for teaching sportsmanship and ethical behaviors through interscholastic sport. Specifically, the call is for defining sportsmanship, emphasizing participation rather than winning, teaching positive values, and educating and involving parents to reinforce these desired outcomes.

Zimmer, D. 2004. "Values and Priorities and Where They Begin." *Coach and Athletic Director* 74 (5): 30–32.

At times, coaches fail to take advantage of the opportunities they have to influence the development of moral values in athletes. The author encourages coaches to use teachable moments in sport to develop sportsmanship and model character.

Ethical Issues in Intercollegiate Athletics

Books

Bowen, W. G., and S. A. Levin. 2003. *Reclaiming the Game: College Sports and Educational Values*. Princeton, NJ: Princeton University Press, 490 pp.

> Using data from elite institutions, this investigative report examines the admissions' advantages, academic performances, and campus cultures associated with intercollegiate athletics. Debunking myths, the authors call for national reform based on their findings of preferential treatment of athletes and their underperformance in the classroom.

Brooks, D. D., and R. Althouse, eds. 2013. *Racism in College Athletics*, 3rd ed. Morgantown, WV: Fitness Information Technology, Inc., 420 pp.

> Contributors explore discrimination in college sports as experienced by college athletes historically to the present. Racism, sexism, exploitation, and limited opportunities are among the topics examined.

Byers, W., with C. Hammer. 1995. *Unsportsmanlike Conduct: Exploiting College Athletes*. Ann Arbor: University of Michigan Press, 413 pp.

> The former head of the NCAA exposes some of the exploitive rules and actions used to further the goals of intercollegiate athletic programs at the expense of athletes. The author expresses concern about several questionable aspects of college sports, especially as played at the highest competitive level.

Carpenter, L. J., and R. V. Acosta. 2005. *Title IX*. Champaign, IL: Human Kinetics, 270 pp.

The authors provide a comprehensive examination of the content and application of Title IX of the 1972 Education Amendments to sports.

Comeuux, E., ed. 2015. *Introduction to Intercollegiate Athletics.* Baltimore, MD: Johns Hopkins University Press, 400 pp.
In an examination of intercollegiate athletics, authors explore ethical issues, financial and business operations, racial and sexual equity issues, athlete rights, academic support, governance issues, recruiting, amateurism, social media, and reforms.

French, P.A. 2004. *Ethics and College Sports: Ethics, Sports, and the University.* Lanham, MD: Rowman and Littlefield Publishers, 193 pp.
The stated role of intercollegiate athletics stands in contrast to the myths of amateurism, character development, equity for both sexes, and financial equity. In reality, intercollegiate athletics at the highest level is in the entertainment business.

Gerdy, J.R. 2006. *Air Ball: American Education's Failed Experiment with Elite Athletics.* Jackson: University Press of Mississippi, 270 pp.
The author argues the current system of intercollegiate athletics has failed. He suggests reform measures for rebuilding this system, but realizes it will take moral courage to enact changes.

King, C.R., and C.F. Springwood. 2001. *Beyond the Cheers: Race as Spectacle in College Sport.* Albany: State University of New York Press, 214 pp.
This book exposes the racism associated with team logos and mascots and the predominance of whiteness in college sports.

Shulman, J.L., and W.G. Bowen. 2001. *The Game of Life: College Sports and Educational Values.* Princeton, NJ: Princeton University Press, 447 pp.

Using data from elite colleges, the authors investigate admissions, academic performance, postcollegiate lives, and whether athletes donate to the institutions they attended. The authors share empirical data to support their conclusions and the ethical implications of their findings.

Sperber, M.A. 2000. *Beer and Circus: How Big-Time College Sports Is Crippling Undergraduate Education.* New York: Henry Holt and Company, 322 pp.

Comparing intercollegiate athletics to Animal House, the author discusses admission scams, cheating, the collegiate party culture associated with intercollegiate athletics, faculty apathy toward athletics, and an overall undermining of undergraduate education. The picture painted about how important intercollegiate athletics has become on some campuses is not pretty.

Journal Articles

Brand, M. 2006. "The Role and Value of Intercollegiate Athletics in Universities." *Journal of the Philosophy of Sport* 33 (1): 9–20.

The author, as president of the NCAA, suggests the role of intercollegiate athletics has been undervalued. He claims intercollegiate athletics make an important contribution to the undergraduate education of athletes and positively contribute to campus culture.

Calvert, C., and R.D. Richards. 2004. "Fans and the First Amendment: Cheering and Jeering in College Sports." *Virginia Sports and Entertainment Law Journal* 4 (1): 1–53.

Using a First Amendment framework and a model of balancing rights and freedoms with good sportsmanship and the rights of other fans, the authors review policies of athletic conferences.

Doty, J., and A. Lumpkin. 2010. "Do Sports Build Character— An Exploratory Study at One Service Academy." *The Physical Educator* 67 (1): 18–32.

The service academies emphasize building character and preparing leaders through sports. In a comprehensive study at students at one service academy, females, first-year students, and athletes in club sports, individual sports, and noncontact sports had higher character scores than comparative groups by sex, year, competitive level, and sport.

Jordan, J. S., T. C. Greenwell, A. L. Geist, D. L. Pastore, and D. F. Mahony. 2004. "Coaches' Perceptions of Conference Code of Ethics." *Physical Educator* 61 (3): 131–145.
Head coaches of college sports teams are asked to identify what should be included in a code of ethics to encourage positive ethical behavior. They rate the ideals of sportsmanship, promotion of values like honesty, integrity, and fair play, a healthy environment, and professional conduct as most important.

Kavussanu, M., and G. C. Roberts. 2001. "Moral Functioning in Sport: An Achievement Goal Perspective." *Journal of Sport and Exercise Psychology* 23 (1): 37–54.
The authors examine the achievement goals, unsportsmanlike attitudes, and judgments about the legitimacy of intentionally injurious acts in male and female college basketball players. Male athletes show lower levels of moral functioning and greater approval of unsportsmanlike behaviors and are more likely than females to judge injurious acts as legitimate.

Lawry, E. G. 2005. "Academic Integrity and College Athletics." *Phi Kappa Phi Forum* 85 (3): 20–23.
Too often money and incentives for winning obscure academic integrity in intercollegiate athletics as academically unmotivated athletes cheat and academic regulations are circumvented to keep star athletes eligible to play. As possible solutions, the author suggests reducing the size and influence of athletic departments, preventing athletic

departments from being responsible for athletes' academic performance, enforcing academic rules, and requiring more disclosure of athletes' academic records.

Lumpkin, A. 2012. "Athletics in Institutions Competing in the Football Bowl Subdivision: Positives, Negatives, and Recommendations for Change." *Journal for the Study of Sports and Athletes in Education* 6: 219–244.
Positive and negatives about intercollegiate athletics, such as amateurism, recruiting, academics, and commercialization, are examined. Fourteen reforms are recommended.

Lumpkin, A. 2012. "Title IX and Financing Intercollegiate Athletics." *Journal for the Study of Sports and Athletes in Education* 6: 275–292.
Using the Equity in Athletics Data Analysis Cutting Tool, the author uses self-reported data in a six-year comparison of FBS athletic programs. Females athletes in FBS institution had proportionately higher participation opportunities and grants-in-aid than female athletes in FCS, Division II, and Division III institutions and especially in institutions without football teams.

Lumpkin, A., R. K. Dodd, and L. McPherson. 2014. "Does a Glass Ceiling Persist in Intercollegiate Athletics?" *Journal for the Study of Sports and Athletes in Education* 8 (1): 33–46.
With females holding a significantly lower number (one-third) of the administrative positions in intercollegiate athletics among NCAA institutions, the perception of the existence of a glass ceiling persists. Males are most likely to be responsible for facility and event management, media relations, and marketing across all three divisions. Females disproportionately work in academic support and compliance.

Lyons, V., and B. A. Turner. 2015. "Examining the Influence of Gender on Athletes' Levels of Moral Reasoning: A Comparison of Intercollegiate Athletes and Students." *Journal of Issues in Intercollegiate Athletics* 8: 28–49.

Using the Hahm-Beller Values Choice Inventory, the researchers examined moral reasoning grounded in Kohlberg's moral development theory. Female athletes morally reason at a higher level than do male athletes; college students morally reason at a higher level that do college athletes.

Thelin, J. R. 2008. "Academics and Athletics: A Part and Apart in the American Campus." *Journal of Intercollegiate Sports* 1 (1): 72–81.

The author discusses the special privileges granted to athletic departments, misbehaviors of coaches, financial issues associated with academics and athletics, and the inclination of some coaches and athletic directors to violate rules. Specific examples are provided in this examination of policy and ethical issues.

Other Types of Print Works

Acosta, R. V., and L. J. Carpenter. 2014. "Women in Intercollegiate Sport: A Longitudinal, National Study—Thirty-Seven-Year Update, 1997–2014." Available at: www.acostacarpenter.org/, 56 pp.

The authors report on a longitudinal basis the status of females in intercollegiate athletics in NCAA-member institutions. The data include number of teams for female athletes, head and assistant coaches of teams for females, athletic directors, head athletic trainers, head sports information directors, and females employed in intercollegiate athletics.

Cheslock, J. 2008. "Who's Playing College Sports? Money, Race and Gender." Available at: www.womenssportsfoundation.org/en/home/research/articles-and-reports/school-and-colleges/money-race-and-gender, 43 pp.

While Title IX expanded opportunities in sports for females, this report concludes increases in expenditures in football and men's basketball are constraining participation opportunities. This study specifically examines high school participation trends as they influence intercollegiate athletics: the impact of rising health care costs on sports with high injury rates; increased number of international athletes; and enrollment management strategies favoring sports played by athletes who are well prepared academically, able to pay high tuition costs, and less diverse in race and ethnicity.

Huma, R., and E.J. Staurowsky. 2012. "The Price of Poverty in Big Time College Sport. National College Players Association." Available at: www.ncpanow.org/research/body/The-Price-of-Poverty-in-Big-Time-College-Sport.pdf, 33 pp.

The study investigates whether football and men's basketball players should be compensated for the billions of dollars in revenues they generate when playing at the highest competitive level. It exposes the exploitation of these athletes whose "full ride" scholarships fall woefully short of covering the full cost of education.

Judge, J., and T. O'Brien. 2012. "Equity and Title IX in Intercollegiate Athletics: A Practical Guide for Colleges and Universities." Available at: http://www.ncaapublications.com/productdownloads/EQTI12.pdf, 256 pp.

The authors provide guidance about how to comply with Title IX. It includes suggestions for dealing with harassment issues, employment issues, gender equity, and case law.

Knight Commission on Intercollegiate Athletics. 1991. "Keeping Faith with the Student Athlete: A New Model for Intercollegiate Athletics." Available at: www.knightcommission.org/images/pdfs/1991–93_kcia_report.pdf, 46 pp.

The commission's original report calls for a "one-plus-three" model. The one is presidential control of intercollegiate athletics directed toward academic integrity, financial integrity, and accountability through certification.

Knight Commission on Intercollegiate Athletics. 1992. "A Solid Start: A Report on Reform of Intercollegiate Athletics." Available at: www.knightcommission.org/images/pdfs/1991–93_kcia_report.pdf, 11 pp.

This follow-up report of its 1991 recommendations commends the NCAA on its progress in addressing the issues of satisfactory progress in meeting degree requirements, grade point average, and school year progress, coaches' income, official visits by prospective athletes, transfer students, presidential control, certification, gender equity, cost containment, financial integrity, and initial eligibility.

Knight Commission on Intercollegiate Athletics. 1993. "A New Beginning for a New Century: Intercollegiate Athletics in the United States." Available at: www.knightcommission.org/images/pdfs/1991–93_kcia_report.pdf, 11 pp.

Although progress had been encouraging, the Knight Commission encourages reforms to address abuses in recruiting, boosters meddling in athletic department decisions, an overemphasis on television revenue, strengthening academic standards, and other ethical issues facing intercollegiate athletics.

Knight Commission on Intercollegiate Athletics. 2001. "A Call to Action: Reconnecting College Sports and Higher Education." Available at: www.knightcommission.org/images/pdfs/2001_knight_report.pdf, 47 pp.

Given the lack of sufficient progress made in achieving the recommended one-plus-three model, the commission a decade later calls for a stronger commitment to academic standards in intercollegiate athletics.

Knight Commission on Intercollegiate Athletics. 2010. "Restoring the Balance Dollars, Values, and the Future of College Sports." Available at: http://knightcommission.org/images/restoringbalance/KCIA_Report_F.pdf, 21 pp.

    In this report, the commission advocated for greater transparency in reporting athletic spending, rewarding making academic values a priority, and treating college athletes primarily as students, not as professional athletes.

National Collegiate Athletic Association. 2012. "The 2004–2010 NCAA Gender Equity Study." Available at: http://www.ncaapublications.com/productdownloads/GEQS10.pdf, 100 pp.

    This report provides data on participation of athletes, number and salaries of head and assistant coaches, recruiting expenses, athletically related financial aid, and overall revenues and expenses for intercollegiate athletic programs. The data are categorized by NCAA division and subdivided in Division by competitive level and whether an institution sponsors a football team.

National Collegiate Athletic Association. 2015. "Student-Athlete Participation 1981–1982 to 2014–2015—NCAA Sports Sponsorship and Participation Rates Report." Available at: http://www.ncaa.org/sites/default/files/Participation%20Rates%20Final.pdf 295 pp.

    This report provides longitudinal and comparative data on the teams and athletes for member institutions in the NCAA. The number of teams and athletes continues to grow as does the number of women's teams competing in NCAA championships. The average number of male athletes (247) per NCAA member institution is higher than for female athletes (190).

Ethical Issues in International Sport

Books

Albergotti, R., and V. O'Connell. 2013. *Wheelmen: Lance Armstrong, the Tour de France, and the Greatest Sports Conspiracy Ever.* New York: Gotham Books, 364 pp.

The Lance Armstrong doping scandal exposes how he defrauded fans, sponsors, and cancer victims by denying he used performance-enhancing drugs to help him win seven consecutive Tour de France titles. Violating the strictures of morality, Armstrong and other cyclists enacted possibly the greatest conspiracy in sports.

Bahrke, M.S., and C.E. Yesalis, eds. 2002. *Performance-Enhancing Substances in Sport and Exercise*. Boston: McGraw-Hill, 373 pp.
    This edited book provides an extensive description of the physiological effects of the use of performance-enhancing drugs. It also includes information on drug testing and the ethical issues associated with the use of these drugs.

Barney, R.K., S.R. Wenn, and S.G. Martyn. 2002. *Selling the Five Rings: The International Olympic Committee and the Rise of Olympic Commercialism*. Salt Lake City: University of Utah Press, 384 pp.
    This historical examination of the Olympic Games emphasizes commercialization, especially from the selling of television rights and obtaining corporate sponsorships. This well-researched book provides in-depth information about the key leaders, processes, and rationales associated with the evolution of the International Olympic Committee as a corporate entity, along with the associated ethical issues that characterized its evolution.

Beamish, R., and I. Ritchie. 2006. *Fastest, Highest, Strongest: A Critique of High-Performance Sport*. New York: Routledge, 194 pp.
    The authors discuss doping in sports and specifically the Olympic Games. They also examine associated ethical issues.

Girginov, V., and S.J. Parry. 2005. *The Olympic Games Explained: A Student Guide to the Evolution of the Modern Olympic Games*. New York: Routledge, 272 pp.

After discussing the history of the Olympic Games, the authors examine topics such as politics, the media, marketing, economics, use of drugs, and the ethics of Olympic sports.

Maraniss, D. 2008. *Rome 1960: The Olympics That Changed the World.* New York: Simon and Schuster, 478 pp.

The author artfully weaves politics, history, and sport in this comprehensive examination of the 1960 Rome Olympic Games. Using unforgettable characters and dramatic contests as context, the author describes how the Olympic Games began to be forever changed, such as through the crumbling of amateurism, doping, and commercialization.

Pound, R. W. 2004. *Inside the Olympics: A Behind-the-Scenes Look at the Politics, the Scandals, and the Glory of the Games.* Etobicoke, Canada: J. Wiley and Sons, 288 pp.

An IOC member provides an insider's perspective about judging scandals, negotiating television rights, doping, securing corporate sponsorships, and bidding scandals. Integrally involved as a leader in growing the Olympic Movement, the author is committed to guarding its integrity.

Voet, W. 2001. *Breaking the Chain. Drugs and Cycling: The True Story.* London: Yellow Jersey, 128 pp.

A former rider in the Tour de France discusses the interwoven nature of drugs and international cycling. The author claims that in pursuit of competitive advantages, most riders have chosen to use performance-enhancing drugs.

Wilson, W., and E. Derse. 2001. *Doping in Elite Sport: The Politics of Drugs in the Olympic Movement.* Champaign, IL: Human Kinetics, 295 pp.

This edited book examines the use of performance-enhancing drugs in the Olympic Games from multiple perspectives from testing to scandals. The chapter authors place the issue of doping in historical, sociological, global, and ethical context.

Woodland, L. 2003. *The Crooked Path to Victory: Drugs and Cheating in Professional Bicycle Racing.* San Francisco: Cycle Publishing, 192 pp.

Professional racing has for decades attracted cheaters who have sought unfair advantages through drugs. Even though many cyclists lie about and deny the use of performance-enhancing drugs, this book describes many forms of their cheating and recounts how some cyclists have paid the ultimate price with their lives.

Journal Articles

Carr, C. L. 2008. "Fairness and Performance Enhancement in Sports." *Journal of the Philosophy of Sport* 35 (2): 193–207.

The author questions from a philosophical perspective whether the use of performance-enhancing drugs represents unfair behavior by athletes. Since all athletes have the freedom to break the rules banning these drugs, it is argued using performance-enhancing drugs is merely a technological innovation in training.

Catlin, D. H., and T. H. Murray. 1996. "Performance-Enhancing Drugs, Fair Competition, and Olympic Sport." *Journal of the American Medical Association* 276 (3): 231–237.

The authors provide an overview of the drug testing process for the 1996 Atlanta Olympic Games, which included testing prior to athletes' arrival in Atlanta, immediately after events, and on short or no notice. Although some athletes claim drug testing violates their personal liberties, most athletes support drug testing for banned substances, including stimulants, anabolic steroids, diuretics, hormones, and marijuana.

DeFrantz, A. L. 2001. "The Future of the Olympic Movement." *Journal of the International Council for Health, Physical Education, Recreation, Sport, and Dance* 37 (2): 37–41.
    The author states that the Olympic Games enjoy global appeal because they affirm universal values like the pursuit of excellence, sportsmanship, international cooperation, peace, and respect for all. The IOC (of which the author is a member), in the role of guardian, must preserve and nurture Olympic values and not permit commercialism to interfere with achieving these values.

Kalinski, M. I. 2003. "State-Sponsored Research on Creatine Supplements and Blood Doping in Elite Soviet Sport." *Perspectives in Biology and Medicine* 46 (3): 445–451.
    Using previously restricted information, the author reveals athletes in the former Soviet Union used creatine supplements and blood doping in the 1970s and 1980s. This evidence shows charges at that time against some successful Soviet athletes for using performance-enhancing drugs and practices could not be substantiated because of the secrecy surrounding Soviet research in exercise biochemistry.

Milton-Smith, J. 2002. "Ethics, the Olympics and the Search for Global Values." *Journal of Business Ethics* 35 (2): 131–142.
    The author states the economic globalization of the Olympic Games has been plagued by commercial exploitation, intense national rivalries, cronyism, cheating, corruption, and a winning-at-any-cost approach. To revitalize the Olympic spirit, suggestions are offered for building a framework of global values to counterbalance naked economic priorities.

Parry, J. 2006. "Sport and Olympism: Universals and Multiculturalism." *Journal of the Philosophy of Sport* 33 (2): 188–204.

The author suggests the Olympics play a significant role in globalization, multiculturalism, and the struggle for universal principles. With the growing interdependency among societies and people, the Olympic Games can help bring about liberal ideals and universal values, such as living together in mutual respect.

Ritchie, I. 2003. "Sex Tested, Gender Verified: Controlling Female Sexuality in the Age of Containment." *Sport History Review* 34 (1): 80–98.
The author explores the sociohistorical construction of the sex test, which was a policy known as sex verification. Female athletes in major international sport competitions from the 1960s to the 2000 Sydney Olympic Games were subjected to invasive verification procedures to prove their sex and eligibility to compete.

Rogge, J. 2003. "Olympian Efforts." *Harvard International Review* 25 (1): 16–20.
Writing prior to the 2004 Athens Olympic Games, the author, as the president of the IOC, reflects on the values associated with the ideals of the Olympic Movement. Founder Baron Pierre de Coubertin in espousing this utopian ideal believed sport could teach the world's youth basic human values leading to friendship and peace among all communities.

Sekot, A. 2011. "Fair Play in the Perspective of Contemporary Sport." *Sport Science Review* 20 (5/6): 175–189.
The author advocated for the principle for fair play in sports. He stressed the Olympic Movement should ensure the preservation of Olympic values and principles of protecting the environment, meeting the needs of young athletes, and enhancing gender equity and equal opportunities.

Tomlinson, A. 2014. "The Supreme Leader Sails On: Leadership and Governance in FIFA." *Sports in Society* 17 (9): 1155–1179.

FIFA has claimed to contribute to intercultural understanding and international relations. Instead, the governance of the international governing body for world football between 1974 and 2013 is exposed for its ethical controversies and lack of accountability for its practices.

Other Types of Print Works

World Anti-Doping Agency. 2015. "World Anti-Doping Code." Available at: https://wada-main-prod.s3.amazonaws.com/resources/files/wada-2015-world-anti-doping-code.pdf, 152 pp.

Adopted by representatives of governments, the IOC, International Paralympic Committee, Olympic and Paralympic sports and national committees, and athletes, this code leads the fight against doping in sport. Through a uniform set of rules, this code harmonizes anti-doping policies, rules, regulations, and enforcements within sport organizations and among public authorities.

Nonprint Resources

Ethical Issues in Sport for All

Sport and Film

Baker, A. 2006. *Contesting Identities: Sports in American Film.* Urbana, IL: University of Illinois Press, 162 pp.

American filmmakers have told compelling narratives about individual athletic achievements, often within the socially constructed identifies of class, race, ethnicity, and sex. Real-life sports figures have made significant impacts on society as they personify self-reliance.

Crosson, S. 2013. *Sport and Film.* New York: Routledge, 205 pp.
The sport film genre has been a commercial success story. The social, historical, and ideological significance of sport films is recounted.

Poulton, E., and M. Roderick. 2008. eds. *Sport in Films.* New York: Routledge, 258 pp.

Sport in films can be used a metaphor for other aspects of life and society. The authors examine issues such as globalization, politics, commodification, and violence while describing heroes and villains, triumph and tragedy, and achievement and despair. American filmmakers use sports to tell compelling stories of conflict, triumph, and individual achievement.

DVDs

A Hard Road to Glory. New York: Eastman Kodak Company. 1988.

Based on Arthur Ashe's book by the same title, the compelling story of African American athletes in the United States is described and the excellence of athletes despite racial discrimination is celebrated.

Concussion. Culver City, CA: Sony Pictures Entertainment, 2015.

Dr. Omalu, a forensic neuropathologist, discovers chronic traumatic encephalopathy (CTE), a football-related brain trauma, in former Pittsburgh Steeler Mike Webster. The NFL attempts to silence Dr. Omalu for exposing the truth about the serious consequences of repeated concussions from youth through professional football.

Playing Hurt: Ethics and Sports Medicine. Princeton, NJ: Films for the Humanities and Sciences, 2005.

A panel of experts representing the Orthopaedic Society for Sports Medicine discusses ethical and medical issues associated with injured athletes.

The Sociology of Sports in the United States. New York: Insight Media, 2005.

This program describes sports as a social phenomenon. In exploring the interface between sports and society, it examines the relationship of sports to religion, social roles, citizenship, morality, class, race, sex, and the institutionalization of sports.

Ethical Issues in Youth Sport

DVD

Give It Your All: Defining Yourself through Sports Participation. Ames, IA: Championship Productions, 2003.

> Former intercollegiate athlete and current athletic director at Ohio State University, Gene Smith delivers a passionate and motivational message directed to athletes and parents. He discusses sportsmanship as the way to handle challenges in sports and life, the importance of achieving academically, the roles of coaches and parents, and how to resist temptation by making values-based decisions.

Internet Sites

The Coach Education Center (www.asep.com) offers educational courses and products for coaches, officials, sport managers, and parents. A range of courses helps volunteer, club, and high school coaches provide athletes with developmentally appropriate skill instruction and values-based learning experiences.

The Institute for the Study of Youth Sports (http://edwp.educ.msu.edu/isys/) at Michigan State University was established in 1978 to address negative practices in youth sports. This institute conducts research on ways to maximize the physical, psychological, and social benefits of participating in youth sport while minimizing detrimental effects.

The Josephson Institute Center for Sport Ethics (http://sports.josephsoninstitute.org/) uses six pillars of character—trustworthiness, respect, responsibility, fairness, caring, and citizenship—to help coaches, parents, and athletes build character. Its "pursuing victory with honor" program emphasizes that character counts as the basis for becoming a true champion.

The Positive Coaching Alliance (www.positivecoach.org) is dedicated to helping youth sport leaders, coaches, and parents ensure a positive playing environment for young athletes. Its mission to develop "Better Athletes, Better People" is achieved through advocacy efforts, publications, and educational seminars that emphasize helping young athletes learn life skills that will serve them well beyond the playing field or court.

Ethical Issues in Interscholastic Sport

DVDs

Blind Side, The. Los Angeles: Alcon Entertainment, 2010.
   Homeless and educationally deprived, Michael Oher's life changes for the better when the wealthy Touhy family help, educate, adopt, and support him in reaching his potential on the football field and in life.

Coach Carter. Hollywood, CA: Paramount Pictures, 2004.
   Based on a true story, this movie recounts how a high school boys' basketball coach, despite intense criticism, benches his undefeated team due to how poorly some of the athletes are performing in their academic work.

Friday Night Lights. Universal City, CA: Universal, 2004.
   H.G. Bissinger's book by the same name, this video chronicles the 1988 high school football season in socially and racially divided Odessa, Texas. Overwhelming pressures are felt by Coach Gary Gaines and the Permian High School Panthers as they try to win the state championship while struggling with real-life issues.

Hoop Dreams. Irvington, NY: Criterion Collection, 2005.
   Two inner-city Chicago high school basketball players, Arthur Agee and William Gates, pursue their dreams of playing professionally.

Power, Passion, and Glory: The Real Story of Texas Football Madness. Ken Heckmann Productions Inc. and Game Partners, Ltd., 2005.

This depicts the real story of the Celina Bobcats, a team that has won more games than any other team in Texas history.

Remember the Titans. DVD. Burbank, CA: Walt Disney Home Video, 2001.

In the context of forced school integration in Alexandria, Virginia, in 1971, the successful white coach, Bill Yoast, is replaced by an African American coach, Herman Boone. These two coaches model how to overcome their personal and philosophical differences in developing a championship high school football team comprised of boys of both races.

Ethical Issues in Intercollegiate Athletics

DVDs

Code Breakers. Santa Monica, CA: Orly Adelson Productions, 2005.

Over 80 cadets are dismissed from the United States Military Academy at West Point for participating in a cheating scandal in 1951. These cadets violated the cherished honor code of the Academy.

Express, The. Universal City, CA: Universal Studios Home Entertainment, 2009.

Ernie Davis, the first African American to win the Heisman Trophy as a Syracuse University running back, endures discriminatory treatment and death threats.

Glory Road. Burbank, CA: Walt Disney Home Entertainment, 2006.

Coach Don Haskins of Texas Western College recruits African American players to this small, remote institution and develops a winning team. In the 1966 NCAA Men's Division I Basketball Championship, Haskins's all-African American starting lineup and mostly minority team defeats the all-Caucasian team from the University of Kentucky.

Junction Boys, The. Burbank, CA: Buena Vista Home Entertainment, 2003.

In his first year as the head football coach at Texas A&M University in 1954, Paul "Bear" Bryant subjects 100 potential players to grueling practices without water in the over 100-degree temperatures of Junction, Texas. One player almost dies and never plays again, while the 35 surviving players form the nucleus of his undefeated team two years later.

Databases

The Equity in Athletics Disclosure Act (http://ope.ed.gov/athletics) requires institutions to annually report data on their intercollegiate athletic programs. The analytical (cutting) tool on this site permits access to institutional and aggregated data for number of athletes by team, number of coaches and their salaries, and revenues and expenses by team and category.

Internet Sites

The Chronicle of Higher Education (http://chronicle.com), a weekly newspaper that covers higher education issues in the United States, frequently includes articles on ethical issues of intercollegiate athletics. Click on athletes to search for topical articles of interest.

The Champions of Character program (www.naia.org/SportSelect.dbml?&&DB_OEM_ID=27900&SPID=117008&SPSID=700608), launched by the National Association of Intercollegiate Athletics in 2000, seeks to help develop character through sport in athletes, coaches, and parents by providing practical tools for modeling the values of respect, responsibility, integrity, servant leadership, and sportsmanship. This educational outreach initiative reaches hundreds of thousands of college students to influence them to live their lives based on the tenets of character and integrity.

The Institute for Diversity and Ethics in Sport (TIDES) (www.tidesport.org) conducts research on issues related to race and sex in intercollegiate and professional sports. TIDES publishes numerous studies, including the NCAA College Sport Racial and Gender Report Card (http://www.tidesport.org/college-sport.html), that provide an assessment of hiring practices and composition of athletic teams, coaching staffs, and athletic administrators.

Ethical Issues in International Sport

DVDs

Chariots of Fire. Burbank, CA: Warner Home Video, 2005.
> The rivalry between an upper-class Jew and a Scottish missionary who become teammates on the British team in the 1924 Paris Olympic Games shows how the passion to compete transcends money, ethnicity, and class.

Invictus. Burbank, CA: Warner Brothers Pictures, 2010.
> With the goal of helping unite apartheid South Africa, newly elected president Nelson Mandela challenges the national rugby team, whose members are half black and half Afrikaner, to win the 1995 Rugby World Cup.

Race. Paris, France: Forecast Pictures, 2016.
> Jesse Owens faced harsh discrimination as an African American in the United States in the 1930. At the 1936 Berlin Olympic Games, he won four gold medals in the 100-meters, 200-meters, 4 × 100m relay, and long jump, forever destroying the myth of Hitler's Aryan supremacy.

Running Brave. Westlake, CA: Trinity Home Entertainment, 2004.
> Emerging from an impoverished South Dakota reservation, Sioux Indian Billy Mills challenges cultural barriers to win the gold medal in the 10,000-meter race at the 1964 Tokyo Olympic Games.

In examining the history of sport from an ethical perspective, two contrasting types of incidents are especially relevant to consider. First, what have been times when athletes and others involved with sports have made choices and acted in ways most people would categorize as unethical? That is, when these individuals gambled, were violent, cheated, lied, or took performance-enhancing drugs, did they adversely affect how the games were played and perceived by fans and other participants? Second, have there been times when athletes demonstrated sportsmanship, fair play, and other praiseworthy actions? That is, did these individuals enhance their reputations because their actions showed striving to win and championship performances can be congruent with ethical behaviors? Following are some examples of unethical and ethical actions in sport that provide evidence of individuals demonstrating or failing to demonstrate principled behaviors.

Examples of Unethical Behaviors in Sport

1880s   Many college baseball players, in the absence of eligibility rules, play on resort teams and local teams during the summer months and receive money. Baseball players being

Western Oregon's Sara Tucholsky gets carried around the bases by Central Washington's Liz Wallace, left, and Mallory Holtman after injuring her knee so she can record her home run during their softball game in Ellensburg, Washington, in 2008. (AP Photo/Blake Wolf)

paid and subsequently playing intercollegiate baseball remains an unresolved issue. Even after colleges establish rules precluding students from retaining their eligibility if they have been paid to play, for years many students use assumed names and receive money and benefits to play summer baseball.

1887   Owners in the National League of Professional Baseball Clubs make a "gentleman's agreement" to exclude African Americans from their teams. This racial discrimination pervades professional baseball until Branch Rickey signs Jackie Robinson to a contract in 1945, and Robinson begins playing for the Brooklyn Dodgers in 1947.

1890s   Intercollegiate football, which is played without helmets and protective pads, becomes increasingly brutal. Teams use mass formation plays, like the flying wedge, hit opponents with their fists, and intentionally inflict physical harm, sometimes with blows to the head causing deaths, until the level of violence results in calls for reform in the rules. In 1906, the Intercollegiate Athletic Association of the United States (changed to NCAA in 1910) is established and begins to change the rules, such as legalizing the forward pass.

1919   Concerns about gambling threaten the integrity of professional baseball from its earliest years. But, after eight Chicago White Sox players accept money from gamblers to fix the outcome of the World Series against the Cincinnati Reds, MLB tries to eliminate this problem. Even though the court in 1921 acquits Eddie Cicotte, Oscar Felsch, Arnold Gandil, Joe Jackson, Fred McMullin, Charles Risberg, Buck Weaver, and Claude Williams of criminal charges, MLB commissioner, Kenesaw Mountain Landis, bans them from MLB for life.

1920s   When professional football begins with the establishment of the American Professional Football Association (changed to NFL in 1922), it is minimally regulated. In addition to poorly paid players jumping between teams for more money, college students using assumed names are enticed to play for pay. College officials, in attempting to enforce amateurism, ban these athletes from intercollegiate teams if their actions become known. During this decade, institutions with the leading football teams generate significant revenues and build massive stadiums, while players fund their college expenses, although some receive under-the-table payments. Major controversies and even breaking off of relationships between institutions characterize a decade when football becomes commercialized while operating under the guise of amateurism.

1948 The NCAA, in an attempt to prevent the awarding of financial aid based on athletic skill, passes the Principles for the Conduct of Intercollegiate Athletics (called the Sanity Code). Even though several intercollegiate athletic programs refuse to stop their practice of making financial awards to athletes, NCAA members fail to expel these violators and enforce this code. As a result, the NCAA establishes policies in 1956–1957 to govern recruiting and awarding of athletic scholarships.

1951 Following an administrative Honor Code investigation, 29 West Point cadets in the class of 1952 and 54 cadets in the class of 1953 admit their knowledge of or participation in a cheating ring. This investigation proves numerous football players, including Coach Earl Blaik's son Bob, and other athletes provide information and copies of some common examinations to other cadets. The USMA dismisses the guilty cadets.

1961 Gamblers and fixers Aaron Wagman and Joseph Hacken entice 37 players from 22 colleges to alter point spreads in 44 basketball games. The players who fixed games play for Brooklyn College, Columbia University, La Salle University, Mississippi State University, New York University, North Carolina State University, Seaton Hall University, St. Joseph's University, St. John's University, the University of North Carolina, and the University of Tennessee, among others. In addition, some evidence points to Jack Molinas's paying numerous other players to fix games. The players escape convictions.

1977 During an NBA game, the Los Angeles Lakers' Kermit Washington punches the Houston Rockets' Rudy Tomjanovich.

This life-threatening blow and his head's impact with the court detaches Tomjanovich's face from his skull, causing blood and spinal fluid to leak into his skull capsule. Washington receives a 60-day suspension without pay for this violent incident.

1980   Rosie Ruiz appears to finish as the first female runner in the Boston Marathon. The Boston Athletic Association strips Ruiz of the title for cheating, because she shows no fatigue, she fails to recall landmarks along the course, and there is no video evidence she actually runs the marathon.

1986   Jan Kemp, an English teacher, receives an award of over $2.5 million (later reduced to $1.1 million) for lost wages, mental anguish, and punitive damages from the University of Georgia (UGA). The court decides UGA wrongfully fires Kemp because of her accusation that the institution passes student-athletes in its developmental studies program even though many of these athletes can barely read and write.

1987   While on NCAA probation for rule violations, representatives of Southern Methodist University (SMU) give money to numerous football players. SMU's football program receives the "death penalty," the harshest penalty ever imposed by the NCAA Infractions Committee, for its persistent rule violations and deceit. The penalties include cancelation of the 1987 football season, banishment from bowl games and television for two years, and loss of athletic scholarships.

1988   Ben Johnson wins the 100-meters race in the Seoul Olympic Games. After Johnson tests positive for the use of a performance-enhancing drug, he loses this gold medal and the world record he set. After a second failed drug test in 1993, he is banned from international track-and-field competitions for life.

1989   Commissioner Bart Giamatti bans Pete Rose, who holds the MLB record for most hits, from baseball for life for gambling on MLB games. The evidence in a 225-page investigative report shows Rose bets thousands of dollars daily on baseball games, even while playing for and managing the

Cincinnati Reds. After years of denial, in 2004, Rose admits in his autobiography to gambling on baseball games. Despite his pleas for reinstatement, Pete Rose's continued gambling and evidence of his betting on baseball games resulted in repeated rejections by MLB commissioners including in 2015.

1994   Shane Stant executes the plan of Shawn Eckardt, Derrick Smith, and Tonya Harding's ex-husband, Jeff Gillooly, to club the knee of rival skater Nancy Kerrigan at the United States Figure Skating Championships. Without Kerrigan competing, Harding wins this competition and qualifies for the Lillehammer Winter Olympic Games. Harding finishes eighth, but then pleads guilty to conspiracy to hinder prosecution of the attack. The United States Figure Skating Association bans Harding from competitive figure skating for life.

1996   After Jim Harrick coaches the UCLA men's basketball team to the 1995 NCAA Division I men's basketball championship, UCLA fires him for lying on an expense report. The University of Rhode Island hires Harrick as its basketball coach in 1997. Christine King, a secretary in the basketball office, alleges that Harrick harasses her, changes players' grades, has term papers written for players, and gives players improper benefits. After moving to the University of Georgia in 1999, Harrick subsequently resigns under pressure in 2003 due to academic improprieties, including the travesty of grades given to basketball players by his son, Jim Harrick Jr., who is an assistant coach.

1997   NBA commissioner David Stern suspends Dennis Rodman for 11 games and fines him for kicking a cameraman during a Minnesota Timberwolves' game. Some people assume the severity of these penalties relates to Rodman's previous behavior problems, such as head-butting referee Ted Bernhardt during one game and his profanity-laced tirade against officials after another game.

Golden State Warriors' Latrell Sprewell chokes, punches, and threatens his coach, P. J. Carlesimo, alleging the coach disrespected him. Initially banned for a year by NBA commissioner David Stern, arbitrator John Feerick reduces Sprewell's suspension to 68 games, and Sprewell loses $6.4 million during the suspension.

1999   The IOC expels six of its members and a seventh member resigns for receiving improper benefits like cash, tuition payments, medical treatment, and lavish gifts in exchange for their votes in the 2002 Salt Lake City Winter Olympic Games bidding scandal. With this admission of improprieties among these and other IOC members, the IOC changes the selection process for future host cities.

U.S.'s goalkeeper Briana Scurry violates the rules for penalty kicks when she moves forward to cut off the angle as Chinese player Liu Ying hits her penalty kick. This tactical move to gain an advantage while violating the rules helps the U.S.'s women's soccer team win the World Cup.

The NCAA penalizes the University of Minnesota with probation for four years and reduces grants-in-aid, official visits, and evaluation opportunities due to serious academic fraud. With the full knowledge and support of the men's basketball coach Clem Haskins, a team tutor writes hundreds of papers for numerous basketball players over a five-year period. The team's violations also include extra benefits, academic eligibility, unethical conduct, and lack of institutional control.

1990–2010   For nearly two decades, Miami University athletics were embroiled in a series of rule violations. First, athletes were provided excessive funds through a fraud of the Pell Grant program led by an academic advisor who helped over 80 athletes falsify their applications. Second, athletes on four teams, with most in football, received thousands of dollars of excessive aid. Miami University booster Nevin Shapiro provides a litany of improper benefits to football players between 2002 and 2010. The NCAA's mishandling of its investigation of the later violations added to perception of unethical behavior compounding other unethical behavior.

2000   The Boston Bruins' Marty McSorley hits the Vancouver Canucks' Donald Brashear in the head with his stick during a game. Brashear suffers a serious concussion and is unconscious and convulsing due to McSorley's vicious hit. In a criminal case, a Canadian court finds McSorley guilty of assault with a weapon, but he serves no prison time. NHL commissioner Gary Bettman suspends McSorley for a full year.

2002   Ed Martin pleads guilty to conspiracy to launder money and admits he gave $616,000 to University of Michigan players Chris Webber, Robert Traylor, Maurice Taylor, and Louis Bullock. The institution forfeits all games in the 1992–1993, 1995–1996, 1996–1997, 1997–1998, and 1998–1999 seasons, including the 1992 and 1993 Final Four games; repays the NCAA about $450,000 received for postseason play; and takes down the participation and championship banners. Chris Webber initially lies to a grand jury, but then pleads guilty to criminal contempt for lying about accepting money from Martin.

Judge Marie-Reine Le Gougne admits to being pressured by the French skating organization to award higher scores to the Russian figure skating pair in the Salt Lake City Winter Olympic Games. The high ratings help the Russian pair receive the gold medal and in exchange for favorable ratings for the French ice dancing team. The IOC awards a second gold medal to the Canadian pair that initially receives a silver medal. Le Gougne receives a suspension for her misconduct.

2003   Carlton Dotson shoots his teammate Patrick Dennehy during a target practice outing. While Dotson claims self-defense and mental problems, in 2005 he receives a 35-year prison sentence. Dennehy's disappearance and the circumstances surrounding his murder trigger an investigation of the Baylor University men's basketball program. Coach Dave Bliss tells his players to lie to investigators and impugn Dennehy's character as Bliss attempts to cover up wrongdoings, such as payments to players and unreported positive drug tests.

2004   Tim Montgomery, Olympic gold medalist in the 4 × 100-meter relay, admits to using human growth hormone and The Clear (tetrahydrogestrinone), an anabolic steroid, supplied by Victor Conte, founder and owner of BALCO.

Indiana Pacer Ron Artest goes into the stands and shoves a fan who he mistakenly believes throws a beer cup at him. Nine fans receive injuries during the resultant brawl. The NBA suspends nine players for a total of 146 games, with Artest receiving the longest suspension of the remainder of the 2004–2005 NBA season.

2006   Zinedine Zidane receives a red card disqualification in the World Cup finals after head-butting Italian defender Marco Materazzi. Zidane claims he struck Materazzi because of insulting comments from Materazzi about Zidane's mother and sister, an accusation Materazzi denies. FIFA, soccer's world governing body, suspends and fines both players.

Miami University and Florida International University (FIU) football players engage in a bench-clearing brawl that leads to the ejection of several players. After reviewing a video of the brawl, the conferences and institutions suspend 18 FIU and 13 Miami players from their teams' next games.

2007   Bill Belichick directs his staff to videotape the defensive signals of the New York Jets. Commissioner Roger Goodell punishes Belichick with a $500,000 fine and the New England Patriots with a $250,000 fine and loss of a first-round pick in the 2008 draft.

2008   University of Oregon basketball fans resent that Oregon native Kevin Love spurns his father's alma mater and chooses to attend UCLA. When his team plays at Oregon, fans send cell phone messages threatening to kill him. When members of Love's family come to the game, they are pelted with cups, obscene gestures, and profane insults.

2009   A class-action antitrust lawsuit (O'Bannon case) against the NCAA alleges an antitrust violation of a restraint of trade because FBS football and Division I basketball players have to relinquish their rights to compensation for the use of their names and images in perpetuity, even after they are no longer college athletes. Even though several rulings have been made, it is likely this case will be appealed to the Supreme Court.

2011 Jerry Sandusky, a former football coach at Penn State University, is arrested and charged with 52 counts of sexual abuse of young boys between 1994 and 2009. He receives a prison sentence to 30–60 years. Formerly revered football coach Joe Paterno, who was known for his integrity, was fired during the season for failure to properly report knowledge of Sandusky's sexual abuse.

2012 Bounty-gate is exposed as a pay-for-performance bonus program among New Orleans Saints' defensive players who seek to injure opposing players between 2009 and 2011. While suspended players win their reinstatement through the efforts of the NFL Players Association, head coach Sean Payton (2012 season), defensive coordinator Gregg Williams (indefinitely; changed to the 2012 season), and assistant head coach Joe Vitt (first six games in 2012) are suspended, and the team is fined $500,000 and loses second-round draft selections in 2012 and 2013.

2014 Baltimore Ravens running back Ray Rice knocks out his then-fiancée and after a video documents this domestic violence NFL commissioner Roger Goodell suspends him initially for two games and later indefinitely. Between 2012 and 2014, 33 NFL players are arrested for domestic violence, battery, assault, and murder, including Arizona Cardinals' running back Jonathan Dwyer, Minnesota Viking's running back Adrian Peterson, San Francisco 49ers' defensive end Ray McDonald, and Carolina Panthers' defensive end Greg Hardy.

2015 FIFA president Sepp Blatter and UEFA president Michel Platini are banned from all football-related activities for six years by the FIFA for a payment deal of 2 million Swiss francs made by Blatter to Platini. Although Blatter denies any ethical misconduct, he and other current and former FIFA officials are indicted for widespread corruption by the U.S. Department of Justice.

2016   No issue in the NFL is more controversial than concussions and their association with CTE. For decades, professional, college, and high school football players ignore concussions and subsequently suffer repeated blows to their heads. Junior Seau, Frank Gifford, Ken Stabler, and Mike Webster are among the 87 out of 91 former NFL players who have shown clear signs of CTE, while numerous other former players report symptoms associated with CTE.

Are there more incidents of unethical behavior in sports today, or do the media simply report and emphasize them? It could be argued there is a greater prevalence of cheating, violence, use of performance-enhancing drugs, and other unethical behaviors at all levels of sport in recent years. It is more likely the intensity of competitions and rewards for winning have contributed to a cheating culture in sport. Not all is bad, however, as the following positive role models for sportsmanship show.

Examples of Ethical Behaviors in Sport

1925   During the U.S. Open, golfer Bobby Jones barely touches his ball as he addresses it, but it moves slightly. No one else sees this, including his playing partner, Walter Hagen. Because Jones sees the ball move, he assesses himself a one-stroke penalty. That stroke puts him into a playoff, which he loses to Willie Macfarlane. Rather than ignoring the rules to claim a victory, Jones states that following the rules is the honorable thing to do.

1940   Dartmouth University outplays nationally ranked Cornell University until Cornell scores a touchdown on a fifth down, which is mistakenly awarded on the next-to-last play of the game. The game ends with the score Cornell 7 and

Dartmouth 3. After reviewing data and pictures from the game the next day, the official admits his mistake in allowing a fifth down to be played. Upon learning this, the president of Cornell sends a telegram to the Dartmouth president, awarding the Dartmouth team the victory.

1947   Brooklyn Dodger Pee Wee Reese stands beside and puts his arm around Jackie Robinson, his African American teammate, as Robinson is mercilessly taunted by racial epithets and slurs by Cincinnati Reds' players. Reese's acceptance of Robinson is revealed when he shakes Robinson's hand in welcoming his new teammate to spring training, declines to sign a petition refusing to take the field with Robinson, and helps smooth the acceptance of Robinson into MLB by befriending him. Reese's support of Robinson stands in dramatic contrast to the widespread physical and psychological abuse and death threats Robinson is subjected to as he integrates professional baseball in the modern era.

1969   Jack Nicklaus, after sinking his putt, concedes Tony Jacklin's two-foot putt, resulting in the Ryder Cup ending in a tie between the U.S.'s team and European team.

1994   Pete Sampras's illness prior to the final match of the Lipton tennis tournament appears to give the victory to Andre Agassi. In a gesture of sportsmanship, Agassi suggests waiting to see, if given time, Sampras will be able to play the match. Sampras wins the delayed match.

1998   The unranked University of Texas football team defeats a highly ranked University of Nebraska team, ending that team's 47-game home-game winning streak. As the Texas players leave the field, the capacity crowd gives them a standing ovation. Texas coach Mack Brown praises this display of sportsmanship.

2006   Norway's cross-country ski coach Bjornar Hakensmoen gives Canadian Sara Renner his left pole when her ski pole breaks during the sprint relay final in the Turin Winter Olympic Games. Renner and her teammate Beckie Scott go on to win the silver medal. Hakensmoen states his action reflects

Norway's belief in fair play as he is reacting like any good sportsman should.

Framingham State University's soccer team needs to win its game against Bridgewater State College to win the Massachusetts State College Athletic Conference regular-season title and advance to the postseason tournament. Even though Framingham's shot for a goal fails to enter the back of the goal, the official awards a point. Coach Tucker Reynolds tells his team to allow Bridgewater to score a goal to tie the game because it is the right and fair thing to do under the circumstances. Bridgewater wins the game 3–2. The players leave the game with something more valuable than a victory as they demonstrate the essence of sportsmanship.

2007   Hayley Milbourn finishes her round at the Interscholastic Athletic Association of Maryland Golf Championships only to discover she has been playing with someone else's ball. Even though Milbourn is the two-time reigning champion, shoots the best score, and no one else notices her mistake, she reports the rule violation. She says she cannot accept a trophy she does not deserve.

2008   With two teammates on base, senior Sara Tucholsky of Western Oregon University hits her first home run as a college softball player. In her triumphant home run jog, she misses first base. As she turns around to tag the base, she collapses with a knee injury, forcing her to crawl back to the base in pain. If her coach replaces her with a pinch runner, she gets credit only for a single. In a remarkable display of empathy and sportsmanship, Central Washington University (CWU) players Mallory Holtman and Liz Wallace carry Tucholsky around the bases, stopping at each base so Tucholsky can touch each base with her uninjured leg. Even though this home run helps eliminate CWU from the playoffs, Holtman states it is the right thing to do because Tucholsky deserves the home run.

2014   Eckerd College's Kara Oberer hit a home run against Florida Southern College, but her knee locked up and she could not walk to secure the 4–2 lead for her team. So, the second baseman Leah Pemberton and the pitcher Chelsea Oglevie who threw the ball hit out of the park carried Oberer around the bases so she could rightfully record her home run.

In the Sochi Winter Olympics, Canadian coach Justin Wadworth gave a spare ski to Russian cross-country skier Anton Gafarrov who had broken one of his skis in a fall. This enabled the skier to enjoy a standing ovation from the hometown crowd when he crossed the finish line.

Glossary

amateurism   Love of, such as a love for playing sports.

arms race   Term used to describe building bigger and more luxurious athletic facilities and paying higher and higher salaries to football and men's basketball coaches, especially by institutions playing in the NCAA FBS.

barnstorming   Term used to describe teams that travel from location to location competing in entertaining exhibitions and sporting events, including with local teams.

beneficence   Playing fairly or doing good.

bidding scandal   During the process of selecting the host city for future summer and winter Olympic Games, representatives of prospective organizing committees provide lucrative benefits to members of the IOC to influence votes in their favor.

blood doping   Occurs when athletes have a portion of their blood removed, which causes the body to replenish the extracted red blood cells; just prior to competition, their blood is reinfused, thus increasing the volume of red blood cells and oxygen-carrying capacity of the blood, which results in increased endurance; is a banned performance-enhancing practice.

boycott   Voluntarily refusing to compete in the Olympic Games to protest some action, situation, or set of circumstances; often associated with political or ethnic issues.

burnout   Occurs when an athlete becomes physically or psychologically exhausted or lacks the motivation or interest to continue participating in a sport.

character   Mental, social, and ethical traits that make each person unique.

character education   Instructing people to know, value, and do what is morally right.

code of ethics   Values, principles, and standards that guide conduct.

cognitive dissonance   Questioning approach through which people examine what is the right thing to do.

death penalty   Punishment assessed by the NCAA against an institution for major, repeated rule violations that disallow a team from competition.

discrimination   Prejudicial mistreatment of an individual or group based on a characteristic such as race, ethnicity, or sex.

drug testing   Process of determining whether the person has used a prohibited drug or method.

eligibility   Requirements regarding academic performance, age, weight, and other stipulations used to determine whether an athlete is permitted to play.

ethical relativism   Each individual determines what is true, with all points of view equally valid.

gamesmanship   Actions not explicitedly prohibited by the rules, but done to gain advantages by whatever means possible to increase the chance of winning.

gentleman's agreement   Unwritten rule in MLB, NFL, Basketball Association of America, and other sport organizations to exclude African Americans, thus discriminating against them based solely on race.

grant-in-aid   Financial award given by an athletic department to an athlete for playing a sport in college.

integrity   Living consistent with a person's moral values.

justice as fairness ethical theory   Advocates guaranteeing equal rights and equality of opportunity while providing the greatest benefit to those least advantaged.

moral callousness   Hardened feelings that lead to rationalizing acting in morally wrong ways.

no pass, no play   Policy in many schools that requires a specified level of academic achievement to be eligible to play sports.

nonconsequential (Kantian) ethical theory   Advocates an absolute moral code of behavior.

Olympic Movement   Collaborative activities of the IOC, national Olympic committees, international and national sport federations, host city organizing committees, and athletes that bring Olympic values and programs to life.

point spread   The publicized difference in the projected scores of two teams before the game is played.

preferred admissions   When an educational institution admits prospective students who does not meet the academic requirements for admission.

punitive damages   Financial awards made by the court for violations of the law as a deterrent to future misdeeds intolerable to society.

racism   Belief that specific human traits produce superiority of a particular race resulting in discrimination against individuals of another race.

redshirting   Keeping a student out of competition for an academic year; in intercollegiate athletics, this approach is used to allow athletes to develop physically, is due to an injury, or occurs because other athletes preclude the likelihood of playing; in interscholastic sports, this approach is used prior to the high school years so a child can gain a physical development advantage.

select teams   Comprised of highly skilled players who focus on winning and advancing to higher levels of competition; often includes playing year-round and competing at regional and national levels; sometimes called travel, elite, or club teams.

sexism   Discriminatory treatment against one sex based on prejudicial attitudes or beliefs resulting in the denial of benefits or opportunities.

sex testing   Process formerly required of female athletes in the Olympic Games and other international sport competitions to prove their sex based on visual appearance or testing protocol to prevent males from competing against females because of their physiological advantages.

shaving points   When athletes are paid by gamblers to manipulate the point spread to enable gamblers to win their bets.

show cause   Requirement that an institution must justify to the NCAA Infractions Committee why a coach who has violated its rules should be permitted to coach in an NCAA-member institution during a designated period of time.

situational ethics   Ethical theory that advocates love is the only absolute law; as long as good intentions are claimed, a person can do whatever is situationally desirable.

spirit of the rules   Sporting behavior that displays conformity to the written and unwritten rules of the game, sportsmanship, and a commitment to not seeking unfair advantage over opponents.

sport ethics   Study of how to teach character and moral values and model making morally reasoned decisions within competitive physical activities governed by rules.

sports agent   Independent contractor who acts on authority of and represents an athlete in negotiating playing and endorsement contracts and performing other agreed-upon services.

sportsmanship   Conforming to the letter and spirit of the rules (sometimes called sporting behavior).

tanking   When tennis players or athletes in other sports put forth minimal effort so they lose.

taunting   Ploys used in sports to attempt to distract and throw off an opponent's game.

utilitarian ethical theory or utilitarianism   Advocates the ultimate standard of what is morally right is dependent on the greatest amount of good for the greatest number of people.

Index

Note: Page numbers with *f* indicate figures; those with *t* indicate tables.

About the Author

Angela Lumpkin, PhD, is a professor and the Department Chair in the Department of Kinesiology and Sport Management at Texas Tech University. She previously served as dean of the School of Education and a professor in the Department of Health, Sport, and Exercise Sciences at the University of Kansas, dean of the College of Education at State University of West Georgia, head of the Department of Physical Education at North Carolina State University, as well as chair of the North Carolina State Faculty Senate, and professor of physical education at the University of North Carolina at Chapel Hill. She also served as women's basketball coach at the University of North Carolina. She holds a BSE from the University of Arkansas, MA and PhD from the Ohio State University, and an MBA from the University of North Carolina at Chapel Hill.

Angela is the author of 24 books, including *Introduction to Physical Education, Exercise Science, and Sport* in its 10th edition, *Practical Ethics in Sport Management* with two colleagues, *Sport Ethics: Applications for Fair Play* published in three editions with two colleagues, and *Modern Sports Ethics: A Reference Handbook*, written for a public audience. She has written 11 book chapters, published over 70 refereed manuscripts, and delivered 24 invited lectures and over 170 professional conference presentations. She has served as president of the National Association for Sport and Physical Education and president of the North Carolina Alliance for Health, Physical Education,

Recreation and Dance. She currently serves as president of the Texas Tech University chapter of Phi Kappa Phi.

Among the recognitions she has received are the Honor Award from the American Alliance for Health, Physical Education, Recreation and Dance, selection as an American Council on Education Fellow, Distinguished Visiting Professor at the United States Military Academy at West Point, Gene A. Budig Teaching Professor in the School of Education at the University of Kansas, Gene A. Budig Writing Professor at the University of Kansas, and recipient of the Order of the Long Leaf Pine presented by Governor James B. Hunt of North Carolina for contributions to the physical fitness and health of North Carolinians.